Rationality and the Study of Religion

ACTA JUTLANDICA LXXII:1

Theology Series, 19

Rationality and the Study of Religion

Edited by Jeppe S. Jensen
& Luther H. Martin

AARHUS UNIVERSITY PRESS

Copyright: Aarhus University Press, 1997
Printed on permanent paper conforming to ANSI
standard Z39.48-1984 by The Alden Press, Oxford, England
ISBN 87 7288 692 7
ISSN 0065 1354 (Acta Jutlandica)
ISSN 0106 0945 (Theology series)

AARHUS UNIVERSITY PRESS
Building 170
University of Aarhus
DK-8000 Aarhus C, Denmark
Fax + 45 86 19 84 33

73 Lime Walk,
Headington, Oxford OX3 7AD
Fax (+44) 1865 750 079

Box 511,
Oakville, Conn. 06779
Fax (+ 1) 860 945 9468

Preface

The study of religion, like the study of anything, would seem to presume rationality. In this sense, it is a child of the Enlightenment. As a rule, this means that generalizations made about the nature and function of religion should somehow be testable with respect to an appropriate corpus of data and that the results be replicable within the community of scholars. In other words, the study of religion is a theoretical enterprise. Even Romanticism's turn to feeling and subjectivity, in reaction to the Enlightenment's appeal to the rule of reason, attempted theoretical formulations and philosophical articulations.

Contemporary anti-intellectualism, however, exemplified though not exhausted by the excesses of 'post-modernism', grants ideological validity to virtually the entire spectrum of subjective fancy. Nowhere is this atheoretical posture more in evidence than in the study of that most fanciful domain of human behaviour, religion. Into its professional academies crowd healers and hermeneutes along with the historians, the pious and the positivists among the phenomenologists, conjurers and creedalists alongside the comparativists — all claiming their own proverbial fifteen-minutes of power. Consequently, when Jeppe Sinding Jensen first proposed a conference to be held in Aarhus with the curiously redundant theme 'rationality and the study of religion', its prospective contributors eagerly accepted his invitation to discuss theoretical matters concerning our field with an international group of colleagues. We do not pretend that the contributions to the conference, revised and published herein, solve all of the theoretical problems of our field; indeed, these contributions themselves represent divergent points of view. The participants are in agreement, however, on the necessary centrality of rationality for any academic study of religion. We do hope, consequently, that this volume will provoke an ongoing discussion of theory and of its place in a field that is notable for its lack thereof.

A workshop for doctoral students from the Nordic countries was held in connection with the conference. The organizers as well as the contributors were keenly set on introducing the future scholars in this field to the issues involved. The students responded enthusiastically through their determined participation, thereby attesting to the central role of the topic in the study of religion.

An executive committee meeting of the International Association for the History of Religions (IAHR) also took place during the conference. This in turn was effective in producing, with the international group of representatives present at that meeting, an awareness of the importance of the conference theme. The conference would not have been possible, however, without the substantial subventions provided by the Aarhus University Research Foundation, which also subsidized the publication of this volume, as did The Danish Research Council for the Humanities. The Faculty of Humanities of the University of Copenhagen deserves sincere thanks for the assistance given to the doctoral students in the provision of the necessary financial support for the workshop, as does Professor Jørgen Skafte Jensen for organizing the workshop. We would also express our gratitude to NORFA (The joint organization of the Nordic Ministries of Education), which supplied travel grants to the students. The helpful cooperation shown by the Department for the Study of Religion and the Faculty of Theology, University of Aarhus, was much appreciated. Professor Armin W. Geertz, Secretary General of the IAHR, organized the conjoint meeting of the executive committee and actively supported the conference project all the way.

In the preparation for publication, Ingrid Mikkelsen assisted in collating the bibliographies, Dr Tønnes Bekker-Nielsen of the Aarhus University Press planned the efficient procedure of production, as did Mary Waters Lund. Her conscientious editing contributed crucially to turning a 'heap' of manuscripts into this finished volume. A final note of gratitude should go to those students from the Department for the Study of Religion whose invaluable assistance, keen interest, and good spirit contributed so much to the success of the conference: Cecilie, David, Dorthe, Jesper and Mette-Marie.

Aarhus, December 1997   *Luther H. Martin and Jeppe Sinding Jensen*

Contents

Rationality and the Study of Religion: Introduction
Jeppe Sinding Jensen   9

Anti Anti-Rationalism: Anthropology and the
Rationality of Human Acts
Michal Buchowski   24

Lévy-Bruhl, Participation, and Rationality
Benson Saler   44

East Asian Rationality in the Exploration of Religion
Michael Pye   65

Religious Models and Problem Solving:
A Cognitive Perspective on the Roles of Rationality in
Comparative Religion
Matti Kamppinen   78

Rationality, Social Science and Religion
Roger Trigg   99

Social Facts, Metaphysics and Rationality in the Human Sciences
Jeppe Sinding Jensen   117

Rationality and Evidence: the Study of Religion as a Taxonomy
of Human Natural History
Gary Lease   136

Rationalism and Relativity in History of Religions Research
Luther H. Martin   145

Rationality in Studying Historical Religions
Hans G. Kippenberg   157

Dissolving Rationality: The Anti-Science Phenomenon and Its
Implications for the Study of Religion
Donald Wiebe   167

Bibliography   184

About the Authors   203

Index of Persons   209

Index of Subjects   213

Rationality and the Study of Religion: Introduction

Jeppe Sinding Jensen

The question of rationality does not often surface in the study of religion. This is remarkable in that it is a fundamental question which has been at the heart of methodological and theoretical controversies since its inception by our forebears: Friedrich Max Müller wanted to instigate a 'science of religion' and Edward B. Tylor envisaged anthropology as 'a reformers science'. Apart from any other criticism which may be levelled against these 'founding fathers' for their evolutionist conjectural history or universal psychological intellectualism, they certainly considered religion a subject matter to be studied rationally.

In this they differed not only from dogmatic positions in religious traditions but also from romanticist or transcendentalist traditions in Western cultural history. The dividing line between apologetics and scientific study was subsequently drawn in the nineteenth century when chairs of the History of Religions were first founded in European universities.

Early attempts to understand religion from a rational point of view, from Xenophanes on, have included such diverse interpretations as, on one hand, the Enlightenment deists' quest for Natural Religion, and, on the other, Ludwig Feuerbach's scathing critique of religion as nothing but human projection. Common to all, however, was the conviction that religion as known and practiced was in conflict with human reason. Then, religion might either be altered and purged of superstition as the deists would have or it could be disclosed as superstition and done away with as rationalist critics would have. If not outright eradicated in the literal sense, religion might at least be explained as being really about something else: projections of the human psyche, of society or whatever.[1] There must be reason somewhere behind the madness and it is to be disclosed by science. As expressed by Emile Durkheim:

The most barbarous and the most fantastic rites and the strangest myths translate some human need, some aspect of life, either individual or social. The reasons with which the faithful justify them may be, and generally are, erroneous; but the true reasons do not cease to exist, and it is the duty of science to discover them. (1965, 14-15)

There is no doubt that science is the master here and religion the servant. Religion is an object to be studied and explained scientifically — a fairly simple agenda, although of course it will always entail a variety of methodological opinions as to: a) the rules of translation from 'madness' into reason, and b) the line of reduction from source to target domain according to theoretical perspective.[2] Now, intriguingly, Durkheim also went on to assert in the next sentence that:

In reality, then, there are no religions which are false. All are true in their own fashion; all answer, though in different ways, to the given conditions of human existence. (ibid.)

Thus, religion contains some kind of potential: cultural, social or existential, which should not be judged by the standards of science alone.

The story of the scientific, or academic, study of religion did not unfold quite as prophesied by the founders, neither in anthropology nor in the history of religions. Most social and cultural anthropologists adhered to explanatory positions, be it in idealist or in materialist terms, but, especially after the advent of the 'interpretive turn' — with its insistence on understanding — an increasing influence of cultural relativism, including cultural protectionism, has landed a good portion of anthropology in a situation of some epistemological perplexity. This is clearly reflected in the amount of literature on the anthropological 'crisis of representation' and self-scrutinizations by practitioners in the field.[3]

For historians of religions the major problem throughout the history of the discipline has been the perception of theological agendas impinging on the conditions of academic scholarship. Religious scholars have seen the study of religion as their 'natural' province — and still do.[4] This, of course, influences the study of religion, which is marginalized, in many cases, intellectually and institutionally in the academic world. Publications by scholars of religion rarely prove influential in other human and social sciences, nor do scholars of religion often figure as prominent intellectuals in their respective societies. In general, their position is ambiguous, because whoever wants either to criticize or propagate religion can do so without the assistance of scholars of religion.

To make matters worse, the general public, along with most of the academy, simply cannot imagine what a critical and rational study of religion might look like: why study religion if you are critical of it? Or, *how* can you be critical of it? Does rationality, as the intellectual bedrock of all science, apply to religion and the study of it — and how? These matters must be addressed if the study of religion is to establish credibility as a scholarly enterprise. Simultaneously, as both the notion of rationality and the integrity of science are currently being criticized from more sides than one, this issue is connected to the general problems of validating rationality and scientific discourse. It is precisely these problems and questions with which the authors of the contributions to this volume are concerned.

Repossessions of privileged opinions

Classical protagonists of the scientific study of religion generally embraced some form of positivist epistomology. Things have changed since then, not only in the study of religion but also in epistemology generally, as demonstrated by philosopher of science Larry Laudan:

These days, social constructionists, epistemological anarchists, biblical inerrantists, political conservatives, and cultural relativists all find in the surviving traces of positivism grist for their mills; for what they find there appears to sustain their conviction that science has no particular claim on us, either as a source of beliefs or as a model of progressive, objective knowledge. Positivism thus transforms itself into a potent tool for resurrecting the very anti-empirical ideologies that it was invented to banish. The multiple ironies in the situation are enough to make grown men weep. (1996, 25)

Laudan set out to show how strong relativism may be conceived as 'positivism's flip side' and his ruminations turn out to be highly recommendable reading for those who are at all worried about the conflations of discourse that thrive in and around the academy.

If no line can be drawn between scientific discourse and religious homily then the academic study of religion goes by the board. In terms of normative epistemology, scientific knowledge simply must be considered cognitively superior to religious thought if the study of religion is to make any sense. The widespread notion concerning the non-cognitivity of religious language should preclude any problem. But, since values are often placed above facts in moral, cultural, social and political situations and since values determine thereby the ways of viewing the world, it becomes apparent that this question is neither trivial nor easily resolved. What is needed then, especially in an intellectual climate which advocates hermeneutic equality, cultural relativism and political correctness, is some set of standards for assessing the problem of demarcation between scientific and other modes of discourse.[5]

We agree that the epistemological arrogance and simple-minded semantic reductionism of logical positivism will not serve us any longer. It is not possible, nor desirable, for the study of religion simply to return to the 'good old days' of theory-independent fact-gathering. It is an established fact that scientists are necessarily under the influence of factors other than strict scientific canons of methodological logic when they grapple with theories and facts. But such necessary socio-epistemological conditions should not be taken to exhaust the problem: it is a mistake to confuse *necessary* with *sufficient* conditions when ascertaining what should count as knowledge of the world — including knowledge of systems of religious belief and action. Descriptions of what goes on in scientists' minds and what causes them to believe and hold true what they do, should not be confused with normative issues in methodology and epistemology. In short, although our knowledge and our modes of scientific pursuit are historically contingent, we should be able to distinguish, normatively and in principle, between what counts as knowledge and what does not. Historicity is not subjectivity. If these are pressing problems in a philosophy of science that deals with matters pertaining to the natural sciences, it demands little imagination to see how urgent it is to find ways of securing the status of the study of religion as a field of scholarly competence. If scholars in the study of religion do not know where to draw the line, who does?

Scholars in the study of religion have often looked to other human and social sciences, such as anthropology and linguistics, as model sciences that display both empirical rigour and theoretical refinement. But now these model sciences also seem to be in quandaries and in search of new orientations. That is, if they do not just attempt to bypass the problems (as some anthropologists do concerning relativism) or have changed their subject matter (as some linguists who study brains and not language).

In most human and social sciences postmodernist ideas about knowledge being social constructs have landed proponents of such ideas right on top of their own hermeneutic pyramids. They completely overlook the fact that postmodernism feeds on critique — including self-critique.[6]

Thus, on the question of rationality in the study of religion we seem to be able to borrow little from adjacent fields which is directly applicable. Although there certainly are sensible contributions to the debate, these must be 'translated' into the terms and contexts peculiar to the study of religion.

One of the effects of the academic marginalization of the study of religion is that it does not easily attract the attention of academics in other fields, such as philosophers of science or critical theorists.

The prevailing climate in and around the study of religion offers a true plethora of opinions about these matters, in a spectrum ranging from latter-day ardent textual positivists, who are mostly non-theoretical, to postmodernist hyper-relativist fictionalists, who are mostly non-critical. A search for good arguments to counter these extremes and present a more balanced view of things should prove a worthwhile activity. Something has to be done if critical theorizing and practice, and not just privileged opinion, is to form the intellectual framework for the study of religion.[7]

Privileged opinions are a function of placing value above fact. The supremacy of values is evident in politics, art, religion and most other areas of human activity. That may cause enough problems, as the history of humankind demonstrates, but our main concern here is the status and function of values in science, and in the study of religion. It has been amply shown that scientific practice is *not* value-free but that observation serves as no justification for the view that any value may then be applied in judging scientific knowledge by anyone. The intersubjectivity of scientific discourse seems quite often to be confused with a kind of intrasubjective opinion bordering on taste, which may be shared with a number of other of the same opinion; thus, cultural consensus is promoted as true — because it is 'intersubjective'. This 'democratization of epistemology' accords well with a marketplace notion of ideology, religion and values where you may own knowledge and protect your copyrights. In a global perspective religious and cultural groups increasingly strive to repossess their semantics, to engage in what could appropriately be termed 'cultural heritage management', with access only for the privileged who may 'sell it' to those willing to conduct research and publish results in compliance with the wishes of the proprietors. This 'cultural copyright movement' is the reverse of anthropology's postmodernist self-doubt. Remarkably, demands for political correctness from, e.g., anthropologists and scholars of religion, do not generally apply to those who themselves set the demands. The non-essentialist and construc-tionist critiques in anthropology and the study of religion are in inverse proportion to the self-assuring essentialism of religious, cultural and social groups. The human and social sciences have become severely politicized from both inside and outside and placed under massive critique from ethnic, minority, religious and other kinds of groups. Scholars' pleas for rational, intersubjectively controllable discourse are being brushed off as the last remnants of hegemonizing, neo-colonialist, chauvinist discourse. Rationality has become relativized and suspect, a thing of the past which is associated with positivism, empiricism and the entire project of modernity.

It is fair to say that the study of religion faces problems if and when academics in the field itself use it to pursue their own religious quests; when other academics, including those who administer funds in high places, fail to understand what it is about; when religious groups consider it the place to promote their own views; when politicians and edifying educators demand values; when students belonging to religious traditions must not be offended by the scholar's presentations; when students with New Age inspiration claim to possess superior epistemologies — then the study of religion is in dire straits.

On values and rationality

Mostly, problems of rationality and value stem from the already noted predominance of values and 'meaning' over science, a preference which we find highly questionable in relation to the pursuit of knowledge. Of course, this critical view reflects in itself a value judgment, so it should be emphasized that we are not *in any way* trying to uphold or revive a positivist fact-value distinction, because that would simply be both naïve and untenable other than as an analytic distinction. What we do claim, in relation to the study of religion, is that the values involved may be, can be, or indeed, *should* be other than religious values. It is a common misconception that religious values should be employed in the study of religion as parallel to the employment of aesthetic values in the study of literature, music and art. The falsity of this view becomes apparent when transferred, e.g., to political science studies of politics — are they to be conducted on the basis of political values or scientific values?

Among the lessons taught by postmodernism is the dissolution of totalizing epistemologies and ideologies and the fragmentation of culture. Thus, when we plead for scientific rationality in scholarly practice is does not follow that we suggest that such rationality must dominate all areas of human activity. It must do so in the pursuit of scientific knowledge, or where such knowledge is applied. In that sense we are thoroughly modern. We accept the fact that modern life is split into various realms and areas, where all human activity may not need to be judged by the same yardstick. And we *do* have values, but these may stem from, and be applied in, differing cultural realms and domains. Some values, however, come with a coverage that crosses domains; e.g. sincerity, without which neither matrimony, language, nor science would work. In short, when scientists have values, it is not only because they are merely human but because science itself needs values and virtues.[8]

At the other end of the spectrum, this also means that there are rationalities of values, otherwise they would not be values, but merely matters of taste.[9] As rational thought is a human product so are values. And, just in order to underscore their historicity: we do not promote a foundationalist view of eternal and unchanging values. However, humans do, and must, act rationally both cognitively and axiologically because as pointed out by Michal Buchowski:

If we cannot assume that people act rationally, that their conduct is somehow related to cultural norms shared by them, we will not be able to interpret the behaviour of social actors. The entirety of social life would appear totally incomprehensible. We would not even be able to act in, or analyze, our own group, not to mention study people in alien cultures. The fact that we can interpret the acts of other human beings, that we can predict most behaviors in everyday relations in our own culture, and, with some effort, actions in cultures alien to us, indicates that there is some regularity in socially conditioned conduct. (1994a, 8-9)

When we conclude that rationality is a systemic property of social and cultural life, we can also acknowledge that rationality is an integral aspect of religion, including religious values. We may consider it a matter of fact that rationality in science, and in social, cultural and religious life have much in common. If not in contents or referents, then in structure and logic. No worldview, of any kind, could function or make sense if propositions, including value statements, were not logically or structurally integrated. As outlined by Michael Kearney:

The organization of worldview assumptions is shaped in two ways. The first of these is due to internal equilibrium dynamics among them. This means that some assumptions and the resultant ideas, beliefs, and actions predicated on them are *logically* and *structurally* more compatible than others, and that the entire world view will 'strive' towards maximum logical and structural consistency. The second and main force giving coherence and shape to a worldview is the necessity of having to relate to the external environment. In other words, human social behaviour, social structure, institutions, and customs are consistent with assumptions about the nature of the world. (1984, 52)

In order to make sense of what other people do and think — in other times, in other cultures and societies — we are compelled to work from 'a methodological assumption that rationality holds the key to Other Minds'. (Hollis 1994, 228)

Rationality in question

All this seems fairly straightforward and we may well wonder what all the fuss is about. With the benefit of hindsight we can discern the basis of common objections to scientific rationality as an outgrowth of the linguistic turn in epistemology. From that basis it has been conjectured that because our knowledge of the world is linguistically mediated, then the world itself is a construction which consists of nothing but language.[10] In such a view natural laws become social constructions because they are formulated by humans — the rest is the now familiar history from relativism to postmodernism. Linguistic determinism has had its say in many fields, e.g., in anthropology, where the dictum 'the limits of my language are the limits of my world' has been believed, by some, to indicate that we humans live in different worlds, in incompatible and incommensurable universes of fabricated facts.[11] Depending upon one's favoured brand of cultural relativism the import of such theses would vary: from moderate descriptive to full-blown ontological relativism — and, perhaps, to cognitive paralysis.[12] Or, as Hans Albert has scathingly and succinctly formulated it in his critique of relativism, when it is, like dogmatics, 'maintained by rigorous cognitive protectionism' in the service of religious purposes:

Apparently, everyman has the right to his own perspective. Thus, religious views have to be seen on a par with scientific views. Every view has its own area of truth which is depending on its framework... We can if we like dogmatize any point of our propositional space, any component of our convictions. (1995, 51)

Now, what has this story of relativism to do with rationality? The answer given by social constructionists is that rationality is context dependent and therefore non-translatable, that there are no fixed, universal standards nor any non-cultural vantage points from which to view the whole affair. There is no longer any 'God's eye view' and 'reality has no key' — all human knowledge is historically contingent and expressed within conceptual schemes and frameworks. Very convincing (or seductive?) arguments have been launched in support of these claims, but they do not make up the whole story.

Although an awareness of the historicity and cultural contextuality of our knowledge of the world is a definite advance over and against former rationalist, scientistic, and empiricist idolatries, there are weaknesses and inconsistencies in the 'Myth of the Framework' — as Karl Popper termed it (1994, 33). If that 'Myth' were true, we would, at the end of the line, have no possibility of understanding anything, including ourselves. That certain things are 'cultural constructions' does not mean that they are less real; most relativists, I think, would concur with that. The metric system, for instance, is certainly a construction — we may even date it — but that does not detract one bit from its scientific status and practical utility.

Rationality, and its (often) perceived opposite, relativism, have been debated in a number of contributions relevant to the study of religion. Many of them in connection with the so-called 'rationality debate' between anthropologists (and other social scientists) and philosophers on the possibilities and problems of 'Understanding a Primitive Society'.[13] One could imagine that the debate would have abated, problems been solved, and some mutual understanding agreed upon. But, it is as if the debate has proved at least one relativist point, namely, that understanding in the scholarly community is a vexed affair. Added to this we find the aforementioned political, religious and other concerns involved. There is no question that rationality has been questioned, along with scientific realism. The degree to which rationality is tied to realism and relativism need not worry us unduly, they may be more compatible than commonly suspected (e.g., Putnam 1992). Simply because cultural relativism exists, there is no need for us to give up our ideas about rationality as a fundamental quality of human communication. Is there such a thing as a non-rational natural language?

Then, of course, there may be different versions of rationality according to the field in which they are employed. Theological and religious semantic systems may be eminently logical from one point of view, but not from another. Scientific rationality may be uniquely applicable in some activities — but not in others. We have no reason to dissolve the concept of rationality altogether simply because logical-empiricist notions of rationality have been proved wanting and plainly non-sensical in other realms of human activity. They have fallen and do not reign supreme anymore.

That scientific rationality (with a capital "R") does not hold the key to, or should be the measure of, all human knowledge and values could come as a shock only to modernist and empiricist fundamentalists. Rationality may not be a product of the universe itself which is then, as some revelation, reverently obeyed and copied by humans, but this does not imply that we are left with irrationalism only. Instead, we are left with rationality as a human property; it is precisely and only as a human property that rationality ensures the possibility of knowledge acquisition on the basis of cognitively and intersubjectively validated criteria. These may then be spelled out in various ways — and with various consequences for the study of religion. Let us proceed, then, from a twofold assumption: that relativism is not the logical opposite of rationality (the case for relativism having been argued rationally) and that rationality should not be uniquely defined by notions of hard-core scientific realism.

Rationality has indeed been questioned. However, the outcome of the critique is not a dissolution but the emergence of a multi-stranded and richer notion of rationality.[14] If the concepts of culture and religion are polythetic, then why should comparable criteria not hold for rationality? As it turns out, rationality comes, as most other things in this world, in a number of varities.

Taking stock: Some current notions of rationality

If there are those who are not in favour of rationality where we think it most appropriate, that is, in science, then it is ironical that their insistence on having good reasons for rejecting rationality could in itself only be judged as rational — because this is what 'having good reasons' means. It seems that rationality is not just an option, but an inescapable and necessary condition for human communication (this, of course, does not preclude the existence of irrational actions, beliefs or emotions). But, insofar as we are not irrational, our choice is limited to the forms of rationality we deem appropriate for various contexts and purposes. But maybe, and this requires some reflection, these forms or modes of rationality are not of the same species?

If rationality is an inherent property of human action and communication, then why not extend the notion of rationality to the animal kingdom? Cats and dogs, we might say, react rationally to a number of signals and stimuli. Perhaps even oysters or bacteria react rationally given certain conditions in their environments. Rationality thus conceived is but a rule-governed mechanism for survival. What we must assume, though, is that although these creatures follow rules that are systemic at some level and in some way, then they do not *know* the rules, nor can they be brought to know rules. Mere non-cognized rule-governed activity does not qualify therefore as an exhaustive concept of rationality. We noticed above that there can be no sense without rules, but rules in themselves do not constitute sense. Thus, the following brief overview of modes of rationality shall be restricted to what pertains to human cognition and culture — and to what is of particular interest to the study of religion.[15] A balanced presentation of modes of rationality is out of the question here, as is the possibility of quoting some 'quantitative' consensus; there are simply too many views about this issue:

As any card-carrying philosopher will tell you, rationality is a many-splendored thing... In one familiar view of rationality, for instance, being rational involves meting out one's degree of belief in accordance with the probability calculus. In another view, it involves basing one's beliefs on legitimate models of logical inference. In still another, it comes down to adopting beliefs which conduce to one's cognitive ends. To make matters worse, "rational" functions both as a normative and as a descriptive concept. (Laudan 1996, 195)

Also, a thorough historical presentation would be out of the question here, since this would require a comprehensive systematization of the use and meaning of the concept, even when restricted to, say, the philosophy of science. Then, lastly, there is the possibility of assembling an eclectic collage for a specific purpose, for example, problems in the study of religion.

To give some idea of what we are facing, a typology of modes of rationality would include such different notions as 'agent', 'systemic', 'purposive', 'practical', 'instrumental', 'value', 'belief', 'epistemic', 'reflexive', 'evaluative', 'critical' and 'scientific' rationality — just to mention some well-known modes. Ordinarily, conceived as modes of actions, 'agent', 'purposive' and 'instrumental' rationality would be opposed to 'value' and 'belief' rationality conceived as modes of thought, e.g., in moral or economical evaluations. Now, the two sides of that typological distinction are obviously linked, and causally so; neither of them would work without the other. Human action, when rational, is so in relation to some system of beliefs. Since Bronislaw Malinowski demonstrated the instrumental rationality of Trobriand magic and Max Weber explained the relations of economic rationality to religious worldviews it has been fair to say that religiously motivated actions can be accounted for as rational, be it in terms of theories based on strain (concerning, for example, conflicts arising from deprivation or political subjection), or on interest, whether this is motivated by economic or salvific concerns. Such forms of rationality can be termed 'emic', that is, they are intrinsic to holistic systems of beliefs and values, such as, for instance, the Hindu Varnashrama-dharma system or the Muslim system of purity, Tahara.[16] The common view of rationality as exclusively linked to practical and scientific procedures is simply misguided. Even when rationality is thinly defined as instrumental, as consisting in ways to match the means to an end, it covers much more than practical and technical acts. To restrict rationality in such a way is to remain trapped in a logical empiricist framework.[17]

Social scientists' game or rational choice theories can be put to use in the study of religion as long as the notion of the utility of actions is not restricted to an evaluation of the material outcome of such actions. They must consider the sum total of beliefs in a religious system in order to have explanatory power. Still, we are considering here types of rationality which I would classify as 'procedural', i.e., concerning the ways in which beliefs and actions are linked and how rules are followed. Different societies play different games with different rules, but they all have rules. And there are rules in religions as there are in science. It is fair enough to say that 'When in Rome, do as the Romans' — but whether one wants to play along is an entirely different question.

The question is whether we can say that rationality in the *study* of religion should consist in following 'the rules of the game' only? It appears that the contrary might apply; that rationality may equally consist in the ability to transcend rules; in making critical and reflexive judgments about rules.[18] This other major category of rationality as rule-transcending can be designated by the term 'reflexive rationality' and it is the more appropriate mode of rationality when it comes to the study of religion as a species of scholarly practice. A quick glance at the history of the study of religion will convince us that the rules of study have changed, and not only as functions of cultural, social and institutional locations, but also because of critical evalutions and reflections carried out by scholars *breaking* the rules and bending the habits. It is this critical and self-reflective mode of rationality which constitutes the epistemological backbone of the study of religion: it is engaged in trial and error, it is fallibilist, it will attempt to refute its own hypotheses and be relentlessly critical of its own assumptions, concepts and theoretical orientations. It will therefore also have a hard time legitimizing itself. Empiricist criteria are hard to defend these days, but rationality in science has to correspond, somewhere down the line, to some form of realism.[19] We may also, along with Joseph Margolis, put it the other way round, when he concludes: 'In short, realism, whether of the externalist or internalist sort, is unintelligible without a counterpart theory of human rationality' (1986, 236). Rational acceptability is ultimately tied to the empirical, to cognitive adequacy and to the sharability of claims. But, the empirical need not be conceived as what is reduceable to the world of physics. Semantics, e.g., is also an empirical matter.

These considerations lead to the question of whether this form of rationality is reduceable? I think not. It seems implausible that reflexive rationality could be 'naturalized', reduced to brainstates or in the form of some specifiable neurocortextual function. Reflexive rationality is, on the other hand, inextricably linked to our language. Karl Popper has emphasized that we:

owe to the third world [of objective knowledge] especially our rationality — that is, our subjective mind, the practice of critical and self-critical ways of thinking, and the corresponding dispositions. (1979, 147)

Rationality, unquestionably, has to do with our being reasonable. We might, in the end, have to consider it a 'primordial intuition' or an 'underived notion', which we are unable to reduce or explain causally, but of which we can, however, present an intelligible geography and demonstrate the implications in the scholarly enterprise.

This is what the authors of the contributions to this volume have attempted — and precisely in relation to the study of religion. They have done so in various ways. They deal with 'agent' rationality, rationality as discerned in religious action and associated theories, and with the varying approaches to the questions of 'scholarly rationality'. As far as we know, this is the first book ever to grapple with these matters in the scholarly study of religion. Therefore, any shortcomings should be considered good reason for future research and reflection.

Notes

1. This is not the place to rehearse the history of the study of religion, others have done so quite admirably, see e.g. Preus (1987) and Morris (1987).
2. The debate on 'reductionism' in the study of religion is by now rather voluminous, if not prolix. An informative volume is Indinopulos and Yonan, 1994.
3. A list of contributions to this debate would be immense, but see, e.g., Lawson and McCauley 1993, the contributions in Nencel and Pels 1991. A now classic is Clifford and Marcus 1986.
4. As an instructive example of this problem in relation to G. van der Leeuw, see Kippenberg and Luchesi, eds. (1991). The continuation of this situation is scrutinized by e.g. Wiebe (1988, 1990, 1991) but there are countless examples, cf. the discussions concerning Mircea Eliade's work (e.g. McCalla 1994, Murphy 1994, Penner 1989a).
5. That it is also possible to publish almost anything in (certain) scholarly journals has recently been demonstrated by American physicist Alan Sokal in his brilliant hoax: 'Transgressing the Boundaries: Toward a Transformative Hermeneutics of Quantum Gravity' (1996). Sokal's experiment was meant to expose postmodernist theorizing as plain gibberish, cf. his own comments (1996a).
6. There are notable, and critical, voices from 'within postmodernism', e.g. Norris 1995 and Eagleton 1996, who redress the caricatured images of postmodernism as 'non-critical'.
7. On the status of current theorizing in the study of religion, see e.g. McCutcheon's (1995) insightful review. That these matters are crucial is apparent from the special MTSR-issue (7-4, 1995) on the plight of the study of religion in North America. Although the situations in Europe are quite different, there are lessons to be learnt.
8. Cf., e.g., Jürgen Habermas' insistence on standards in science being connected with practical, moral, and hermeneutic stances (e.g. 1973).

9. In his *Validity of Values*, (volume II of *A System of Pragmatic Idealism*) Nicholas Rescher conludes in a note (1993, 186, n. 18): 'Morality is, as we have seen, inextricably bound up with rationality, since moral validity calls for a justification of certain sort (in terms of protecting the interests of people). A "value" whose adoption one cannot justify with reference to cogent principles is no real value at all but merely an arbitrary preference.'

10. In a critique of the 'sociological turn' (which in many ways parallels the 'linguistic turn') in the philosophy of science, Larry Laudan has aptly termed this form of argument 'the fallacy of partial description': Typically, the argument runs like this: "Science is a social activity, therefore it is best understood and explained in sociological terms". (1996, 201) As Laudan points out, one might as well say that science is a psychological activity to be studied by psychologists or that it is a biological activity because it is carried out by human animals... (ibid.). It seems to be forgotten that the study of science is not what science itself studies.

11. Or, in Nelson Goodman's wonderful phrase: 'One might say that there is only one world but this holds for each of the many worlds', which is often taken to indicate that Goodman must be a hyper-relativist. Not so, he 'takes science at full value' (1978, 4), but respects the differences between worlds of watercolour and worlds under the microscope.

12. On modes of relativism cf. Hollis (1994, 224-47) including a concise overview and discussion (in tune with the present author's convictions).

13. As was the title of Peter Winch's seminal paper from 1964. It is reprinted in the first anthology in the debate (Wilson 1971). In 1982 another volume appeared (Hollis and Lukes). Since then a number of works have carried on the discussion (e.g..: Bernstein 1983, Geertz 1984, Gellner 1985, 1992, Margolis et al. (eds.) 1986, Krausz (ed.) 1989, Tambiah 1990 and Kamppinen and Revonsuo 1993).

14. Cf. the volume with the inviting title: *Rationality in Question. On Eastern and Western Views of Rationality*, Biderman and Scharfstein, eds. (1989)

15. On 'animal rationality' see, e.g., Davidson 1985. The question is whether animals entertain beliefs and have propositional attitudes? Davidson's answer is: No, for the reason that although we have no better way to explain animal behaviour than to sometimes 'summon up propositional attitudes' (477), then 'The conclusion of these considerations is that rationality is a social trait. Only communicators have it' (480). Admittedly, some animals are social and communicate, but they do not command the 'subjective-objective contrast, as required by belief', and 'Communication depends, then, on each communicant having, and correctly thinking that the other has, the concept of a shared world, an intersubjective world. But the concept of an intersubjective world is the concept of an objective world, a world about which each communicant can have beliefs.'(ibid.)

16. Cf. Penner's conclusion on a view of rationality, which 'allows ritual action and belief into the domain of rationality. It may well be that the [religious] beliefs are mistaken, but we must insist... that such mistaken beliefs do not entail irrationality or sheer non-rational expressiveness. Moreover, once we begin our analysis from this view we shall note that beliefs and actions are to be explained from within a massive network of rational beliefs and actions. Ritual beliefs and actions will have to be explained holistically as elements within a rational system.' (1989, 24)

17. Consider how often rationality comes in a 'package deal' in a series of paired analogies (but often treated as homologies): Rationality/Irrationality; Objectivism/Relativism; Objectivity/Subjectivity; Realism/Anti-realism.

18. Bernstein (1983, 57) approvingly quotes Alisdair MacIntyre's point that: '...rationality is therefore to be found not in rule-following, but in rule-transcending, in knowing how and when to put rules and principles to work and when not to.' So, 'The teaching of method is nothing other than the teaching of a certain kind of history.'

19. See, e.g., Putnam 1994, 352ff. Robert Nozick (1993, 101*) has a pointed remark on rational belief vs. religious bias:

    'Some writers on physics report to us that physics support a spiritual view of the universe, but what is the non-expert to think if these writers themselves thirst for such spiritual lessons? To what extent do their reports result from what the facts most plausibly show and to what extent from their own wishes and desires? What would be impressive is some physicist reporting *in distress* that, despite what he wished were the case, against his own personal materialist preconceptions, he had been forced to conclude that contemporary physics pointed to the lesson that the universe is at base spiritual. (To my [i.e. Nozick's] knowledge, that has not yet occurred).'

Anti Anti-Rationalism: Anthropology and the Rationality of Human Acts

Michal Buchowski

In this paper I will outline a view on the problem of rationality of actions from a perspective which I call both anthropological and pragmatic. I will examine how the rationality issue can be perceived in the light of actual ethnographic practice and an historically contextualized, contingent view of culture. In order to present and justify this view I will first delineate the principles of contention between universalists (absolutists, rationalists) and particularists (relativists), and the way the controversy was approached by prominent anthropologists and religious scholars. This explication will allow me to exhibit the most important inconsistencies of the philosophical assumptions of existing theories and the limitations of justified anthropological claims. Finally, I shall give my own account of the controversy discussed.[1]

Universalism versus particularism: an outline of the controversy

Ton Lemaire writes that:

For about 25 years anthropology has been rediscovering and rethinking its philosophical dimension. The process of decolonization transformed the traditional anthropological object and thereby gave rise to epistemological reflection. (1991, 23)

In order to situate properly the discussion on rationality of beliefs we should start with a synoptic description of the roots of the encounter. The whole spectrum of viewpoints on the problem of rationality can be reduced to the two extreme poles: usually called rationalist and relativist, but later often described as universalist and particularist.[2]

Karl Popper may be regarded as the godfather of the *universalist* approach. This stance can be rendered as follows: There are some universal rules of reasoning, and these can be spelled out within modern European (scientific) discourse. The acceptance of universal features is necessary if one wants to consider human behaviour as being rational at all. Among several justifications for such universally shared rationality let us indicate some of the most important ones. The first argument refers to the common core of human experience. External reality constrains practical and conceptual responses; otherwise the human species would become extinct (Horton 1982). This argument is bolstered by the claim that human biological endowments are generally identical and therefore perception of the world has to be similar (Sperber 1985, 35-63). The whole idea of innate human universals is strongly supported by cognitive anthropology (Berlin and Kay 1969, and many others).[3]

For universalists, from an epistemological point of view, the necessity of assuming some universal forms of reasoning through which we all encounter the same world in order to interpret other cultures is obvious. Hollis put this point succinctly:

Hence he [the researcher] must assume that the Other Mind perceives very much what he perceives and says about it very much what he would say. For his only access to the phenomena of the Other's Mind experience is through interpreting behaviour and utterances. If he had to get to the phenomena before he could interpret and had to interpret before he could get at the phenomena, there would be no way into the circle. (1977, 147)

That is to say, if we did not share some common principles of reasoning, alien meanings would remain inaccessible and incomprehensible for us.

There is no full agreement about the scope of these shared logical principles, but most often the laws of identity, non-contradiction and negation are invoked (Hollis 1977, 150; Lukes 1973, 238). These kinds of *logical universals* are accepted not only by proponents of rationalist doctrine, but *also* by scholars who declare themselves adherents to such relativizing traditions as Kearney's Marxist (1984), or Hanson's (1975, 51) contextualist, approach.

The *particularist* theories are founded in Wittgenstein's (1953) ideas of 'forms of life' and 'language games', ideas applied to the social sciences by Peter Winch (1970; 1987). Adherents to the particularist approach distrust the attempts of their adversaries to attribute an objective value to scientifically oriented culture and its norms. Nobody can prove that our logic is a 'gift from God'. Science makes up one among many existing ways of describing and conceptualizing the world, a mode governed by appropriate 'game rules'. Relativists claim that we cannot use any criteria of measurement other than that used in the context of a given culture. However, this gives rise to the problem, of *whether we can* correctly *identify* the 'language game' of any alien culture. The particularist standpoint is consequently defended by the creators of the 'strong programme' in the sociology of knowledge (Barnes and Bloor 1982):

We possess no rationality criteria which universally constrain the operation of human reason, and which also discriminate existing belief systems, or their components, into rational and irrational groups. Variability in institutionalized beliefs cannot be explained by a conception of external causes producing deviations from rationality. (Barnes 1974, 41)

In short, in the universalist approach we deal with a kind of normative, intrinsic, epistemologically evaluative understanding of rationality. This notion is articulated in a scientist's own culture and its criteria are used as the common yardstick of the 'rationality' of actors in all cultures. The particularist attitude denies the possibility of arriving at common standards of rationality, particularly those established within science. Every rationalistically inspired attempt is treated as a case of absolutization of modern European conventions.

Anthropological transcriptions: the modernist fashion

In anthropology and religious studies the philosophical controversies about rationality usually translate into conflict between intellectualist and symbolic approaches;[4] quite often it takes the form of an argument concerning the rationality of science versus the rationality of magic. Therefore, before we discuss theories in which a *via media* between objectivism and relativism is pursued we should sketch two classical standpoints which have defined the area of discussion. These theories are represented by Ian C. Jarvie and Joseph Agassi, on the one hand, and John Beattie, on the other, both attempting some form of compromise.

John Beattie (1964; 1970), as a symbolist, harshly criticizes the intellectualist position epitomized by Frazer's work (1922). Beattie assumes that ritual acts in tribal cultures cannot be assessed literally in terms of modern European thought. One should not apply logical norms to everyday behaviour, particularly those in indigenous societies where symbolic and pragmatic domains are meshed. Modern scientific thought can adequately address only the practical aspects of culture, and is not able to unravel the complex activities of this twofold sort. Failure to take account of the symbolic dimension of the vast number of native activities thus deprives their subjects of rationality. The actors of magic instrumentalize their symbolic activity:

technical effectiveness, appropriate to practical acts, is ascribed to expressive acts. I think that 'symbolist' theory grasps the essential nature of magical and religious beliefs, i.e., the synthesis of instrumental and symbolic values.

Intellectualist critics of the symbolist trend — Jarvie and Agassi (1987a; 1987b) — suggest that in the whole symbolist tradition the notion of rationality (of the individual or the belief system) is simply substituted by the notion of symbolism which is effective due to social convention. This is a thesis on the instrumental power of symbols which portrays magical systems as inferior to the scientific one. Intellectualists identify the category of symbolism as nothing but an *Ersatz* version of the Frazerian category of irrationality. The act of *splitting* the acts into those amenable and those non-amenable to direct rational evaluation is arbitrary and obliterates the attribute of the rationality of human agents. What solution, then, do Jarvie and Agassi suggest? Their perspective can be called *monism*, because it presumes an existence of a universal gauge of rationality, independent of social context. In general Jarvie (1984)[5] adopts as such the standard explicated in the latter writings of Popper (cf. 1966) — an openness to critique of one's own convictions, which are held as a result of rational choices and decisions. The 'critical spirit' permits the growth of knowledge and objectivity. Modern science embodies this critical ethos, systematically enhances the 'truth content' of its statements, and decisively contributes to the technological efficacy of societies applying scientific principles. This is tangible proof of the highly rational character of scientific practice. It is also a rationale for the evaluation of alien systems of beliefs from the privileged stance of a culture born in modern Europe.

But the 'spirit of criticism' is not the only relevant point in the intellectualist theory. The acts of individuals can be evaluated on the basis of the assumption of rationality. This assumption claims that every individual will undertake acts which will lead to the preferred goals according to his/her knowledge. Analysis carried out in terms of the assumption of rationality is called *situational logic*. This kind of rationality is defined by Jarvie and Agassi as being 'relatively strong'.[6] It is, then, a goal-oriented rationality informed by particular cultural standards.

However, this not fully-fledged type of rationality ought to be distinguished from 'very strong rationality'. It is characterized by the presence of critical thinking in a given intellectual tradition, a thinking 'which pertains to the highest standards of rationality known anywhere...' (Jarvie and Agassi 1987b, 392). Strong rationality implies skepticism in regards to the dominant beliefs. The emergence of critical thinking is determined by social factors. Because traditional beliefs constitute generally closed systems which lack alternatives to the dominant way of thinking, an individual is unable to break out of the vicious circle of group images.

Although I cannot agree with some of the philosophical foundations of the 'intellectualist programme' I think it has a well-founded formulation of rationality of the behaviour of human subjects. This assumption of rationality requires correction only when it attempts to apply the notion of the 'highest criteria' elaborated within modern European culture to all systems of beliefs. Also, the idea of critical thinking is taken from the universally understood epistemology of science. Within science it is an 'ethical' imperative as well as an integral part of the investigative ethos. The question is, however, whether this criterion can be transposed to the realm of studies of beliefs?

Even if we confine ourselves within the conceptual limits of the intellectualist approach discussed, objections can be raised due to the obscurity of the notion of 'criticism'. What allows us to define a specific attitude, found in tribal cultures as well as in the 'culture of science', which fulfils the requirements of Popperian 'critical thinking'? Does every act of skepticism about existing beliefs prove rationality? Have people in indigenous societies not introduced certain innovations into their lives? Does this mean that they have fulfilled the requirements of the criterion typical of science? It seems that, in accordance with Jarvie and Agassi's ideas, a rational practitioner of magic has non-rational magical convictions. But this view makes sense only if one is ready to acknowledge a Popperian standard as a universal criterion of rationality.

Anthropological transcriptions: postmodernist fashion

Some scholars assume that the issue of rationality has become old-fashioned. One may sense a 'rage against rationalism', as Bernstein put it (1992, 31). This feeling can be traced in many anthropological writings, with Geertz's (1984) article on anti anti-relativism in the forefront. However, Geertz made the notion of rationality an easy prey. In the polemics with rationalism he connects it with foundationalists' desire for some objective criteria. He seems to treat rationality as universalists' property, a concept assigned exclusively to those who, like Jarvie, Horton, Spiro and Sperber, worry about the possibility of 'spiritual entropy, heat death of the mind' (Geertz 1984, 265). But is it really the case that rationality should be inherently tied to rationalism? Can we resign from the notion of rationality of human agents? I understand and appreciate the reasons for the critique of anti-relativism, but do not agree with the implicit aversion to the concept of rationality itself, with a denial of its presence in anthropological and religious studies.

Geertz expressed in a very shy form a view which those who would claim to have gone beyond him, e.g., postmodernists, take for granted as an intellectual imperative: *strong anti-rationalism*. Postmodernists (Clifford and Marcus 1986, especially Asad 1986) connect the concept of rationality not only with a foundationalist menace but with Western domination and colonialism as well. This 'ethical' commitment has led to the denunciation of the notion. In effect, postmodernists have denied any cognitive value to the conception of rationality and have discarded it. As Stephen Tyler put it: 'Rules and criteria are not necessary guides to action, knowledge, and belief, as much as they are posterior excuses and justifications for them' (1991, 80). In a postmodernist view: 'Reason has either colonized every other discourse or, those whose irrationality it could not digest, it has consigned to a kind of shadow life as superstition...' (Tyler 1991, 92).

However, I am convinced that by rejecting the notion of rationality itself anthropologists have thrown out their own baby with the bathwater. The baby's name is 'rationality of every human being'. As I will show, the idea of rationality comprises also a premise of any interpretive activity.

One may perceive a history of anthropology and religious studies as a continuous struggle with ethnocentric presumptions (Buchowski 1989). Malinowski, Evans-Pritchard, Leach, even Frazer, tried to convince their public that there is something worthy in alien cultures. Many of those classical writers, with Ruth Benedict and Melville Herskovits in the past, and postmodernists today, want not only to explain, but also to understand the meaning and relevance of other cultures. I take this, despite many differences, as the essence of all these scholars' efforts. Anthropology, as Geertz tirelessly points out, seeks comprehension and mutual cross-cultural interpretation utterly devoid of fixed cultural, not to mention ontological, premises. It may sound paradoxical, particularly in relation to postmodernists' rejection of the same notion, but this is *the* reason why the rationality question is inherently important for the discipline. It is indispensable in our attempts to understand human actions.

In *Postmodernism, Reason and Religion* Gellner (1992a), in turn, ravages postmodernism. In his opinion, the postmodern movement is a transitory fashion which presents a radical form of relativism. Its version of relativism is so extreme that it disavows anthropological practice. Postmodern authors indulge in a 'meta-twaddled' analysis of their own and other scholars' texts. Postmodernists are so afraid of possible distortion of meanings of cultures studied, says Gellner, that they prefer to write about themselves and the inaccessibility of the Other. This excludes any comparative assessment of rationality. For postmodernists the issue evaporates!

For Gellner (1992), rationalism comprises a contingent product of history and one which is irreversibly ingrained in Western culture. It defines the nature of our socially shared values, such as the search for truth, and criticism. 'Rationalism is our destiny ... it is of the essence of *our* culture that it is rooted in the rationalist aspirations' (Gellner 1992, 159). In modern European culture the only absolute idea is the critical method even-handedly applied to every phenomenon and every proposition. This approach has enabled us to make real progress in conquering nature. The fact that other cultures must subscribe to this vision of the world, under the threat of perishing, confirms the pre-eminence of Western rationalism.[7]

Of course, it is easy to trace which of the traditional attitudes, i.e. rationalistic or relativistic, Gellner and postmodernists defend. It is also obvious that the first seeks some foundations in reality and objectivity for rational claims, while postmodernists' ideas are 'based' on quickly shifting dunes and refer to subjectivity. Recent writings indicate that with postmodernism the pendulum has swung very far in a direction of relativism. This evokes a zealous reaction from the advocates of rationalism of whom Gellner is a prominent exponent. Thus we may consider the last few years as a period in which the views in the rationalist/relativist debate have been radicalized. Clearly, the issue of rationality is still on the agenda, and there are pragmatic reasons vital for scholarly practice which make the problem unavoidable. These reasons should be made explicit.

In search of a compromise

In the fervour of radical polemics, one should not forget that anthropologists and, at the same time, scholars in religious studies, often have searched for some kind of compromise between particularism and universalism. These searches suggest at least three underlying motives. First, it is held that neither of the extreme positions — rationalist or relativist — can sustain critique; in this way some measure of credibility in both views is acknowledged. Second, actual anthropological practice contradicts both kinds of radicalism. The acceptance of extreme relativism undermines the possibility of cross-cultural studies since it assumes that we are not able to grasp alien meanings. As Spiro claims:

Epistemological relativists can't have it both ways. They can't at one and the same time argue that cultures are incommensurable while also claiming that ethno-graphers... are able to understand the cultures and minds of alien people. (1992, 21)

On the other hand, radical rationalism excludes the possibility of cross-cultural understanding, co-existence, and, as Rorty (1991, 208) put it, weaving strands taken from the web of beliefs of another culture into our own web. Third, rationalists hope for a judicious compromise which will counter the accusation that, by claiming the triumph of Western rationalism, they disdain people living in other societies.

Philosophical theories elaborated by Willard V. Quine (1960), Donald Davidson (1984), Steven Lukes (1982), Mary Hesse (1980), Alasdair MacIntyre (1989), Ian Hacking (1982), Richard Rorty (1991), Hilary Putnam (1990) and many other scholars can be considered as attempts, however divergent from each other, to find a 'third way'. It would be fascinating to confront all these attempts. However, this discussion will be confined to hypotheses which (1) exemplify a major attempt to search for a *via media* between the two opposite views, (2) tie in directly with anthropological practice, particularly in the study of beliefs, and (3) illuminate issues important for my proposed interpretation of rationality. The views presented by Robin Horton, F. Allan Hanson, and Stanley J. Tambiah seem most instructive to me. In what follows I will examine how far these conciliatory standpoints are philosophically justified and logically coherent.

The theory presented by Robin Horton (1967) may be called *parallelist* because he presumes that traditional belief systems are the counterparts of modern science. In this sense his position is strongly intellectualist. Religious ideas are treated as conceptualizations of the world. Their main difference from science is that the magico-religious concepts about the world are personified, while scientific ones are de-personified. Explanations are either spiritual or natural in character.

The differences between the two systems is caused by social factors. In his analysis Horton refers implicitly to theories that apparently remain at variance with each other. Similar to Jarvie and Agassi, he employs the Kuhnian ideas of the 'closeness' and 'openness' of a given system to intellectual influences from outside; these are determined by properties of the whole social system, not mental capacities of individuals. The closeness and tradition-bound nature of native beliefs are results of the lack of alternatives to the existing views, which, in turn, makes it impossible for 'the spirit of criticism' to emerge. This argument fits into the Popperian paradigm. In summary, Horton suggests the following view: people in all societies strive to conceptualize the world in abstract terms, but in traditional societies the concepts are spiritual, and the choice among such concepts is extremely limited.

In more recent writings Horton (cf. 1982; 1993) alludes to symbolic tradition and to Lukes' (1970) assertions about two disparate categories of phenomena — 'material' and 'ritual' (conventional). They are addressed by two kinds of theories: primary and secondary. Primary theories directly describe the physical world. These are like positivistic observational sentences, are interculturally intelligible, and they serve as a bridgehead for cross-cultural communication. Starting with the perception of the rudimentary facts we may finally arrive at more abstract symbols and meanings. Secondary theories form complex world view systems which are devised to conceptualize universally experienced phenomena. Horton's distinction between traditional and scientific theories applies to the domain of secondary theories.[8]

Now let us turn to Tambiah's (1990) *dualistic* theory. His position follows a symbolic orientation in discriminating the kinds of actions and beliefs that can be evaluated with regard to their rationality. In this respect Tambiah not only agrees with Horton (whom he criticizes for 'intellectualism') and obviously with Beattie, but also expresses prevailing anthropological opinion. However, this kind of split is unsubstantiated, at least as far as the rationality question is discussed. First, there is material reality, where the instrumental type of rationality, as practiced in science, governs. This kind of rationality is easily amenable to cross-cultural evaluation. Second, there is a conventional reality of social customs, morality, rituals, etc. which cannot be measured by universally applicable standards. A different ordering of things asks for different modes of interpretation. According to Tambiah nothing prevents us from reconciling relativism in regard to culturally regulated facts with a 'unitary philosophy of science which holds that in a certain core sense there can only be a *single science*' (ibid., 130). The latter pertains to domains such as physics, biology, medicine, mathematics, etc. This way of reasoning enables Tambiah to declare that he is 'neither a relativist nor an anti-relativist in an absolutist or blanket sense' (129).

The last standpoint I shall exercise is labelled *contextualism* by its proponent, F. Allan Hanson (1979). He draws heavily on R.G. Collingwood's (1940) and C.I. Lewis' (1929) theories of truth and meaning, and I, in turn, will draw extensively on some of Hanson's ideas. He says that 'truth and knowledge may vary from one culture or mode of discourse to another', while maintaining 'the notion that all people inhabit in a single world which exists in determinate form and independently of what people say or think about it.' (Hanson 1979, 517) Truth about the world is the result of the relation of reality to statements about it. Neither reality nor statements can be grasped in a pure form; each possesses a kind of negotiated quality, which emerges from the encounter between reality and cultural description of it.

Meaning is probably the most important constituent of Hanson's theory; meaning determines the cultural character of actions. However, he distinguishes between two types of meanings: intentional and implicational. The analysis of the first sort refers to the individual's motives and intentions. Because intentional meaning is interpreted on the basis of the individual's convictions, it is an example of situational logic. But when it comes to the implicational meanings of socially determined concepts, 'their meaning and truth is to be found in their logical relations with other propositions, beliefs, institutions' (Hanson 1975, 21). In other words, intentional meaning is discovered through situational analysis; implicational meaning through analysis of social institutions and their influence on the actor's beliefs and actions.

Implicational meanings exist independently of individuals' consciousness and can be reconstructed in a research on culture which does not have to resort to empathy or other hermeneutic methods. In order to reconstruct these meanings, a fluent knowledge of rules of cultural interpretations suffices. At the same time, this means that the truth and rationality of culture should always be contextualized within the institutions of a given society. The echo of Wittgenstein reverberates here. Subjects in various cultures are rational according to different types of rationality.

But, as mentioned above, Hanson makes a clear concession to objectivists, and this is the reason why I classify his theory into the group of median ones. He admits that some fundamental standards of logic *have to* be universal, i.e. laws of non-contradiction, identity and negation. Otherwise a given system of beliefs could not be considered as such, but merely as an unintelligible conglomeration of judgments. Hanson appears to be a believer in the external, adjudicative power of objective reality and inherent, universal laws of logical thinking.

Critical assessment of previous theories

I will not make a detailed appraisal of every theory discussed but merely indicate the points most pertinent to the analysis as well as those shared by all (or almost all) of the scholars described.

As we have seen, the main issue of the rationality debate revolves around the question whether it is feasible to establish some universal standards of rationality. For the relativists, this is unattainable because the truth for each culture is determined by its particular 'rules of the game'. Objectivists maintain that universal standards do exist. The reasons given by them are twofold: (a) the unity of the world presupposes the unity of truth, and (b) some universal standards are *sine qua non* for cross-cultural communication and translation.

The question whether we can establish some criteria of rationality has been variously approached. Nevertheless, in my opinion, one line of reasoning is particularly salient. It has its roots in the symbolic orientation. Many scholars, vide Beattie, Horton and Tambiah, decided to divide the universe into two 'ontologically' disparate spheres. On the one hand there is the tangible, hard, physical world of natural phenomena, and on the other, the realm of flexible and arbitrary customs and habits. We can assess universal rationality in the first sphere, but not in the other.

This dualistic approach presents a kind of mechanical amalgamation of rationalistic and relativistic views. But it is intrinsically incoherent. 'Reality' is cut into two domains. In this separated world two radically different discourses prevail, and one of these discourses, namely empirical science, is privileged as far as it deals with the 'harder' part ('material reality') of the world 'out there'. In fact, all of these theorists claim that our beliefs are culturally bound (relativism), but at that same time the scientific beliefs are most objective (rationalism), therefore somewhat less culturally bound. In other words, there are no privileged beliefs, nevertheless beliefs of a specific subculture of the West, in a specific realm of reality, are just that. It is like saying there are no exceptions, except ...! The whole dualistic idea can be easily translated into the old problem of the division between sacred and profane. It was put explicitly by Malinowski (1948, 27) in the form of question: 'do the natives distinguish the two domains and keep them apart?' Malinowski, who wanted to prove the rational nature of 'primitive people', exhibited that 'they' draw the line exactly as 'we' positivists do, so the division is held universally. He was a person of his time, as most of us are. But Tambiah and Horton follow in his footsteps a half century later. They represent, even if in a sophisticated form, an *ordinary man's* popular view.

The above issue is closely related to the next one. *Every* theory discussed, whether rationalist, symbolic or median, assumes the *universality* of certain rudimentary logical principles. For the rationalist, this conviction is sustained by the following one: reality discerned in modern European culture is objectively universal and legitimate. In both cases, we deal with an *absolutization* of the findings defined in modern European culture, in which science comprises one of its domains. Of course, the rationalists' claim is much stronger than the compromising relativists'. However, even the latter (including Hanson), share the conviction of the existence of some universals, either cognitive or logical, which are, in fact, determined within the Western tradition. In this respect, the inconsistent character of this kind of assertion still holds: there are no universally valid statements, except ...!

I do not think one can offer any spectacular answer to this eternal conundrum in which religious studies and anthropology are trapped. On the one hand, we have no choice but to describe native beliefs in our own categories. On the other hand, claims that these categories should be treated as universally valid assign to them an ontological, transcendent status. However, a view which at least does not contradict the declaration that meanings are culturally constructed is possible.

How are we to avoid absolutization and solve the conundrum? In our studies we can only identify statements which are not questioned in a given culture. We can assume that our sentences are merely heuristic devices for sorting out these kinds of statements. The description of these never-questioned beliefs is done in our own sentences. Both judgments, i.e. ours and those described, are somewhat 'logically' related. However, this contention cannot be justified by an allegedly universal mode of perceiving and conceptualizing reality. Thus, we contextually define the semantics of a given culture utilizing our own concepts. Unquestioned cultural judgments assert such states of affairs which are addressed by our sentences as well. In this way we unavoidably impute our logic and perception of reality to the culture studied, but we commit this crime with a full awareness that these imputations are implemented in the name of cross-cultural cognition. It is most important, however, that we no longer ascribe any absolute validity to our own, or any other, statements.

The above problem almost directly coincides with the common *confounding* of anthropological and philosophical discourses (Buchowski 1993, 94). This means that an epistemological status is ascribed to anthropological statements, and vice versa. Such confusion takes place whenever one claims that a certain type of culture, e.g., scientific, renders reality in the best way, or that particular types of judgments, e.g., logical principles, have objective status. Epistemological judgments, evolved within a particular domain of culture and devised to validate procedures and statements within it, serve as an appraisal in cultural studies. And this is a cognitive evaluation applied to non-scientific domains.

What is the difference between cognitive evaluation and the modern philosophical reflections called epistemology? Cognitive evaluation does not belong to the domain of epistemology which merely represents one of the possible reflection on science as a domain of modern culture. Scientists commonly use conclusions reached within epistemology to justify their judgments beyond epistemology. This practice is routine among both relativists and rationalists. The relativists declare that every culture creates a cognition which is, in its own way, epistemologically adequate or inadequate. The universalists maintain that modern science yields an epistemologically adequate cognition. In this way cognitive evaluations serve as proofs in epistemological verdicts.

This is an erroneous stance. The explanation of cultural determinants of cognitive judgements has nothing in common with the epistemological 'meta-question' as to whether a particular cognition is epistemologically valid. It is so because epistemology deals solely with 'the rules of the game' of science, norms and directives of scientific cognition, and not with the questions of how this, or any other form of belief has been established. In other words, epistemology deals with criteria for producing scientific knowledge, whereas cognitive evaluations are made on non-epistemological grounds. It is essential for anthropologists and religious scholars to avoid forms of discourse which unconsciously oscillate between epistemology and cultural studies. It is erroneous when cultural relativists discuss epistemological problems; in this case epistemological conclusions are reached *via* cognitive evaluations. It is also erroneous when philosophers use cognitive evaluations to ground epistemological claims.

One may ask, how the issue of confounding epistemology with cultural studies is related to pragmatists' — or postmodernists' — claims that we do not need any epistemology and specific scientific method, and that there is no real difference in the nature of various forms of cognition (Rorty 1991, 63-77). These claims are only loosely related to the issue discussed. When Rorty says that we do not need epistemology, he does not mean we do not have any. Social practices have some rules of the game. The question Rorty raises is whether rules of scientific practice differ from rules in other domains of life. I can agree with several points he makes, but it does not mean that a description of the cultural determinants of the rules of 'language games' coincides with a description of the rules themselves.

The last problem produced by our discussion concerns the *scope* of rationality. To put this another way, what should we understand by rationality? Meanings attached to this concept are so divergent that many times it is difficult to find their common denominator. At this moment let us assume with Hanson (1981) that one can indicate two of them: intentional and institutional.

Intentional rationality converges with Popperian/Jarvian situational logic. It is parallel to the formal theory of rationality espoused by Jon Elster.[9] Analysis carried out in the terms of this form of rationality addresses beliefs, knowledge, values and aims of individuals in particular situations, and is prevalent in philosophy.

Institutional rationality refers directly to Hanson's implicational meaning. It is determined through consideration of relations between various social institutions — belief systems, norms and patterns of behaviour, etc. Studies on mutual ties within cultural institutions should enable us to elicit the meaning of rationality proper for a given culture. This kind of approach to rationality is prevalent in anthropology and religious studies.

The two understandings of rationality cannot be totally convergent. As Hanson (1981) noted, intentional rationality is concerned with the Popperian 'second world' of human reasons and motivations, while institutional rationality refers to the Popperian 'third world' of belief systems existing independently of the individual's consciousness. Within a philosophical paradigm one addresses the problem of the rationality of an individual in a given situation, whereas in an anthropological paradigm one is concerned with the rationality of the system of beliefs. Although the two perspectives are interdependent, the distinction between rationality of action and rationality of beliefs is clear, but this has not always been recognized.

According to universalists we can set objective criteria for both types of rationality: of actions and beliefs. Medianists, like Horton and Tambiah, hold that criteria of rationality apply in the discourse concerned only with 'objective reality'. Extreme relativists, such as postmodernists, do not bother about rationality at all, but we can say that they always particularize their stories, put them in a form of unique communication of subjects sharing and exchanging meanings.

Hanson, as a moderate relativist, holds that we should contextualize the rationality of a belief system to a given culture, and describe a rationality of actions against these beliefs. However, for cognitive reasons he seeks some kind of external grounding (universal logical principles) which would enable us to identify local criteria of rationality. Although I agree with this perspective on the research procedure itself, i.e. a necessity to discern cultural rules (implicational meanings), I cannot agree that it has to have a foothold elsewhere, in some universals. Moreover, the idea that we can figure out the criteria of rationality of beliefs, proper for a culture studied, is wrongly posed. At this very moment, as Peter Winch (1970, 86-94) convincingly showed, we impose a concept of rationality alien to the system.[10] Inevitably our criteria pop up and serve as seemingly contextualized criteria of the beliefs depicted. According to Stephen Tyler, a discourse, like a critique:

can impose no criteria that are not already domesticated within the discourse or situation it is concerned to set apart and sift through. It can judge then, only within the context it presupposes to be within the interest it shares with what it criticizes. (1991, 91)

In other words, for me the reconstruction of implicational meanings does not equal the assessment of the rationality of an alien belief system. For all these reasons, I maintain that in cultural studies we can justly characterize only the rationality of actions contextualized to the meanings, but not the 'rationality', of a given culture.

Contextualism and the rationality problem

Let me highlight my own attitude to the question of rationality in anthropology and religious studies and add some glosses. My position flows from some premises of so-called historical epistemology (Kmita 1988; 1991; 1996), the pragmatic stance in philosophy, and anthropological practice. What follows, on the one hand, comprises some points sufficient to disentangle the study of religion and anthropology from needless metaphysical snarls, and, on the other hand, mirrors something that necessarily pervades what anthropologists really do and respect.

First, a distinction should be made, more fundamental than Hanson's division of the notion of rationality into implicational and intentional. Despite the common core of the root ratio involved, rationalism as a philosophical doctrine (as opposed to empiricism), should be distinguished from rationality understood as the rational character of human beings. The philosophical theory is 'an epistemological doctrine, a normative definition stating what has, or does not have, a cognitive value', while the second meaning of rationality 'is the relationship between goals and means within the limits of available knowledge' (Kolakowski 1990, 192). Thus, rationalism in the epistemological sense entails some philosophically established criteria of rationality; rationalism in a behavioural sense does not presumes such criteria at all, but is related to the context of a culture in which an individual acts.

Second, we cannot prove in our cultural studies that objective standards of cognition exist. The modern European perspective is one among many and we cannot guarantee that science renders reality in an objective way and that scientists' statements have ontological legitimacy. Cognitive evaluations made on the assumption that scientific concepts have privileged relations with reality, or that some kind of logical principles are objectively valid, cannot serve as an argument in cultural studies. I do not think that, in Rorty's words, social scientists need to ground their statements in 'objectivity' or in 'objective reality'.

Third, there is no reason why we should retreat from intersubjective verifiability in social studies. I do not think postmodernist subjectivity offers a viable option. Hanson with his idea of implicational meanings rightly wants to avoid it, and, inter alia, de Sardan (1992) convincingly argues against empathetic 'methods' as applied in the domain of religious phenomena by, for example, Stoller and Olkes (1987). One may describe this norm of disciplinary consensus in pragmatic words as 'the desire for as much intersubjective agreement as possible' (Rorty 1991, 23). Thus, to use Rorty's term, the objectivity of anthropological findings boils down to the solidarity of a given 'interpretive community'.

At the same time anthropologists and religious scholars should take the 'humanistic coefficient' into account in their descriptions of other people's desires and beliefs, in their attempts to 'weave them together with beliefs we already have' (Rorty 1991, 26). This is one of the ways in which extremist rationalistic 'objectivism', i.e. objectivism grounded in metaphysical postulates, can be avoided.

Fourth, the premise of taking the 'subjective factor' into account can be achieved by means of *humanistic interpretation*. The objects of our analyses are undoubtedly manifold. Provided that we accept the aim of anthropological analyses postulated here, i.e. the interpretation of cultural beliefs and actions, humanistic interpretation becomes the principal object of our interest. According to its procedure, the researcher should try to reconstruct the social system of norms and directives of a given culture on the assumption of rationality. In other words, the implicational meanings should be analyzed (but not the rationality of those meanings). By referring to this system, reconstructed in an abstract way, it can be argued that one is able to carry out an analysis of the rationality of a given individual in terms of an agreement between the subjects' activities and convictions with their social 'models' or 'patterns'; the effectiveness of actions in relation to assumed goals can be determined with reference to possible alternative modes of conduct, and so on. In this way one makes a kind of concretized humanistic interpretation.

But the *assumption of rationality* is the essential element of the whole procedure of humanistic interpretation. The assumption of rationality implies, let me repeat, that every individual undertakes an activity which is guided by his/her convictions concerning the possibilities of accomplishing intended goals. These convictions consist of a hierarchy of values and knowledge concerning ways of accomplishing goals (Kmita 1971, 24-30). In other words, human beliefs consist of norms and directives.[11] Making an idealized assumption about the acts undertaken by the individual in the conditions of certainty, it can be argued that a given individual aiming at the accomplishment of a certain goal will act in a way which, according to his/her knowledge, will lead to the attainment of that goal. In other words, humanistic interpretation also involves situational logic and intentional meanings. I think that, up to this point, people on both sides of the fence can agree.

This also means that Hanson's intentional and institutional analyses are intrinsically connected. In light of all these findings the problem of rationality appears in a different perspective. Our formula of the rationality of acts refers to one of its Weberian meanings: *the consistency of actions with regard to shared convictions* (e.g., Hollis 1994, 147-151). I believe that anthropological tradition encourages us to accept this view, and nothing more can really be done in this field. The rationality of individuals acting as taught by the cultures in which they live is also a denominator common to universalists and relativists. My 'definition' is partly similar to Elster's definition of 'thin rationality' (as contrasted to 'thick rationality'):

Consistency, in fact, is what rationality in thin sense is all about: consistency within the systems of desires; and consistency between *beliefs and desires* on the one hand *and* the *action for which they are reasons* on the other. (Elster 1983, 1; emphasis added)

One may argue that this is a narrow or even banal meaning of rationality: humans always act in a way they believe they should. But I maintain that this standpoint has its justification. In Mongin's (1991, 31) words, 'Weberian "subjective rationality" should suffice for nearly all the historical or ethnological explanations'.

The ground for such a stance is evident. The most important issue contested by relativists is allegedly the ontological (objective, foundational, transcendent, transcultural, criterial) status of scientific assertions or logical rules of reasoning. The idea of science as the embodiment of rationality in every, or at least some respects, is shared by universalists and most medianists; the belief that there are logical universals is accepted by all scholars discussed. The charge that both these presumptions objectify ('transcendalize') modern European categories proves to be correct. Such a stance, as I showed, does contradict the claim that meanings are socially established. One cannot consistently say that in some domains of life relativist ideas apply, and that in others rationalist foundationalism is king.

In the field of cross-cultural studies, the anthropologists' task ends with the description of relatively strong/intentional/subjective/thin rationality. In the critique of other scholars, they should refer to current norms of internal scientific rationality. The clues for this restrained attitude can be found in anthropological tradition (cf. Firth 1985; Roth 1989; Carrithers 1992).

However, this modest view means also that not every achievement of the rationalists' tradition deserves condemnation. I would call this standpoint *rationality relativized*. And I think that transcendental, criterial rationality is a cultural creation which plays some role in the worldview of Western societies. Anthropologists and religious scholars, as members of this modern European culture, became involved in the issue and tried to contribute to the idea. But when they tried, consciously or not, to combine strongly relativistic disciplinary experience with their rationalistically permeated cultural bias, they inevitably committed some logical errors. As we have seen, they either become inconsistent, or uphold some metaphysical postulates which should not be identified in cultural studies. These postulates can be identified in the philosophy of science and applied in science.

Nevertheless, one should not throw out the notion of rationality, as postmodernists encourage us to do. We do not have to, or to be more precise, we *cannot* desist from the notion of rationality as such. In the mold presented above, the assumption of rationality of acting humans comprises an axiom which is necessary for any research of culture. If we do not presume that humans act rationally we will not be able to describe and to understand their behaviour, even in terms of situational logic. We will be unable not only to figure out the actions of members of other cultures, but also people from our own community. The conduct of other people will appear totally incomprehensible, not to mention unpredictable. Social life would be impossible. I do not claim, of course, that participants of any culture need to consciously assume this kind of rationality. However, it is implicit in the process of interpersonal communication, coexistence of individuals and groups, social practice as a whole. And this is a *cognitive and epistemological* aspect of the issue. But there is also a *moral* one, which, after all, concerns all anthropologists, particularly postmodernists. The assumption of rationality enables us to treat other people as equally reasonable. It is the starting point of any understanding and interpretation.

One may ask at this point, what is it about human emotions which, traditionally, in Western culture, have been treated as contrary to reason (cf. Solomon 1992). My answer is that there is no contradiction between rationality and emotion. Emotions related to caring for, let us say family, religion or sex, for satisfying one's desires, are culturally resolved as well. It is culture which teaches us what we should care about and how. Culture equips us with goals and instructs us how to achieve them. It is an entirely historical coincidence whether, say, the prescribed way of communicating with deities is through ecstatic shamanistic ritual or solitary, silent deliberation. Either way is rational for the people who think this is the best way to approach the sacred. Within the framework of my discourse it is not important whether emotions, like ways of reasoning, are humanly universal; they may or may not be. It is enough to conclude that they too are conditioned by cultural norms, and as such can be studied and made comprehensible. This Durkheimian view of culture allows us also to grasp idiosyncratic behaviours. Even eccentrics follow some patterns of conduct and our attitude to them is defined by social norms. Finally, one may ask about deviant behaviours in a given culture. Let us note that psychiatrists describe and explain them according to criteria that are 'already domesticated', i.e. in terms of deviation from social norm or from behaviour regarded by them as rational.

This is, I think, what underlies ethnographic encounters whether we articulate it or not. Individuals' behaviour is placed in a cultural setting. By token of rational acts contextualized within a given culture, we return to the dialectic of institutional and intentional analyses. And this limited notion of rationality is, in fact, accepted by both rationalists and relativists.[12] 'Universally' valid, the non-transcendent but transcultural notion of rationality is relativized historically within a cultural context. But this kind of 'metaphysical' justification does not have to be expressed explicitly by scholars. What is at stake is a pragmatic challenge of cross-cultural translation, comprehension and mutual enrichment. This is what anthropologists and religious scholars promote independently of how their efforts are interpreted, e.g. in terms of the debate between universalists and particularists.

Some scholars may claim that this is a mainly descriptive project of cultural and religious studies. It may appear as too modest and not challenging enough. Explanation and understanding is limited to the analysis of situational logic. One may want to criticize others, and ask, let us say, whether we shall not disparage a tyrant who is very effective in achieving his/her horrible goals and, thus, rational within a given cultural context. My answer is as follows: of course we can, or even should, criticize behaviour which we, after critical reflection, consider condemnable. And as a matter of fact, we do it all the time. Nevertheless, this is an ethical evaluation carried out in terms of our own moral standards. This issue goes beyond the question of the rationality of actions and is yet another story.

Notes

1. I would like to thank F. Allan Hanson, Jerzy Kmita and Richard Rorty for their comments on the first draft of this paper. The project on the rationality problem in anthropology and philosophy was supported by the Kosciuszko Foundation

while I was at the University of Kansas in Lawrence. The final version of this paper was prepared when I was an Alexander von Humboldt Foundation Scholar at the Humboldt University in Berlin.

2. I think that these terms describe the division more adequately because, as it turns out, none of the adherents of either attitude denies some degree of variously defined rationality of individuals or cultures. The whole controversy seems to revolve, at least in anthropologically tinted theories, around the universalistic or particularistic character of the rationality criteria.

3. Sperber (1985, 44) put it plainly: 'Cross-cultural psychology is generally not relativist.' Donald E. Brown (1991), formerly a staunch relativist, advocates the idea of human universals which underlie the surface of human diversity.

4. John Skorupski (1976) provides a very accurate analysis of the philosophical backgrounds of both traditions and of "literalism".

5. For a relativist's critique of Jarvie's book see Hanson 1986.

6. I only discuss here issues pertinent to my criticism. Besides the two types described, Jarvie and Agassi distinguish also weak rationality, i.e. rationality of action as explained by given goals. This is, I think, an empty notion since one cannot evaluate an individual's rationality without taking into account his or her beliefs.

7. For my critique of Gellner see Buchowski 1994.

8. For my critique of Horton see Buchowski 1995.

9. 'The *thin theory* of rationality explains action by reasons — beliefs and desires — the content of which it does not examine.' (Elster 1983, 1).

10. Let me recall that in his discussion on Evans-Pritchard's study on the Azande, Winch (1970,93) writes: 'Azande notions of witchcraft do not constitute a theoretical system in terms of which Azande try to gain quasi-scientific understanding of the world. [...] the forms in which rationality expresses itself in the culture of a human society cannot be elucidated *simply* in terms of logical coherence of the rules according to which activities are carried out in that society.' (emphasis in original)

11. We have to point out that this assumption of rationality can be fully applied only to post-traditional, conventional — in Habermas' (1973) terminology — societies in which knowledge and values are distinguished. In the case of societies presenting a religious form of consciousness only a very generalized version of this assumption can be utilized — the version referring to the consistency of individuals' acts and shared beliefs. A recognition of the status of the assumption of rationality in different types of societies, and an awareness of its limitations in various cultural situations are crucial, because it is not in all cultures that knowledge and values, or norms and directives, are differentiated. For more details on this see Buchowski 1990, 190-95.

12. For example, Beattie (1970, 247) writes that 'part of the fieldworker's task is to record the goals which people seek by means of their rites.' In other words, he accepts that an assumption of 'relatively strong rationality' is a *sine qua non* of anthropological practice.

Lévy-Bruhl, Participation, and Rationality

Benson Saler

Our concern with rationality in the study of religion invites a number of questions about 'rationality.'

First, What do we — or what should we — mean by 'rationality'? That question is obvious, and easy to frame. But it is not easy (or perhaps even possible) to find a simple answer to it that all scholars of religion would accept. Some persons, for example, prefer to identify rationality with conformance to the fundaments of standard (two-valued) Western logic: Identity (A is A), Excluded Middle (either A or not-A), and Non-Contradiction (not both A and not-A). Others, while not necessarily abjuring the formalisms of Western logic, are inclined to stress pragmatic instrumentality, whereby rationality is to be judged in terms of the selection of appropriate means to accomplish recognized ends. And still other persons may be given to emphasizing other possibilities. These include various kinds of posited coherences among human activities or between human activities and other things, and sweeping normative or prescriptive assertions to the effect that rational beliefs are those that we ought to hold and rational acts are those that we ought to perform.

Postmodernists, however, suggest a rethinking of the question. They generally maintain that criteria of rationality are largely or entirely cultural formulations, and that transcendental standards of rationality proffered by different theorists either cannot be supported or are so abstract as to be vacuous unless they are culturally situated and coloured.

A second question about rationality to be considered here is this: what tends to be associated with our understandings of rationality? That question is not as obvious as the first, and it is in greater need of explication. To reframe it: if we operate with some understanding of rationality, what other understandings might accompany that understanding?

Lévi-Straussian structuralists have sensitized us to 'homologies of thought.' We are prepared, in consequence, to countenance the possibility that in Western discourses each member of the paired distinction 'rationality/irrationality' may be associated with discrete members of other paired distinctions.

Deconstructionists, moreover, have alerted us to the probability that in expressing paired distinctions, the first expressed member of each pair is likely to be privileged over the second. Participants in a discourse, furthermore, may not always realize that they tend to commit themselves to preferences or biases by committing themselves to conventional expressions of distinctions.

In the English-speaking community to which I belong, for example, one normally says 'rationality and irrationality' rather than 'irrationality and rationality.' And one normally says 'thought and emotion' rather than 'emotion and thought,' and 'thought and action' rather than 'action and thought.' Catherine Bell (1992) calls our attention to the role played by the privileging of thought over action in theorizing about religion, and we would do well to consider the possible consequences of the other two examples just given.

In this paper I explore the two questions posed above — what might we mean by rationality?, and what tends to be associated with our talk about rationality? — by relating them to the theorizing of Lucien Lévy-Bruhl (1857-1939) respecting so-called 'primitive mentality.' That French scholar played an influential role in supporting and disseminating the idea that there are distinct modes of thought among the peoples of the world.

Lévy-Bruhl held that the members of some small-scale, nonliterate societies can be characterized as operating with a distinctive mind-set, one that differs significantly in rationality from that found in what he broadly thought of as modern Western civilization. Among the most salient features of that mentality, he supposed, are an unconcern for, or veritable indifference to, 'contradictions'(which he eventually modified in his final writings to a tolerance for physical impossibilities rather than logical contradictions); an absorption in the 'mystical', by which he meant a realized disposition to suppose that the world is filled with powers and entities that are not usually accessible in any direct way to normal human vision, hearing, or other senses (albeit 'primitive' peoples may find what they take to be evidence for the existence and activities of suprasensible realities, including what might be remembered of dreams); and a certain marriage of what we call the cognitive and the affective in which the latter is much the dominant spouse, so that many of the ideas of so-called primitives are more felt than thought.

Lévy-Bruhl: Myth and Reality

When I was in graduate school, there was a popular legend — or, if you will accept the term, a popular myth — about Lévy-Bruhl that was recited around academic campfires to hordes of note-taking anthropology students.

According to that narrative, Lévy-Bruhl published six imaginative but flawed books on the mentality of so-called primitive peoples between 1910 and his death in 1939. Those works, it was alleged, challenged widely held (if somewhat variegated) anthropological opinions about the 'psychic unity' of humankind. The substance of that challenge, the myth continued, was evaluated and refuted by numbers of anthropologists, including such masterful fieldworkers as Bronislaw Malinowski and Edward E. Evans-Pritchard, who knew 'primitive' peoples at first hand. In consequence of their criticisms, it was claimed, Lévy-Bruhl came to see the errors of his theories, and he more or less recanted them. In eleven posthumously published notebooks, he abjured much of what he had previously affirmed, thus drawing closer to, if not actually endorsing, opinions widely held by anthropologists.

This inspiring story pleased me and many of my fellow graduate students. It helped to rescue so-called primitive peoples from seeming inferiority. It drove home the importance of ethnographic fieldwork, for which most of us were then preparing, as antidote to armchair theorizing. And it resonated strongly with an ancient and powerful parable in Western traditions, that of the Prodigal Son (see, for example, *Luke* 15).

The Lucien Lévy-Bruhl of the myth that I encountered as a graduate student was, in effect, anthropology's adopted prodigal son, worthy of a fatted calf because of his posthumously published recantation. But while it is the case that he altered his views in the *Notebooks*, the scope and significance of the changes entered were greatly exaggerated. As Robin Horton points out, what Lévy-Bruhl:

retains is more significant than what he withdraws. Thus, although his final picture of primitive thought allows a good deal of common sense in alongside the mystical, and although his final picture of modern thought allows a good deal of the mystical in alongside common sense, his characterization of the mystical remains unrepentantly the same. (Horton 1973, 257-258)

Horton (1973, 258, n.1) adds that the greater part of the *Notebooks* 'is taken up, not with recantation but with clarification and development of the two key concepts' that Lévy-Bruhl advanced in his first book on primitive mentality in 1910: mystical orientation and participation.

In my reading of Lévy-Bruhl's works on 'primitive mentality,' the views that he expressed in 1910 are continually under his own critical review in the succeeding years. He elaborates on some, modifies others, and eventually withdraws still others.

Thus in the *Notebooks*, Lévy-Bruhl caps more than twenty years of retrenching from the notion of 'prelogical mentality, (1975 [1949], 39, 47) by finally abandoning it as 'a badly founded hypothesis' (1975 [1949], 47). He does so for several reasons: 'prelogical' had confused or distracted many of his readers; it was a crude way of pointing to something that can be better explicated as the expression of a 'mystical orientation'; and, as his critics had suggested, it lacked balance in characterizing the socially formulated mentations of 'primitive' peoples. Indeed, in the *Notebooks* he acknowledges that such peoples 'no more support a formal contradiction than we do,' but that while they reject what is *logically* impossible, they do not reject what is physically impossible (1975 [1949], 62), and they are relatively tolerant of 'incompatibilities.'

Lévy-Bruhl's final abandonment of the notion of a clearly marked and crucial distinction in *logic* between modes of thought is perhaps the most important retrenchment in the *Notebooks*. Lévy-Bruhl disavows a difference in mentalities — and hence in rationalities — based on formal differences in logic. It is worth quoting him on that point:

I no longer speak of a prelogical character of the primitive mentality, even when clarifying the misunderstandings which this term has occasioned. From the strictly logical point of view no essential difference has been established between the primitive mentality and ours. In everything that touches on ordinary, everyday experience, transactions of all sorts, political and economic life, counting, etc., they behave in a way which involves the same usage of their facilities as we make of ours. (1975 [1949], 55)

In the *Notebooks*, moreover, while Lévy-Bruhl makes extensive use of 'the affective category of the supernatural,' a construct that he had made the subject of his fourth book, *Le Surnaturel et la nature dans la mentalité primitive* (1931), in one section he appears to drop it. (The *Notebooks*, we need to remind ourselves, are not a book, and inconsistencies in them might have been eliminated or otherwise resolved had they been turned into a book by their author.) In any case, Lévy-Bruhl affirms in one section (1975 [1949], 106) that he no longer needs 'the affective category of the supernatural' because his mature understanding of participation now renders it unnecessary. 'The affective category of the supernatural,' he writes in the *Notebooks*, 'is participation' (*ibid.*).[1]

In the *Notebooks*, indeed, Lévy-Bruhl virtually exults in a more profound understanding of participation. He abandons what he once called 'The Law of Participation', but he affirms strongly that 'What exists is the *fact* (not the law) that "primitive man" very often has the feeling of participation' between himself and other objects, so that at one and the same time he may be both a human being and something else. No less frequently, Lévy-Bruhl maintains, primitive man 'imagines similar participations' between other objects (1975 [1949], 61).

Different commentators trace the development of Lévy-Bruhl's thought in different ways, depending on what they find especially interesting. Maurice Leenhardt, for example, sees 'a great gap' between the first book and the sixth, *L'Expérience mystique et les symboles chez les primitifs* (1937), in which, Leenhardt opines, Lévy-Bruhl 'qualifies endlessly' (1975, xiv).

Robin Horton (1973, 256-7), however, groups together the sixth book and the *Notebooks* because they both respond positively to a major criticism voiced by anthropological fieldworkers. Lévy-Bruhl, some complained, had slighted common-sensical thought among 'primitives', and had characterized such peoples as more absorbed with the mystical than is actually the case. 'Mystical', as Lévy-Bruhl describes it in his first book, 'implies belief in forces and influences and actions which, though imperceptible to sense, are nevertheless real to "primitive" peoples' (1985 [1910], 38). In the sixth book and in the *Notebooks* Lévy-Bruhl accepts the criticism of ethnographers, and he takes pains to present 'primitive' thought as oscillating between the common-sensical and the mystical.

Jean Cazeneuve separates the first three books from the last three because the fourth book, *Le surnaturel et la nature* (1931), advances some important refinements and qualifications of the earlier theories. In the early works, Cazeneuve remarks, the matter of differences in mentality was posed 'in terms of logic', and 'at the very least the hypothesis of different mental habits was adduced' (1972 [1963], 22). Lévy-Bruhl, in describing 'primitive mentality' as 'prelogical' had not meant that it was illogical or irrational, but, rather, alogical and non-rational. Prelogical, as he himself characterizes it in his first book, is preeminently a mentality that 'does not bind itself down, as our thought does, to avoiding contradiction' (1985 [1910], 78). But in his later works, Cazeneuve writes:

The discovery of the affective category [of the supernatural] even modifies the way of problematizing 'primitive mentality'. The description of archaic mentality is no longer so much that of specific characteristics of the mind, constituent or acquired, *as that of the role of affectivity in thought.* (1972 [1963], 22, emphasis added)

Lévy-Bruhl himself, we might note, groups together the last two books because he opines that their treatment of participation marks a more sophisticated stage in the development of his theorizing than the earlier works (1975 [1949], 108-109).

In what follows, I try to clarify certain aspects of what Lévy-Bruhl came to understand by participation, and to connect those understandings to our interests in rationality in the study of religion. While Lévy-Bruhl's theories have been deservedly criticised over the years, we continue to refer to them. We do so, I think, for two major reasons. First, Lévy-Bruhl played an important role in establishing questions about modes of thought, questions that we continue to address. Second, some of Lévy-Bruhl's claims resonate with later findings. I will point to such a resonance by referring to some of the work of two contemporary anthropologists, the Norwegian Unni Wikan, and the North American Catherine Lutz. I relate their understandings to Cazeneuve's important remark about Lévy-Bruhl's shift of emphasis from 'specific characteristics of the mind', as exemplified by the notion of 'prelogical mentality', to 'the role of affectivity in thought', as exemplified by a more profound conceptualization of 'participation'.

Participation

'Participation' is an ancient construct in Western philosophy and theology, where it is often conceptualized as an ontological function invoked in efforts to answer two broadly posed questions: What is the justification for grouping different individual objects together into one *genus* or class? And how do we account for the fact that the things of our experience exist and manifest the qualities that they apparently do? 'Participation', Charles Bigger writes, 'is the name of the "relation" which accounts for the togetherness of elements of diverse ontological type in the essential unity of a single instance' (1968, 7). And Durkheim remarks that 'Today, as formerly, to explain is to show how one thing participates in one or several others' (1965 [1912], 270).

The Plato of the Middle Dialogues held that when a multiplicity of individuals are conceived as constituting a *genus* or class by virtue of some common attribute, that attribute exists independently in perfection in a superior realm, that of the things that are (τὰ ὄντα), the realm of Being. The realm of Being consists of the transcendent Forms or Ideas. They can be apprehended only by the mind, and they are incorporeal, unchanging, and eternal. Another realm, that of the things that become (τὰ γιγνόμενα), the realm of Becoming, is the inferior realm of the sensibles, the particulars of our experience. They are apprehended by the senses, and they are finite, mutable, contingent, and dependent.

Participation relates these two realms. The relationship, however, is asymmetrical. The sensibles, the entities of the realm of Becoming, exist and have their apparent qualities because they participate, if only for a brief time, in the realm of Being, the realm of the intelligibles. And the realm of Being exists independently; it does not presuppose the realm of Becoming. If we deem a flower beautiful, it is because it participates fleetingly in Absolute Beauty. And although our flower will fade and wither, the Idea of Beauty will remain.

While Plato modified his views in later works, thus giving grounds for the quip that Plato was the first Neoplatonist, the ontology of Forms of the Middle Dialogues and the ontological function of participation were invoked in later traditions, both in philosophy and in theology. Various Christian writers, for example, identified God the Creator with Being and creation with Becoming, and they explained the continuing existence of the latter by positing its continuing participation in the former.

Participation figured into the debate that occupied the Council of Nicaea in 325. Alan Kolp (1975, 101), indeed, remarks that 'Without noting it the Arian controversy is a struggle over the correct use of Platonic philosophical categories'. Thus while Alexander and Athanasius maintained that the Son is God by nature rather than by participation, 'true God from true God', Arius denied it. He is charged with claiming that although the Son be called God, he 'is not truly so (οὐκ ἀληθινός ἐστιν), *but by participation of grace* (ἀλλὰ μετοχῇ χάριτος), he, as others, is God only in name' (Athanasius, *Orations Against the Arians* 6 [PG 26, 21-24], emphasis added).

Other examples of such Platonic uses of participation could be cited. And, to be sure, various divergences from Platonic formulations by mystics and others can be noted. Mainstream Western philosophy and theology nevertheless maintained certain core uses. But these differ in important respects from the participation that Lévy-Bruhl attributes to so-called primitive peoples.

First, in mainstream Western traditions, one normally forms representations of two or more distinct things or elements, and then one posits a participation between them. But according to Lévy-Bruhl, this is not what happens among 'primitives'. For such people, he tells us, participation 'does not come after these representations, it does not presuppose them; it is before them, or at least simultaneous with them. What is given *in the first place* is participation' (1975 [1949], 2). For the 'primitives', he goes on to claim, what is given is a complex, not elements between which one may come to see relations.

Second, in mainstream Western traditions there is always a recognized difference, and often an explicitly attributed inequality, between participating things. This crucial awareness of difference is put succinctly by Justin in his *Dialogue with Trypho* (6 [PG6, 489]): 'that which partakes of anything is different from that of which it partakes'. But 'primitive man', according to Lévy-Bruhl, 'feels...a participation that forms for him a duality-unity of which, *first and foremost*, he feels the unity' (1975 [1949], 4).

Third, in mainstream Western philosophical and theological traditions, efforts are made to put participation on a rational footing. That is, at a minimum, analytical distinctions are specified among elements, and such conceptual exercises are often implicitly or explicitly related to, just as they are requisite for, attentions to the fundaments of standard logic. And even where certain of the details of posited participations are so exceptional as to escape the normal limitations imposed by what we deem the logical and the rational — as, for example, in the case of Cyril of Alexandria's doctrine of *communicatio idiomatum*, whereby predicates pertaining to each of Christ's two participating natures apply to the other — efforts are typically made to explain exceptions in such a way as to preserve the structure of rationality that they might otherwise subvert. But in 'primitive mentality', according to Lévy-Bruhl, concerns for rationality, and even considerations that we would enter respecting conceptualization, symbolization, and experience, are of little or no consequence. Participation, he writes, 'is not represented but felt' (1975 [1949], 158).

That point of view, reaffirmed in the *Notebooks*, is put in an interesting way in the 1910 book. In a concluding chapter entitled 'The Transition to the Higher Mental Types', Lévy-Bruhl maintains that among such peoples as the Arunta and the Bororo, where participations are directly felt, all life might be said to be 'religious', and yet we do not really find what we understand by 'religion'. He writes:

Our own way of thinking makes us imagine the objects of their thought in the attitude of divine beings or objects, and that it is by virtue of this divine character of theirs that homage, sacrifice, prayer, adoration and all actual religious belief is directed towards them. But to the primitive mind, on the contrary, these objects and these beings become divine only when the participation they guarantee has ceased to be direct. The Arunta who feels that he *is* both himself and the ancestor whose *churinga* was entrusted to him at the time of his initiation, knows nothing of ancestor-worship. (1985 [1910], 367-8)

With the development of individual consciousness prompted by changes in social institutions, Lévy-Bruhl supposes, mentality becomes more sensitive to experience, collective representations become truly cognitive, and participations, now realized rather than directly felt, become ideological. It is among peoples such as the Huichol, Zuñi, and Maori, who have made such a transition, Lévy-Bruhl claims, that we find such things as ancestor-worship, hero cults, gods, sacred animals, and so forth. 'The ideas which we call really religious', Lévy-Bruhl opines, 'are thus a kind of differentiated product resulting from a prior form of mental activity' (1985 [1910], 368).

Affectivity in Thought

Jean Cazeneuve (1972 [1963], 14) opines that 'Lévy-Bruhl brings an important modification into philosophy which, since Aristotle, has limited categories of thought to the intellect, disregarding whatever comes from affectivity.'

While this statement may be somewhat overblown, it does call our attention to possibilities beyond the conventional reach of traditional Western theories about 'categories of thought' and related matters of 'rationality'.

It has long been a convention in Western traditions to distinguish between thought and emotion. While both thoughts and emotions are viewed as similar in some respects — both, for instance, are thought of as private until expressed — they are for the most part distinguished, and Western languages normally include well established vocabularies for doing so.

This occasioned some difficulty for Lévy-Bruhl in his attempts to conceptualize, and to convey to us, what he deemed distinctive of the so-called primitive mentality. Thus in the 1910 book he tells us that the collective representations of 'primitive' peoples are not really representations as we understand them. That is because our classificatory system distinguishes between the 'emotional', the 'motor', and the 'intellectual', and we place 'representation' in the last category. But representations for the 'primitives' are more complex affairs, 'in which', he writes:

what is really "representation" to us is found blended with other elements of an emotional or motor character, coloured and imbued by them, and therefore implying a different attitude with regard to the objects represented. (1985 [1910]: 35-36)

However critical we may be of some of the things that Lévy-Bruhl claims, I think it fair to say that in these passages he prefigures some contemporary anthropological findings. Ethnopsychological research — that is, the systematic exploration of the psychological theories and classifications of diverse peoples — demonstrates that at least some non-Western peoples do not make the distinctions that we do between the cognitive and the affective. Rather, like Lévy-Bruhl, and to borrow an expression penned by Cazeneuve, they make great allowance for 'the role of affectivity in thought.' Unni

Wikan, for example, reports that the:

Balinese regard feeling, thought, will, and desire as inextricably linked, truly one concept. In their native language they do not distinguish among them; all are summed up in the concept *keneh*. (1990, 95)

Wikan glosses *keneh* 'feeling-thought'. She remarks, moreover, that 'Balinese laugh when they hear that some Westerners regard feeling as "irrational"' (1990,36). Catherine Lutz reports something similar for the Ifaluk, a Micronesian people. She writes:

At the core of Ifaluk ethnopsychology is a set of beliefs about the structure of persons which portrays them as basically undivided entities. In marked contrast to Western ethnopsychology, sharp distinctions are not made between thought and emotion, between the head and the heart, or between a conscious and an unconscious mind. (1988, 91)

Wikan and Lutz are among a growing number of anthropologists now studying emotions in novel and promising ways. Many of them suppose, as does Lutz, that:

concepts of emotions can more profitably be viewed as serving complex communicative, moral, and cultural purposes rather than [be viewed] simply as labels for internal states whose nature or essence is presumed to be universal. (Lutz 1988, 5)

Viewing emotion as, in Lutz's words (1988, 5), 'an emergent product of social life,' they focus on how people talk about emotions, how discourse constitutes emotions as social objects, and how people employ or deploy emotions in social interactions. This orientation is part of a larger orientation, one that marks a shift from an emphasis on language as semantics to an emphasis on language as social action (Lutz 1988, 8). Among other things, it assigns hermeneutical functions to emotions, whereby emotions are viewed, in part, as interpretations that people put on situations.

These newer orientations, while often offered as correctives to narrow conceptualizations of the emotions as essentially precultural, psychobiological phenomena, do not always incorporate well informed distinctions between Western folk theories of the emotions and Western scientific understandings. The latter are decidedly more complex and nuanced than the former. Charles Darwin (1872), for example, deemed learning to be of great importance for expression of the emotions, and scientists who followed after him widened and deepened his insight as well as going beyond it in various ways.

Members of the more traditional scientific community (e.g., Spiro 1984; n.d.) have offered thoughtful and informed criticisms of some constructivist claims about the emotions, and a healthy debate has ensued. But in attending here to the question of what we might mean by rationality, particularly in the light of other understandings that often accompany widespread notions of rationality, studies of Western folk discourses about the emotions seem relevant.

In analyzing Ifaluk folk theory about emotions, Lutz compares it to a broadly conceptualized Euro-American or Western folk theory. Not only does the Western theory tend to associate thought with rationality, and emotion with irrationality, but it loads thought and emotion — and rationality and irrationality — with other associations as well. Focusing on emotion, Lutz describes this contrast set:

Emotion is to thought as energy is to information, heart is to head, the irrational is to the rational, preference is to inference, impulse is to intention, vulnerability is to control and chaos is to order. Emotion is to thought as knowing something is good is to knowing something is true, that is, as value is to fact or knowledge, the relatively unconscious is to the relatively conscious, the subjective is to the objective, the physical is to the mental, the natural is to the cultural, the expressive is to the instrumental or practical, the morally suspect is to the ethically mature, the lower classes are to the upper, the child is to the adult, and the female is to the male. (1988, 56-57)

Lutz also describes another Western contrast set, one that puts a higher valuation on the emotions. It values emotion as 'the seat of the true and glorified self' (1988, 56), and as standing 'against estrangement or disengagement' (1988, 57). There are thus two folk contrast sets regarding emotions in the West, and they speak to an ambivalence in Western discourse about emotion, and a perdurable cultural paradox respecting the place of thought and emotion and, *inter alia*, rationality and irrationality, in Western life.

Exploring Affectivity

In his final reflections in the *Notebooks*, Lévy-Bruhl attempts to clarify his earlier claims that the 'primitive mentality...is not conceptual like ours' by affirming that at one and the same time it is both conceptual and affective (1975 [1949], 127-128), though he continues to emphasize its affectivity. And he insists that he has long believed that although a mystical mentality 'is more marked and more easily observable among "primitive peoples" than in our own societies', it is nevertheless *present in every human mind* (1975 [1949], 101, emphasis added).

Despite what some of us might regard as overstated or unnuanced formulations, Lévy-Bruhl begins to suggest the resolution of an old problem. Examining the affirmations of so-called primitives solely in cognitive or intellectual terms tends to nurture questions such as these: Why do 'primitive' peoples seem to affirm seemingly irrational beliefs? Why, indeed, do they not test their beliefs against evidence or subject them to reasoned analysis? These can prove to be invidious questions, for they may well suggest a sharp divide between 'us' and 'them' — to the detriment of 'them', to be sure, but perhaps also conducing to a unidimensional (and therefore misleading) consideration of 'us'. To the extent, moreover, that we dwell on the presumed falseness and irrationality of beliefs, we may sometimes loose sight of more interesting avenues of research. For the sociologists of knowledge, Barnes and Bloor (1982, 23) advise that inquiries into *why* something is 'believed' may prove more rewarding than a focus on whether or not the purported belief is true.

Lévy-Bruhl's efforts to transcend the gratuitously invidious take this form: he begins by affirming that the beliefs of 'primitive' peoples are largely social. They are, or they crucially pivot on, 'collective representations'. And collective representations among 'primitives', he affirms, should not be thought of as primarily intellectual. Rather, they are in great degree affective. As such, they answer to the emotional needs of those who affirm them. Since, moreover, Lévy-Bruhl claims that a mystical mentality is 'present in every human mind', he suggests that *our* thought, too, is sometimes coloured by affectivity. If we accept his suggestion, we may conclude that a purely intellectualist approach to our thought would also be inadequate. As Spiro (1984, 338) suggests, 'Many apparently arbitrary cultural propositions make sense in terms of emotion'.

The obvious and immediate conclusion to be drawn is that scholars should attempt to explore the *affective* as well as cognitive significance of beliefs for those who affirm them. For brevity of exposition I pose the matter in terms of the still regnant categorical distinction between cognition and affectivity, although we have increasing reason to suppose that the border between those analytical domains is unstable or fuzzy. Such exploration would include, to the extent possible, the probing of experiences and ideas associated with statements that we take to be statements of belief, for those experiences and ideas are contextualizing and so affect how the affirmers understand — and respond to — their affirmations.

The study of affect, to be sure, is extremely difficult. Many suggest that sympathy and empathy are important, on the supposition that emotions are precultural and universal, and that we can come to recognize the emotional expressions of others on the basis of their similarities to our own. But putting aside the question of the universality of emotions, ethnographic and psychological testimony strongly suggests that the *expression* (and, indeed, *control* or *repression*) of emotions relates to cultural considerations and individual variables. While monitored and judicious empathy and sympathy can sometimes be useful in research, more is clearly required.

Insofar as the cultural exploration of affect is concerned, efforts should be made to learn local category terms for emotions and local cultural theories about their nature and expression. While it will prove as difficult to be certain about how a given individual may actually feel as it is to be certain about what that individual 'really believes', we can have more confidence in our abilities to determine what people say about feelings and the expression and experience of them in different circumstances. Further, case studies, to the extent that such can be made, will be useful. One technique, by way of an ethnographic example, is to ask different informants to analyze some social transaction with respect to the possible deployment and probable experiences of emotions; while there is no guarantee that informants will be accurate, there is a good likelihood that what they say will prove culturally informative.

The above relates to what I deem a potentially rewarding set of methodological strategies and tactics for exploring the affective significance of cultural propositions. But now we might ask what larger lesson respecting *our overall scholarly perspective* on the study of religions might be drawn from Lévy-Bruhl's insights about the role of affectivity in thought. That question becomes even more intriguing when we couple it with a growing recognition that talk about 'rationality' is likely to be freighted with the baggage of multiple homologies.

Rationality, Reflexivity, and Experience

The 'modes of thought' problem addressed by Lévy-Bruhl was inspired in large measure by reports of seemingly odd 'beliefs': that, for example, some individuals can be in two places at the same time, that rain dances bring rain, that certain people are both human beings and parrots, that the sun is a white cockatoo, and that while a cucumber can be an ox, an ox is never a cucumber.

A question was raised about the rational status of such assertions. Like the first question about rationality that introduces this paper, that question was an obvious and easy one for Western scholars to pose, yet difficult for them to answer in a manner that inspired wide agreement. Some attempts at answering are iterated or reiterated in three widely known anthologies edited, respectively, by Bryan Wilson (1970), by Robin Horton and Ruth Finnegan (1973), and by Martin Hollis and Steven Lukes (1982). But there are other attempts also. These include (but are not limited to) the so-called paleologic of Ernst von Domarus (1954) and Silvano Arieti (1974),[2] David E. Cooper's (1975) invocation of the tri-valued logic of Jan Lukasiewicz,[3] C.R. Hallpike's (1979) appropriation of Piaget's schema of cognitive developmental stages,[4] Richard Shweder's (1977) essay on the wide distribution of 'magical thinking'[5] and the classicist G.E.R. Lloyd's book, *Demystifying Mentalities* (1990).[6]

The wide fan of interpretations advocated in those sources testifies to a lack of scholarly consensus about the rational status and significance of many expressions of conviction and other behaviours among the peoples of the world. But that has had some positive consequences. Awareness of the lack of consensus has been one of several factors prompting some of us to develop greater sensitivity to the roles that our own categories and discourses play in attending to the world. And as we have become reflexively aware of our hitherto unrecognized commitments, commitments disposed and supported by those same categories and discourses, many of us have sought to transcend their limitations.

Current anthropological thinking about the socio-cultural roles, including the hermeneutical functions, of the emotions, is an example of such efforts at transcendence. In rethinking the matter of emotions, indeed, some anthropologists have not only begun to reconceptualize the category, in an effort to understand 'emotion' in novel ways, but to recognize and reflect critically on the categories and assumptions that tend to be conventionally associated with more traditional understandings of affectivity and cognition. This has not only promoted significant alterations in their views, resulting, for example, in a blurring of traditional boundaries between 'thought' and 'emotion', but it has made them all the more aware of intellectual options. Partially in consequence of the observations of their critics, indeed, they have become increasingly aware of some of the consequences of choosing to attend to the world through a set of emerging categories as compared to adhering to more traditional alternatives.

There is a wider lesson to be drawn from this respecting reflexivity and the matter of rationality in the study of religion. The philosopher Theodore Schatzki (1995, 154) characterizes reflexivity in terms of 'self-knowledge, openness to self-criticism and change, and dialogue'. These are qualities that he chooses to view as constitutive of objectivity and as hallmarks of rationality in intellectual practices. They ought to be, I believe, of crucial importance for our concern with rationality in the scholarly study of religion.

Rationality, as I prefer to conceptualize it with specific reference to scholars, is not the property of one theoretical or methodological approach as contrasted to some other. Rather, it is expressed above all in our critical monitoring of what we do and in our willingness to make serious efforts to understand and evaluate alternative possibilities. Rationality in that sense is realized in the actualized conjoining of open-mindedness with critical dispositions in the pursuit of knowledge. And in pursuing knowledge, a rational humility suggests that we acknowledge that what we offer the world are knowledge-claims rather than fixed and eternal verities. In pursuing knowledge, moreover, the exposure and elimination of error in standing knowledge-claims are at least as important as the formulation of novel claims.

Rational intellectual practices require us, in my opinion, to acknowledge that there is a world that exists independently of the self. We might well endorse a long-standing claim: that when we close our eyes in sleep, the world does not disappear. And just as we sometimes test our claims about the world, so, too, in a manner of speaking, does the world test us (and sometimes awards us flunking grades, as when we seek to transcend with inadequate means its physical realities).

But while there is a vast world that exists independently of the self, our *access* to that world is inevitably mediated by our categories and by our sensitivities and insensitivities. We cannot understand the world in any profundity or sophistication, nor can we convey our understandings to our fellows, outside of language. And language, semioticians cogently argue, is incapable of full transparency. At the very least:

in any rule-governed sign system arbitrariness, the principle that expressive vehicles are not formally determined by the meanings they stand for, is constrained by systemic motivation, the principle that meaning combinations are predictable from sign combinations (regular grammatical proportionality, for example). As a result, no sign system can be internally cohesive and still be transparent to the meanings it is created to express. (Parmentier 1985, 372)

Some might nevertheless suppose that experience, when coolly considered, could provide the touchstone for an objective overview, one that offers the possibility of transcending the colourations of culture and their encodings in language. There are, I believe, serious arguments against such a view. Given the subject matter of this essay, however, it must suffice to consider only one such argument here: that of Lucien Lévy-Bruhl.

In his sixth book, *L' Expérience mystique*, Lévy-Bruhl considers the question of why so-called 'primitives' might impress Euro-American observers as sometimes taking for 'experience' what we identify as 'belief'. This, he remarks, is partially explainable 'by the ambiguity inherent in the use of the terms "belief" and "experience"' (1938, 125). While the distinction between them seems clear to us, it is nevertheless a convention 'gradually acquired by our psychology and our theory of knowledge', and it thus bears 'the mark of our civilization.' To impose it on the study of 'primitive mentality', he adds, is to make of it 'a cause of hinderance and a source of errors'. To do so, indeed, is to suppose imprudently that there is 'a definition of experience that is uniquely and universally valid' (*ibid*).

Rodney Needham appreciates the importance of Lévy-Bruhl's point. He explicates it as suggesting that:

The concept of experience, which is commonly treated as though it denoted a constant possibility of apprehension and a permanent background to the varieties of categorical thought, is itself an idiocratic and problematical construct'. (1972, 171-72)

That is, it is a complex concept for us, and it is 'not a neutral and undifferentiated background against which cultural concepts can be set up for inspection' (1972, 172). In support of that position, he quotes (1972, 172, n. 9) Alfred North Whitehead's remark that 'The word "experience" is one of the most deceitful in philosophy' (1927, 16). For Lévy-Bruhl, Needham notes, our concept of experience is prepossessingly 'cognitive' (1972, 173). But such a concept, he points out with respect to Lévy-Bruhl's views, 'cannot be applied as it stands to the experience of primitives, which is predominantly "affective"' (1972, 173). Lévy-Bruhl, Needham opines, has successfully invalidated our own concept of experience as a universally applicable instrument for 'the comparative analysis of alien concepts' (1972, 175).

In short, then, there is no escaping the problems posed by language and culture in attending to the world. This need not be a cause of despair, however, even when we take into account the impossibility of achieving utter transparency in language and the complexities and vagaries of our categories. *Taking those considerations into account*, indeed, is the beginning of wisdom. And with wisdom, we may hope to improve our categories and, through their instrumentality, our claims to knowledge. We may hope to do so even though the world to which we attend is inescapably a participated world.

We are saddled with an irony that the admirably reflexive Lucien Lévy-Bruhl helps us to appreciate: that for those of us who aspire to a rational account of the world, the most troubling participation is the participation of the observer in the observed.

Notes

1. Lévy-Bruhl (1975 [1949], 108-112) distinguishes between two major sorts of participation. First, a 'community of essence', whereby an identity is felt between things, as between an animal and its footprints, an image of a person and the person, or, broadly put, 'between symbol and what it represents'. Second, a participation that equals an imitation, as when Australian aborigines, in order to bring rain, imitate what occurs when they are in the midst of a downpour. This, says Lévy-Bruhl, 'is not a prefiguration of the rain'; rather, the imitation 'effectively *realizes* the rain which will fall soon...the imitation is a felt participation, and, as such, independent of time' (111). This second sort of participation, he remarks:

   has a metaphysical significance: it does not express a relationship between given things and objects; it founds an existence (legitimation, as we have seen in so large a number of myths of the aetiological sort [Volume V]). Imitation (μίμησις) is the *raison d'être*, not by way of causality but by way of consubstantiality, that is to say of essence, communicated and divided; in brief it is a participation (μέθεξις) and from this point of view it is nearly no longer distinguishable from the first sort. (112)

   In declaring on the same page, and in classical Greek, that 'Μίμησις = Μέθεξις', 'imitation equals participation', Lévy-Bruhl, we may suppose, was aware that he was not the first to equate those two Greek terms. The French scholar, whose Chair at the Sorbonne was in the *History* of Philosophy (Leenhardt 1975 [1949], xii), and who in 1880 published an edition of *The Nicomachean Ethics*, was very likely to have known that Aristotle also pointed to a connection between them. According to Aristotle, when Plato maintained that sensible things exist by participation in the Ideas that share their names, 'Only the name "participation" was new; for the Pythagoreans say that things exist by "imitation" of numbers, and Plato says they exist by participation, changing the name.' (*Metaphysics* 1.6.10) In this sense, then, imitation equals participation.

   One wonders what, if anything, Lévy-Bruhl might have made of this had he written the seventh book for which the *Notebooks* were a preparation. Pythagoras, a legendary and influential pre-Socratic, was both mathematician and mystic, and something of a transitional figure in the history of Greek philosophy and science. Note that in Peter Rivière's 1975 English translation of the *Notebooks*, μέθεξις is consistently misprinted as μέθεζις. Rather than faithfully reproduce that error while condemning it with a '*sic!*', I have taken the liberty of correcting it above, and noting what I have done here.

2. Von Domarus and Arieti regard the 'paleologic' as a distinctive form of reasoning, a precursor to our 'normal' secondary process or 'Aristotelian' logic. Secondary process logic is called Aristotelian, Arieti (1974, 229) writes, because 'Aristotle was

the first to enunciate its laws'. According to the Principle of Von Domarus, while in Aristotelian logic identity is accepted on the basis of an identity of subjects, the paleologician accepts identity on the basis of an identity of predicates. Thus in a case cited by Arieti (1974, 230-231), a psychotic patient reasons, 'The Virgin Mary was a virgin; I am a virgin; therefore I am the Virgin Mary.' Von Domarus and Arieti attribute paleological reasoning to schizophrenics, who adopt it, they claim, as a matter of teleologic regression, in order to shield themselves from an unbearable awareness of reality and ego-destructive anxiety. The psychotic, they maintain, will focus on all sorts of coincidences, in a veritable 'orgy of identifications'. More broadly, they hold that the Principle of Von Domarus lies behind Freudian symbology. Thus, for example, a cigar might symbolize the penis because the same general shape can be predicated of both. And in a case cited by Arieti (235), a cigar symbolized Jesus, for the patient predicated 'encirclement' of both (cigars are usually banded by a ring of paper, and in images of Jesus halos often encircle his head — as, I might add, do crowns of thorns). Von Domarus and Arieti also attribute the 'paleologic' to young children and to so-called primitive peoples. But, they hold, while young children and 'primitives' have a *propensity* to reason paleologically, they are not driven to doing so by internal compulsions, as are schizophrenics.

Anthony Wallace (1961, 136) points out that the force of Von Domarus's distinction between Aristotelian logic and the paleologic depends on the analysts's ability to posit at least one predicate distinctive of one of two compared objects but not the other. If the analyst could not, then formally speaking the two objects would indeed be identical. Wallace concludes that the paleologic appears to be 'the same old [Aristotelian] formal logic, operating in psychotic thinking with a drastically limited range of predicates', and he deems the attribution of it to children and to 'primitives' to be 'even less justified than its attribution to schizophrenics' (1961, 136).

3. Jan Lukasiewicz (1878-1956), a Polish logician, developed a three-valued logic in 1917, the values being 'true', 'false', and 'possible.' He built on this work, as did various of his students (e.g., Mordchaj Wajsberg and Jerzy Slupecki), devising multi-valued logics, and so demonstrating that in propositional logic there are viable alternatives to bivalent 'standard' logic (Aristotelian logic). Lukasiewicz's work (e.g., 1964; 1974) has proven useful to a diversity of persons, including the physicist Hans Reichenbach in dissolving certain apparent anomalies in quantum mechanics, the electrical engineer Lofti Zadeh in developing fuzzy set theory, and the mathematician Iván Guzmán de Rojas in writing algorithms for the computer-aided analysis and modeling of Aymará grammar. David E. Cooper, a British social anthropologist, also makes use of Lukasiewicz's three-valued logic, and argues that 'Primitive magico-religious thought incorporates an alternative logic to our "standard" one within the terms of which the apparent inconsistencies [noted by anthropologists in certain famous statements made by non-Western peoples] are not inconsistencies at all'. (1975, 241)

In a Reichenbachian variant of three-valued logic, Lukasiewicz's third value, 'possible', is conceptualized preeminently as *indeterminate*. Propositions that are indeterminate cannot be either verified or falsified logically, although we may know or believe them to be true or false on other grounds. Thus, for instance, in accordance with the quantum principle of complementarity, some paired propositions complement one another because determining the truth of one renders it impossible in principle to determine the truth of the other. Where verification and falsification are ruled out in principle, a proposition must be assigned some value other than true or false. Cooper holds that when applying three-valued logic in an effort to dissolve anomalies in magico-religious thought, two conditions must be satisfied: First, it must be demonstrated that if 'primitive' thought does incorporate this alternative logic, the anomalies do indeed disappear. Second, it must be shown that 'primitive' thought actually does incorporate it. If we fulfil the first but not the second condition, we only show that certain troublesome propositions can be interpreted *by us* in such a way as to render them less troublesome, but we do not save the authors of those propositions from the charge of being inconsistent (and thus, perhaps, irrational). Cooper then goes on to argue in favour of this claim:

The magico-religious thought of a people is a highly theoretic explanatory system, within which propositions occur that, while meaningful in terms of the system, are not capable of any verification or falsification within it. Such propositions are not counted by the people in question as being either true or false, but as having a third truth-value. The anomalies arise because the people explicitly reject the consequences of propositions they appear to accept. However, in every such case, we find that at least one of the propositions is counted by the natives, in virtue of its untestability, to be neither true nor false — hence, despite appearances, the people do not regard as *true* a number of inconsistent propositions. (1975, 244)

Cooper's thesis elicited a small number of published responses, for the most part negative. His major examples of non-Western propositions are those that others have also given opinions about, thus lending support to a complaint voiced by Michael Kenny:

The recent contributions to the rationality discussion have a pronounced lack of empirical referent, and depend rather heavily on the question of the logic of Azande witchcraft and on Nuer propositions that 'twins are birds'. (1976, 116)

Cooper's interesting thesis, I think, deserves evaluation in fieldwork specifically intended to explore it. Insofar as I am aware, such evaluation has not been undertaken.

4. Jean Piaget (1896-1980), biologist turned psychologist, and self-styled 'genetic epistemologist', played a major role in establishing developmental psychology as a scientific enterprise. He continues to be respected for his efforts even though many contemporary developmental psychologists — probably, indeed, the great majority of them — reject various of his claims about cognitive ontogeny and deem certain of his experiments to be flawed. Piaget holds that children creatively struggle for cognitive mastery. They are, in fact, cognitive constructivists, engaged in actively developing their abilities to understand, their capacities to abstract, and their other cognitive skills. He concludes, moreover, that the European children whom he and his associates studied go through four distinct stages of cognitive

self-development: the sensori-motor, the pre-operational, the concrete operational, and the formal operational. These stages, he maintains, form sequential phases in the normal cognitive trajectory of the children studied (Piaget 1929; 1972; 1977).

The British social anthropologist, C.R. Hallpike, applies Piaget's developmental stages on a societal level, even though Piaget and various of his followers warn against going from findings about the development of individuals to characterizations of social groups or, alternatively, going from crystallized cultural products to claims about the cognitive skills of individuals. Hallpike, however, holds that collective representations must reflect the cognitive development of most adults in small-scale or so-called 'primitive' societies. Grounded in that assumption, he goes on to argue that the collective representations of nonliterate, non-Western peoples in a number of small-scale societies indicate pre-operational processes of thought. That is, the thought processes of 'primitive' peoples are of the sort that Piaget attributes to European children between the ages of two and seven. Hallpike attempts to account for the reason why many 'primitive' peoples would remain, as it were, at a pre-operational level of cognitive skills. Accepting Piagetian constructivism, whereby increasing cognitive sophistication is largely a matter of progressive self-development, Hallpike suggests that the socio-cultural environments within which 'primitives' grow up and live do not stimulate or challenge them to develop other cognitive skills. Hallpike's thesis has been attacked strongly by anthropologists and psychologists. One of the most well informed critiques was penned by the anthropologist Richard Shweder (1982). (See also Shweder's 1981 comments on a paper by Allan Young that makes use of Hallpike.) Shweder (1982) notes that Hallpike takes little or no note of some important post-1966 developments in the field of cognitive developmental psychology. These break with Piagetian psychology: they move away from the advocacy of broad stages in thinking, they hold that various operational structures are available to young children and that individuals are not frozen at some one level of thought for all of their tasks, and they suggest that the contents of what people think about are of great importance for how they think.

5. Like many others, Shweder addresses the possibility of a significant distinction between contemporary Western *science* and some other extant mode of thought. But his essay differs from numbers of such exercises in three ways: (1) Shweder is personally skilled in, and lucidly explicates, an important form of mathematical/statistical reasoning in the sciences; (2) he draws on a richness of experimental and clinical studies accomplished by psychologists who addressed the matter of how people actually think; and (3) he argues that 'primitive' peoples *and most of the rest of us most of the time* think 'magically', basing our inferences on perceptual or conceptual *likeness*, whereas scientists *qua* scientists attempt to base inferences on co-occurrent *likelihood* (probability assessments, as modelled by the four-celled contingency table). The latter cognitive effort, he points out, is normally achieved only after sustained tutoring; most of us are neither trained to use it nor are we motivated to do so.

6. Lloyd analyzes various weaknesses in the idea of 'mentalities', the notion that distinct modes of thought can be attributed to social collectivities of persons. He finds reasons to advocate that we move away from efforts to characterize mentalities as such. Rather, we should consider the contexts of communication,

the natures and styles of different sorts of interpersonal exchanges, and the explicit categories available to persons and the ways those resources are used. 'The all-important contrast', he argues, is not between different mentalities, but between 'situations of communication where certain types of challenge, concerning meaning or belief, are possible and expected, and others where they are not' (1990, 15). Individuals in any society, he maintains, may exhibit diverse modes of reasoning, and those modes of reasoning, not mentalities, should constitute the locus of our investigations (1990, 145).

Lloyd faults Lévy-Bruhl for, among other things, never acknowledging 'that the uniformity of primitive thought is a mirage, the product of the distance from which it is viewed' (1990, 144). And in considering the development of argumentation among the Greeks, from whom we have derived many of our analytical categories, he draws on his considerable erudition as a classicist to argue that developing Greek philosophy and science favoured polemical contrasts, and that such contrasts were often overdrawn (1990, 8). Thus, for example, the contrast between the literal and the metaphorical arose out of polemic, and we ought not to impose it on the statements of non-Western peoples, Lloyd maintains, unless we find that they make use of a similar contrast.

East Asian Rationality in the Exploration of Religion

Michael Pye

Prolegomena

The fundamental assumption of this paper is that human beings are able to explore, rationally, their own imaginative constructs and behaviour, and that this applies among other things to those matters commonly designated as religion. Such rational exploration of religion may very conveniently be designated by the German term *Religionswissenschaft* (literally 'science of religion')[1] and its equivalents in other languages such as Danish (*religionsvidenskab*) or Polish (*religioznawstwo*). Equally acceptable equivalents are to be found in Chinese (*zongjiaoxue*), Korean (*chongkyohak*) and Japanese (*shukyogaku*), for all of which the same Chinese characters are employed.[2] In English there is the well known difficulty of the relative diffuseness of the term 'religious studies', and at the same time the lack of institutional backing for the term 'science of religion', in spite of its having being used by Max Müller.[3] This latter phrase has however occurred more recently as the title of the widely distributed bibliographical journal *Science of Religion*.[4] Other terms used in English are 'the academic study of religion' or more briefly 'the study of religion', which is a little like the German alternative *Religionsforschung* (literally 'research into religion') or the East Asian equivalents mentioned above. The word 'exploration', in the phrase 'rational exploration of religion' is intended here to refer to a cluster of related operations including, in particular, the following spectrum: documentation, elucidation, characterization, comparison, theoretical analysis and explanation. At one end, this spectrum takes account of the criterion, established notably in phenomenological studies of religion, that the self-understanding of believers or actors within the system has a certain priority in determining our perception of the system in question. At the other end, comparison, theoretical analysis and explanation may stand in tension to this self-understanding of the believers or actors, that is, of the insiders. The precise relations between these need not be pursued here. Issues of wider debate about religion, such as questions of truth or falsity, value or otherwise, though interesting and in some cases important for various reasons, lie beyond the immediate range of the science of religion. Examples of such issues would be: 'Is Anglicanism rational?' 'Is Tibetan Buddhism politically progressive?' 'Is Manichaeism true?' 'What is the cultural value of Saint Paul?' or 'Is Sufism compatible with post-Modernism?' However such questions fall into a wider range of debate than is envisaged here and certainly go beyond the scope of the *science* of religion.

We are supposed to be thinking here, I suppose, about two problems only. First, we may be thinking about ways in which the concept of 'rationality' might be applied, if diversely, to various religious systems in so far as they function in terms of specific rules of their own; in other words the internal rationality of specific systems. Second, at a meta-level, we may be considering the rationality of the academic study of religion, an enterprise which above, for a change, has been called 'the exploration of religion'. (This expression reflects the close relationship between the German words for researching (*forschen*) and exploring (*erforschen*). My contribution here is intended to lie in the second of the two kinds of question which fall within our range. That is to say, it has a bearing on the general rationality of the academic study of religion, or the science of religion.

For such 'scientific' purposes, the subject matter of *Religionswissenschaft* is to be defined operationally (and not normatively) by means of an open set of characteristics understood as family resemblances (Pye 1972, 1982). The discipline of *Religionswissenschaft*, or as we might say here 'the academic study of religion' achieves its identity through a clear understanding of the relationship between its specific subject matter and the operations selected for the exploration of this subject matter. In this sense, but only in this sense, it is appropriate to speak of the study of religion as an autonomous discipline (Pye 1972, 1982, 1991). At the same time it will be obvious to most people that such a discipline itself stands in a family relationship to various others. The meta-questions of *Religionswissenschaft* or 'study of religion' therefore have much in common with those of history, anthropology, and others. In many cases, such differences in these disciplines as can be delineated in a worthwhile fashion arise only because of the variations in the character of the socio-cultural phenomena upon which the investigators are focusing. Thus depending on their personal emphasis, some investigators conclude, for example, that religion should be studied in principle by means of the historico-philological method with the addition of comparative reflection (Rudolph 1981, 1992) while those trained as anthropologists, working less historically, naturally have different methodological concerns.

For examples of closer integration of methods see Armin Geertz on 'ethnohermeneutics' (Geertz 1990, 1992), or my own interest in the problem of 'access' in the study of contemporary Japanese religions (Pye 1990) which firmly links philology with fieldwork. I do consider that the study of religion should not be locked into any one method which is derived from a single parent discipline. But poly-disciplinarity does not exclude the possibility of a kind of selective integration of methods, carried out according to the requirements of the specific object of investigation. Indeed this is the most desirable approach. So much for general orientations.

The roots of the rational exploration of religion

The specific argument of this paper is that the rational exploration of religion has strong roots not only in the western intellectual tradition but also, independently, in the East Asian tradition. This shows, significantly, that the thrust towards the rational exploration of religion is not a European construct or, as some people patronisingly say, a 'project' of one intellectual culture alone, which has then been adopted by or thrust upon other civilizations. The rational exploration of religion is not of course of interest to all people, and the relevant thought processes may not be documentable in cultures all and sundry. But the same is true of complex mathematics. For example, the mathematician Andrew Wiles has solved a long-standing problem of which I was unaware.

Intellectual traditions and developments are themselves conditioned by all kinds of factors. Nevertheless there seem to be widely available routines in the history of human thought which lead, under the right cultural and intellectual circumstances, into recognizable forms of proto-*Religionswissenschaft* or indeed *Religionswissenschaft*.

Let a couple of such routines now be noted. A most important example is the attempt to deal in some way intellectually with the perception that religions are more than one in number. In other words, when the situation demands, people develop an interest in reflecting on religions in their plurality. Another example of such a routine is what happens when people attempt to re-establish or recreate prior or supposedly original forms of their own religion. This leads to disagreement and eventually to a radical questioning of religious authorities in favour of independent reflection on the development of religious tradition. It should not surprise us therefore to discover that there are intellectual bases for the rational exploration of religion in various cultures. Quite frequently, however, people do not wish to know this. They prefer to think that the rational exploration of religion is something developed in and restricted to so-called 'western' thought patterns. In 'other' cultures, so the argument runs, people think differently and therefore could not possibly have come up with something like *Religionswissenschaft* except under 'western' influence. Proponents of this view sometimes seem to think that 'western' science is superior, and in this they are supported by those products of various cultures who run after the latest jargon in European languages. Alternatively, they undergo a psychological inversion and praise supposedly non-western ways of thinking as an escape from rationality. Support for this variant is often gladly provided by exponents of Asian religious systems or of reinvented primal religious cultures who play the market in exoticism.

As far as Europe is concerned, the modern study of religion is widely supposed to have derived in large part from the interests of the Enlightenment. Note incidentally that there have been alternative views about this. Eric Sharpe, in his influential book on the history of comparative religion (1975) regards Darwinism or evolutionism as the major trigger for the development, at any rate, of comparative religion. Peter Harrison (1990), by contrast, sees the emergence of the 'science of religion' as occurring in the late seventeenth and early eighteenth centuries, i.e. with Deism and the Enlightenment. In general I concur with the latter view. While there is something to be said for both presentations in that much turns on the definitions applied, it is notable that both of them are *entirely eurocentric* (Pye 1996; 1997).

However, the European Enlightenment does not stand entirely alone. There are interesting, independent parallels from approximately the same period at least in Japan. For our purposes, the most important figure is Tominaga Nakamoto who lived between 1715 and 1746. Tominaga's writings offer a critically reflective and historically judicious discussion of the major religions known to him at the time, namely Buddhism, Confucianism and Shinto. Key characteristics of his approach parallel those of the European Enlightenment, in particular the rejection of supernatural or religiously anchored authority in his investigations. Moreover his writings display a strong awareness of the historical relativism of various phases in the development of religions and at the same time of the plurality of religions expressing diverse claims. In 1973 I set out these parallels in some detail, on the basis of information then available to me. In an article entitled 'Aufklärung and religion in Europe and Japan' (Pye 1973), I explored the parallels between Tominaga and his slightly younger European contemporary G. E. Lessing (1729-1781), a comparison whose fascination lies not least in the fact that the two thinkers were of course completely unknown to each other. A comparison had also earlier been made between Tominaga and Voltaire

(Kato 1967), though it must be said that Tominaga was not as decidedly *anti-religious* as Voltaire. In my own experience, reference to the potential significance of the parallel with aspects of the European Enlightenment has not infrequently been met with either thoughtless scorn or worried suspicion, and for this reason I went to the trouble of preparing a full English translation of the relevant writings by Tominaga. This work took several years, and the texts eventually appeared under the title *Emerging from Meditation* (Pye 1990).

I believe that knowledge about these writings is important in the interests of correcting widely held, but erroneous assumptions about the uniqueness of the European intellectual tradition and, in a convoluted psychology, about the supposed inapplicability of ideas derived from that tradition to religions whose centre of gravity lies elsewhere. Of course I am not thereby assserting the propriety of merely transferring analytical concepts from one place to another without any cultural sensitivity. The point is, however, that the rational exploration of religion may fairly be regarded as a shared intellectual enterprise for which there are more starting points in cultural history than is often supposed. This lends the rational exploration of religion a broad strength which is often underestimated. It cannot be written off patronisingly as 'An Enlightenment project', as if this were some isolated European blind alley best closed off for ever.

Naturally, the study of religion today has to be, and indeed is, more than the employment of eighteenth century ideas. It has important roots in that period, both in Europe and elsewhere. It has also had other roots however, for example in the so-called Ancient world, and again in the various features of Indian and Chinese intellectual history. In an attempt to understand the provenance of Tominaga's ideas I have attempted to discern some of the conditions conducive to their emergence. One is the recognition that religions are plural in number. Another is the recognition that a religion now (i.e. at any one time) is no longer the same as the religion that it in earlier times has been (historical relativism). These two perceptions have not always been available to all people but they became clearly available in the complex cultures of East Asia. On this basis, the emergence of rational reflection about religions did in fact take place in East Asia. The overall story of this emergence is very complex and probably cannot yet be authoritatively told. India, China and Japan all have a major part in it, and other countries such as Korea, Vietnam and Thailand should be considered at least in certain respects. All of these countries have experienced in some sense their own 'emerging from meditation' (to use Tominaga's phrase) or rational awakening.

Leading strands in Tominaga's thought

It may be helpful at this point to mention briefly the leading strands in Tominaga's thought about religion or religions. It is quite important to notice, first, that he was independent of any religious institution and was not writing as an apologist on behalf of any particular religion. Concluding his discussion of the classic Chinese problem of the relations between 'the three teachings' he wrote 'I am not a follower of Confucianism, nor of Taoism, nor of Buddhism. I watch their words and deeds from the side and then privately debate them.' (Pye 1990,168). Note the strands of discourse here, and their hierarchy. First, he is independent of any particular religion or, so to say, he is methodologically agnostic. Second, he observes the ideas and the practices of the religions mentioned. Third, he allows himself to form a judgment, but this comes after the process of observation and can be distinguished from it.

In general, Tominaga deconstructed religious authorities. He argued that new schools and sects appeared because new leaders wished to go one better than their predecessors. He had a special term for this: *kajo*. Unpacked, this term consists of two Chinese characters which mean 'adding and [thereby] going above'. I have translated it as 'superseding', which sounds simple enough, but the point lies in the identification of psychological motivation on the part of the actors in the development of new phases of religious tradition. Not only did he thus relativize the position of historically intermediate representatives of the Confucian, Buddhist and Shinto traditions, he also relativized their foundation myths. This is particularly dramatic in the case of Buddhism. He pointed out that the Buddha himself was one teacher among many and that Buddhism began as one teaching among the various 'heresies'. He also pointed out that the normative scriptures (sutras) of Mahayana Buddhism, were not expounded by the Buddha personally but composed many years later. He was the first person to argue, and indeed to prove this.

It is important to notice that Tominaga lived in Osaka, even then a very large commercial city, as the son of a successful manufacturer of soya sauce. In terms of the sociology of knowledge, he enjoyed intellectual independence from the political and religious authorities of the time. In this respect too, therefore, a parallel with the thinkers of the bourgeois European Enlightenment may be seen. He was not a Buddhist monk, just a bright pupil in a private school in Osaka who got himself kicked out because of his critical views. His writings are those of a private scholar. He died very young of disease. For more information about the intellectual and social background see Tsunoda 1958 and the introduction to the English translation of *Emerging from Meditation* (Pye 1990).

Recent reactions to *Emerging from Meditation*

There has as yet hardly been enough time for wider, intellectual reactions to the appearance of Tominaga's writings in English. Hubert Durt's lectures entitled *Problems of Chronology and Eschatology* made use of the translation (with reference to the original) to reflect on some of the themes which Tominaga investigated (Durt 1994). On the whole, however, Durt treats these themes as interesting areas to explore in themselves and does not dwell very much on Tominaga's *method* which, I believe, is where his main significance lies. This learned work might therefore be regarded by some as being a distraction. Durt discusses questions of Buddhist chronology, Buddhist eschatology, and the relations between various versions of the Nirvana Sutra in their own right. These can be discussed by themselves on the basis of modern scholarship. On the other hand, Durt's essays have the merit of showing in considerable detail that there is significant consonance between the kinds of critical questions asked by Tominaga and by modern scholars. Though Tominaga's resources, especially regarding knowledge of Indian history and culture, were of course much more limited than those which scholars enjoy today, the point lies in the fact that historically critical, and therefore in principle relativist presuppositions were unequivocally present in his writings.

Another, somewhat curious reaction to the presentation of Tominaga's writings in English is to be found in an article by T.H. Barrett entitled 'Tominaga our Contemporary' (1993). This article contains about two pages of text by Barrett himself and an alternative translation of just one chapter, *Shutsujo Kogo* ('Emerging from meditation and then speaking'), namely Chapter 24, which deals with the 'three teachings' in China. It is this particular reference to China which drew Barrett's attention; he does not seem to have been interested in the rest of Tominaga's writings or in the reasons for translating them in the first place. One or two necessary corrections are offered, which are entirely acceptable. It is certainly true that the text (composed in what might be called derived classical Chinese by a Japanese) is extremely difficult, and any further improvements can only be welcomed. On the other hand, many of the alternatives offered serve little more than to identify it as a different translation, and in some cases might be viewed as less appropriate. These minor questions of translation will not be pursued further here. A different understanding of Tominaga's ideas does not arise because of them. Instead of going into these details, therefore, what

I would like to offer in the present context is a kind of footnote to the 'orientalism' debate — which Barrett's article suggests. This in turn will lead back to general reflections on the wide cultural base which I see emerging for the rational exploration of religion.

As already noted, people often feel uncomfortable when confronted with the idea that similar ways of thinking may be found in cultures which are distant from each other. It is more fashionable to emphasize the differences between cultures. Of course there are differences and these are fascinating. However at a more boring level, there are also similarities and indeed commonalities, as can be seen in the widespread acceptance of the natural sciences in the context of diverse cultures. Why should we obstinately assume that there are no commonalities in the rationality of other 'sciences', including the science of religion? Orientalist and exoticist yearnings die hard. Indeed, there is still something of an orientalist battle going on with respect to East Asia, as will be illustrated below. But it is important not to be locked into the cultural oppositions created by neo-orientalism if we wish to stabilise rational discourse about religion in an intercultural perspective. Taking Tominaga's *ideas* seriously, rather than being caught on superficialities, may help us to escape from these perennial traps.

Tominaga did not speak Chinese

This matter will now be illustrated by reference to T. H. Barrett's contribution, about which two main points may be made. First, his introductory observations are somewhat patronising in view of the fact that he has provided no more than a *second* translation of less than one twenty-fifth of the whole text (the concluding chapter, Chapter 25, is significantly longer than any of the others). One wonders, if such easy competence is available in the sinological world, why this extremely significant text was not brilliantly translated into English, or some other European language, long ago? The reasons are probably twofold. For one thing, no western specialist in Chinese or Japanese studies ever showed any signs of understanding the wider significance of Tominaga's writings before they had been set by the present writer into a relationship of parallelism with the European Enlightenment. For another thing, the longer text, *Emerging from Meditation*, is in fact linguistically very difficult. The Chinese classics, and the Chinese versions of Buddhist texts which are frequently quoted by Tominaga are on the whole more pungent and transparent.

Barrett refers in particular to a somewhat dated edition of the text which also contains responses to Tominaga's writings from the eighteenth and nineteenth centuries. He comments that while the part which he has translated comes to no more than three pages in that edition, the rest of the ten volumes (edited by Washio Junkei) by various authors 'are, I would guess, just as relevant to Japan's shift to modernity' (252). This is a dubious judgment, for the main responses were pious religious defences against Tominaga's critique. The main positive take-up of Tominaga's ideas was by the important Shinto writer Motoori Norinaga, who commended his analysis of Buddhism but ignored his attentions to Shinto which in *Okina no fumi*, 'Writings of an Old Man', had been quite cutting. Professor Barrett writes, 'I do hope that others will see the need to push on with this sort of work.' Indeed, it would be very helpful for those of us specialising in religion if sinologists such as Barrett would himself get on and translate the rest of those ten volumes for us, instead of just picking over the bits that have already been done by others. The valuable time of specialists in religion, who perhaps have some idea of the wider significance of the contents, should rather be spent in analyzing those contents, and perhaps checking up on one or two minor points of translation on their own account.

Of course the motivation of sinologists must also be considered. This is the second point. What seems to have started Barrett off is his annoyance with the transcription of Chinese names in Japanese pronunciation, even though he admits that my justification of this is 'eminently reasonable'. I will return to this apparently superficial but in fact profoundly important point. As far as can be detected, Barrett has no particular interest in Tominaga's main ideas about Buddhism, Confucianism, Taoism or Shinto (and no reference is made to the discussion of his ideas by others). The avowed aim of his retranslation (of one chapter) 'is simply to restore to our long-lost Japanese colleague a measure of sinological sobriety sufficient to enable his talents in this field to be more widely appreciated.' Why we should be interested in the relative competence in sinology of just one writer, among hundreds who wrote during the Tokugawa Period in Japan, is not explained. However, for this chapter alone, Barrett wants to turn Tominaga into a sinologist who uses the Wade-Giles transcription system.

The non-sinological reader must be informed at this point that European scholars have used several different transcription systems for Chinese. German, French and Anglo-American scholars have had their own versions which all look excruciatingly different and have made the lives of students in western countries even harder than they would otherwise have been. In Anglo-American sinology the leading system was for long the Wade-Giles system, which in itself is quite usable. It has, however, not been self-evident for sinologists of other nationalities, who have produced substantial works. Not surprisingly Chavannes (1967) and Couvreur (1966) used the French system, while Forke (1964) and Franke (1965) used the German system, just to name some obvious examples. This colonialist and later neo-colonialist tug-of-war over transcription systems was effectively neutralised by the Chinese government in Beijing, who managed to obtain international diplomatic recognition for their own 'pinyin' transcription system. This has several advantages: in particular it avoids the usage of changing the value of consonants by the mere addition of an apostrophe (the worst feature of the Wade-Giles system), it avoids long clusters of consonants as in the German and French systems, and it is not geared to any one particular European language. As a result of the introduction of this system for the international designation of Chinese place names, the bottom dropped out of the second-hand market for copies of the *Times Atlas of China* printed in the Wade-Giles system. Chinese personal names (as far as the mainland is concerned) have long since followed suit. Western sinologists are in the process of adjusting to this change. Durt, for example, though interested in very traditional questions, has adopted 'pinyin'. Barrett, however, has not.

This might seem to be an insignificant excursus, but indeed it is not. Tominaga was of course blissfully ignorant of all alphabetic transcription systems for Chinese. He simply wrote down the characters. But note: Tominaga was not himself Chinese, and moreover he did not speak Chinese. He pronounced the characters in a Japanese way. The Japanese readings of Chinese characters used in my translation of *Emerging from Meditation* are themselves independent (of modern Chinese) and consistent. Barrett is not happy with them. Addressing this point, he writes as follows:

The overall effect of reading Tominaga on China in Pye's version is therefore very much that of coming across him at the end of a long evening in the pub, still discoursing as brilliantly as ever, but speech slurred beyond all recognition by several hours of conviviality.

Well, there are various ways of looking at this. For one, if Tominaga were to read Barrett's translation of Chapter 24, ripped out of context, and using the Wade-Giles transliteration of Chinese names, he would think that it was Barrett who had been in a pub! Anyone with significant experience of Japan will know that, whether they are inebriated or not, the pronunciation of the names of Chinese people by Japanese people remains constant. For example, hardly any Japanese people know the Chinese pronunciation even of modern Chinese names such as Mo Takuto (Mao Tsetung). To illustrate it in another way, how many British people know the Chinese pronunciation for Confucius or Mencius (known in Japanese as Koshi and Moshi)? As a matter of fact, even specialists today hardly know how Chinese was pronounced in the early centuries. It is quite certain that Tominaga and *his* contemporaries had even less knowledge of ancient Chinese pronunciation.

More importantly, however, not only was Tominaga *not* trying to recreate the Chinese pronunciation of bygone times, it would have been quite contrary to his *thought* to do so. He was aware himself that Chinese characters have historically been pronounced in various ways in China (this knowledge arises because of various phases in the importation of Chinese terminology into Japan, so that in many cases the same character now has two different phonetic values in Japanese). At the same time he was very scathing about those Confucianists in Japan who made a special point of trying to copy Chinese ways, but only selectively, when it suited them. Here Section 3 of *Okina no fumi* ('Writings of an Old Man') must be read. It is so very apposite. Tominaga argues here that those who give themselves airs as Confucianists should raise cattle and sheep for consumption (not usual in Japan at that time), fix their menu in accordance with the relevant passages in the *Book of Rites*, wear Confucian costume and a Confucian hat (which would have made them look ridiculous in the Japan of the time), and 'read Chinese characters in their Chinese pronunciation'. Moreover, 'Since there are various kinds of Chinese pronunciation they should copy the pronunciation of the state of Lu in the Chou period.' Is this what British sinologists should do! Not even the Wade-Giles transcription of *modern* 'mandarin' Chinese should be used; instead our sinologists should draw on the resources of Bernard Karlgren's studies in Chinese phonology (1915-1919) and see where that leads them in transcription policy.

The point may be further illustrated by reference to Tominaga's discussion in a preceding passage. Here he pointed out, scathingly, that while Buddhists copy Indian manners, they do not actually preach in Sanskrit! For this reason it would have been quite wrong, when translating his relatively extensive writing on Buddhism, to turn all the Indian terms and names back into Sanskrit (except insofar as a small number of terms and names have been effectively Anglicised). Such a policy would simply make everybody dizzy, with or without drinking *sake*. But why should Chinese names be treated differently?

This discussion about choice of transcription systems is intended to illustrate how deeply ingrained are the assumptions with which people frequently go to work, and how far some orientalists are from really letting cultures speak autonomously. In Chapter 24 of *Emerging from Meditation* Tominaga was not writing about China, as in Barrett's phrase 'Tominaga on China'. To present it like this is to push Tominaga into the mould of western sinology. All the other chapters are based on Chinese texts (translated or written in China), but since they are Buddhist sources they do not, apparently, count as sinological. If such a 'sinological' approach is taken seriously, almost all Japanese writings up until recent times would end up by having to be rendered, in part, in transcribed Chinese ('mandarin' dialect, Wade-Giles system)! Tominaga was not even trying to be a 'sinologist'.

Implications and conclusions

If Tominaga was not writing about 'China', what was he doing? In the chapter in question, he was writing about an intellectual problem arising out of the fact that religions are plural in number, pointing out that mere assertion of an inner synthesis (which had been popular in China) is not intellectually satisfying. As argued above, it is becoming increasingly clear that one of the basic motors of modern reflection about religion is the perception that religions (or analogous sets of teachings with competing claims) are more than one in number. And indeed, we see that Tominaga, too, treats this problem in a critical rather than in a religiously enthusiastic manner. If we take the arguments in his writing seriously, we will go on to reflect more extensively about the way in which this problem of religions in their plurality has been conceived in China, in Japan, and perhaps elsewhere in East Asia. We will learn more about the ways in which, in East Asian cultures, religiously creative and normative viewpoints are jostled by critically reflective ones, thus leading into writings on religion with significant analogies to those current in Europe at about the same time. Then a start can be made on rewriting the history of the history of religions all over again. This does not mean that Europe is somehow taken as a norm. Not at all. In future, a history of the history of religions will not be restricted to Europe and North America, but will have to take several, diverse cultural developments into account. The diversity of the cultures and the diversity of the models of religion which compete for our attention will add to the fascination of the subject. At the same time, the commonality of some rather important presuppositions and consequences drawn from them is also coming into view. This will eventually confirm the view that the rational exploration of religion as an enterprise is more than the arbitrary construct of any one culture.

It has come into view that some East Asian rationality in the exploration of religion shares in significant ways the characteristics of Euro-American work. At the same time, of course, there are culturally rooted models of religion which shape the discussion in interestingly different, though yet relatable ways. Getting to know these culturally rooted models is a task in itself and at this point only a few bibliographical references can be given

(Bianchi 1994, Platvoet 1996, Pye 1989; 1991; 1996). Some understanding of this state of affairs is important for the widely shared development of the discipline of the study of religion in the future. We should not allow ourselves to be distracted from it by the remnants of orientalism.

Notes

1. Cf. http://www/uni-marburg.de/fb11/religionswissenschaft
2. Regarding the absence of diacritical marks: the transcription systems for various East Asian scripts are printed without these marks for technical reasons. These do not in themselves affect the argument and it is assumed that specialists will understand what is intended from case to case.
3. E.g. in the introduction, dating from 1867, to his *Chips from a German Workshop* (Müller 1894). He used the term in a manner analogous to 'science of language' and 'science of thought'. The German background of this terminology is evident.
4. This choice of title was made partly for the sake of distinctiveness and partly to reflect the Dutch word *godsdienstwetenschap*, because *Science of Religion* came into being (in 1976) as an Anglo-Dutch venture.

Religious Models and Problem Solving: A Cognitive Perspective on the Roles of Rationality in Comparative Religion

Matti Kamppinen

Introduction

In what follows I will explicate the notion of rationality, its ontological and methodological nature from the viewpoint of the cognitive study of religion. My cognitivist framework is rooted in philosophy: Daniel C. Dennett's theory of intentional systems (Dennett 1987); in cultural anthropology: Robin Horton's intellectualist anthropology (Horton 1970, 1982) and cognitive anthropology (Dougherty 1985, Holland and Quinn 1987). I will also make some strategic references to two classics of comparative religion, William James and Émile Durkheim.

In the Orientation I will introduce the cognitivist framework, and two central notions which are especially relevant for the purposes of comparative religion, namely those of the religious model and problem solving. I will also provide an anecdote from my own fieldwork experience which illustrates the roles and problematics of rationality. Following the Orientation I will proceed to the arguments themselves. In the *first argument* I propose that rationality is a systemic property of cognitive systems; therefore its ontological status is neither more nor less problematic than the properties of such other systems as cells, ecosystems, or galaxies. In the *second argument* I claim that rationality has a definite explanatory role in making sense of human behaviour. This is the case especially in those fields of research where we deal with human persons (conceptualized as cultured actors living in cultured societies). A point worth emphasizing is that since rationality is the unifying aspect of almost all human behaviour, the burden of explanation is shifted onto structured systems of meaning, especially religious models. The *third argument* explicates the assumption of rationality embedded in explanations of religious phenomena. I will argue that our view of rationality and human behaviour is strongly affected by folk psychology and other commonsense theories. The *fourth argument* moves into the specific problematics of comparative religion. Religious phenomena appear to challenge the assumption of rationality; supernatural entities, justification by faith, and other hallmarks of religion are not easily fitted into rational explanations. The strategy I recommend is to look at their abstract properties in order to find the universal structures behind them. The specific religious models to be scrutinized more closely are the ontological model and the functional model, which I will link with William James's ideas about the structures of religious experiences. These religious models are important in providing the *homo religiosus* with the commonsense ontology (or naïve physics) of supernatural entities. The theme of naïve physics and rationality is then further traced to Emile Durkheim. Finally, the *fifth argument* tackles the problem of multiple rationalities. Since we attribute rationality to our study objects, and yet at the same time profess to exemplify rationality ourselves, there is a possibility of clashing belief systems. The relativist and post-modernist ethos in comparative religion has been that we should not try to solve the issue of apparently incompatible beliefs, but rather let them bloom. But the bottom-line is that we cannot do research and at the same time claim consistently that some other, contradictory methods of problem solving are as valid as ours.

Orientation: The roles of rationality in comparative religion

In comparative religion, rationality has a twofold presence. On the one hand, we may inquire how the study of religion is itself rational. The scientific study of religion purports to be rational by adhering to the rules of rationality of science in general. As the history of comparative religion shows, this has not always been so self-evident, considered desirable or easy to achieve (Wiebe 1991). On the other hand, rationality is a constituent property of the people we study. It is this second instance of rationality that will be studied below. The twofold nature of rationality poses an immediate question which will be tackled as well: since both our study objects and we ourselves are rational, how should we react when our respective belief systems clash. The difference between belief systems (concerning, for example, the furniture of the world) is obvious if we treat our objects of study as intentional systems — as they should be treated in the cognitive paradigm — and take their beliefs and other representations seriously.

The cognitivist framework

The basic thesis of the cognitivist framework is that, among other cognitive and intentional systems, *persons* are rational systems, guided by cognitive processes, that is, by processes in which meanings become embodied. By means of identifying and explicating these processes and their structural properties, human thought and behaviour, as well as other cultural items, can be systematized and understood. The dynamics of cognitive processes and related aspects of human and cultural systems form the substance of rationality.

Meanings are clustered into various meaning-systems, or models, which have a central function in shaping human thought and behaviour. Accordingly, they have a prominent role in the explanations utilized in science of religion. *Religious models* — a subset of cultural models — will be of specific interest. Another central notion useful in capturing the role of rationality in comparative religion is *problem solving*: the construction, interconnecting, assessing, and acting upon courses of events and related possible worlds. Possible worlds are best understood as those states of affairs which are referred to by the systems of meaning.

Problem solving is aptly characterized — for the purposes of comparative religion — as a process of thought and action with three constituents: (1) the initial state, (2) the legal operations, and (3) the goal state (Kamppinen 1986, 1988a, Simon 1957, 1981). Problem solving involves the increase of information: as the system moves in time (thinks and acts), the number of possibilities (uncertainty) is diminished. Religious models guide problem solving by means of constraining these three aspects. The initial state or configuration is a combination of beliefs and desires which includes a problem. The problem may be either *epistemological* ('How do I know that there is a God?'), *practical* ('What should I do in order to attain inner peace?'), or *evaluative* ('How valuable are the feelings of my close relatives in comparison with eternity?'). The legal operations include the transition rules like norms of inference, which are constrained by basic beliefs, values and norms. For example, in a belief system where the Bible is considered an unquestioned authority, rules which question it, are not admissible. The goal state is a further combination of beliefs, desires and actions, which then functions as a springboard for a new initial state.

The cognitivist viewpoint is not a novelty within the field of comparative religion. There are at least two areas where the cognitivist viewpoint can be found: Husserlian phenomenology and its sociological offspring, and, surprisingly, the comparative study of religions in the style of Mircea Eliade.

Edmund Husserl's *phenomenology* was largely concerned with the meaning structures (noemata) of the world of experience (Sajama and Kamppinen 1987). Modern cognitive anthropology is fairly much trying to chart the same area of reality (Dougherty 1985, Holland and Quinn 1987). Whereas Husserl was mostly studying the structures of his own experiences, Husserlian sociology — Alfred Schütz, Peter Berger and Thomas Luckmann — operationalized his terminology for the purpose of studying the meaning systems of other peoples. The phenomenology of religion, as practiced by scholars of religion, is more problematic with respect to its location in relation to cognitivism. We can distinguish three kinds of phenomenology of religion:

1) the taxonomic study of religious phenomena, which underlies all comparative religion. Most scholars in the field perform this type of phenomenology without seeing themselves as phenomenologists.

2) the study of religious experiences and the related meaning systems. In this category we could put scholars as diverse as Rudolf Otto, Peter Berger and Thomas Luckmann. The methods of collecting the data on experiences vary from introspection to ethnographic interview.

3) the Hegel-inspired phenomenology of religion, which organizes and grades religious phenomena on a scale of perfection, holding some specific religious system as a norm for 'genuine' religion.

Phenomenologies (1) and (2) are well suited for theoretical and practical purposes. Type (3) remains an ever rarer curiosity, which may now be considered to be a phenomenon in the history of the study of religion (Wiebe 1991).

Mircea Eliade's comparative studies are relevant from the cognitivist perspective as well, since they deal with the fundamental categorizations of religious phenomena. Shared religious models should be built upon some very general distinctions like the ones proposed by Eliade (sacred and profane, time and space, etc.). His ideas consequently can be fruitfully operationalized as empirical hypotheses concerning religious models. It is true that he did not test his generalizations rigorously enough, but if we treat them as empirical hypotheses about the religious models, then we can go on and assess their empirical worth.[1]

Encountering rationality and religion in the wild

Before getting into the argument itself, a short biographical anecdote is mentioned here in order to provide the reader with some activating intuitions. I was educated in analytic philosophy, studying the philosophy of cognitive science and phenomenology. I was especially keen on Daniel C.

Dennett's theory of intentional systems, that is, systems whose behaviour can be understood by means of attributing cognitive states like beliefs and desires to them. While tracing the phenomenological roots of cognitive science in Graz, reading through Alexius von Meinong's manuscripts on the general logic of entities, a question dawned on me: Are there intentional systems out there in the real world? I went to the Peruvian Amazon to find out, and to collect material for my doctoral degree in Comparative Religion on the topic of folk religion and ethnomedicine (Kamppinen 1988b, 1989a and 1989b).

What I discovered was that there is no way to assess the hypothesis of whether people are intentional systems, i.e., whether they are rational. The research question was not *whether* people are rational or irrational, but rather *how* they are rational.

The twofold nature of rationality — namely, how to assess other rationalities by the standards of our scientific rationality — was crystallized as well. There were two instances which undermined my firm belief in the sole authority of the scientific rationality.

The first was that I encountered several systematic, explanatory, science-like belief systems. My key informants were local folk healers, *curanderos*, who were specialists in ethnomedicine and its religious background. Their explanatory systems, methods of data collection, and so on, were so close to our scientific ideals that it left no grounds for arguing that they were epistemologically inferior. The conclusion to be drawn was that their explanatory systems were best understood if treated as science-like, that is, if their systematic and science-like properties were emphasized.

The second instance was a disturbing experience I lived through when participating in a healing session. A psychoactive potion called *ayahuasca* was consumed as usual. The drink causes visual, auditory, tactile and other hallucinations, and its effect wears off in about six hours. The morning after the session — when the effects were supposed to have worn off — I was walking with two friends when I saw a demon engraved on the trunk of a tree. My friends saw it as well. It was a standard demon, horns and evil eyes and all the rest. We just walked on since it was very early in the morning and still quite dark. Later that day, I went to check the demon, but it was not there. Supposedly the experience had been caused by the psychoactive drink. Still, alternative realities can be generated *so* easily and they are *so* real, that the question is: how much may we trust in our privileged realities of commonsense and science? Other supernatural entities I encountered were restless spirits who flew by in the dark — or that was how they were identified. I think they must have been birds or bats... weren't they?

The arguments:

1) *The ontological character of rationality*

From the viewpoint of ontology, rationality is a systemic property of cognitive systems — the mode of operation of human beings. It appears to differ from other systemic properties found in the universe in that it is normative, even though other systems (populations, galaxies, plants etc.) can also be evaluated on the basis of how they should operate.

The ontological character of rationality is found by means of questions like: What is rationality? Is it a property, a process, or a thing? How is it situated in the world? Where do we find it?

On the basis of social scientific theories of rationality, it is obvious that rationality is a property. Moreover, it is a property of complex, functioning entities, that is, of systems. Human beings and other semantic engines (systems that process meanings) are the bearers of rationality. The primary locus of rationality is in the patterns of beliefs, desires and action. Rationality could be more or less identified with these patterns. More precisely, rationality is a subset of all possible combinations of beliefs, desires, and action.

Human action, which is caused and made intelligible by the background beliefs and desires, produces and sustains cultural items like rituals, buildings, texts, contracts, gifts, and so on. These items reflect their origins, and hence the patterns of rationality can be traced here as well. Cultural and social reality can be called the secondary locus of rationality. Most hermeneutical principles of interpretation which seek to make sense of cultural texts, assume that there is some intelligible pattern to be discovered. This pattern is not psychologically experienced in the same way as the primary locus of rationality, but still their mutual dependence warrants us to call them both by the same name (Kamppinen 1993).

Is rationality different from other systemic properties found in the universe? Plants and animals, ecosystems, planet systems and the universe itself all have systemic properties which emerge when suitable building blocks are assembled together. Do we treat the different systems in the same way? The bearers of rationality can be evaluated on the basis of how well they match the ideal type of rationality.[2] The same holds for other systems, whose performance can be assessed by their systemic properties. Ecosystems, for example, have their specific lawful ways of functioning; individual ecosystems differ from one another in the details of performance.

Both ecosystems and human intentional systems can change so radically that it is not worth applying the high-level description to them anymore. In such case a lower-level theory is needed for the purpose of explaining and understanding the behaviour of the system. In the terms of Dennett (1987), we move from the intentional stance to the design stance, and all the way down to the physical stance.

However, human beings have one demarcating feature: they can decide to act irrationally (for a while, and in a limited area of life). Therefore the sense of obligation included in 'should', when applied to human beings, is different from the 'should' which is applied to non-human systems. It could be argued that this is the characteristic feature of human beings: the construction and acting upon different possibilites.

2) *The methodological status of rationality*

Rationality has a definite methodological role in the explanations of human behaviour and cultural formations. Especially so-called intentional explanation by means of beliefs and desires, and other varieties of cognitive explanation assume that the object of explanation is rational.

When ascribing beliefs, desires and other meanings to people in order to account for their behaviour we assume that they are rational. This means that we expect them to behave (in thought and action) in certain specific ways. The assumption of rationality is comparable to other nomic generalizations used in science: it connects sayings, gestures, doings and other evidence to one another; it systematizes the observed phenomena. What is actually included in the assumption of rationality, is another, more complicated matter. Adherence to the rules of formal logic is not the issue. Rules like $((p \supset q) \& p) \supset q)$ tell us very little if it is not specified what sense of implication we have, or what aspect of reality p and q pertain to. A more promising candidate for the substance of rationality is beliefs concerning, for example, naïve physics of the material world. We will have a chance to look at that matter in the next section.

Everyday life is a project that deals with problems and possibilities. We get up in the morning and start preparing breakfast even though the toaster could malfunction. We go on investigating the material and social universes even though it could be the case that there is a Superior Being whom we should worship before everything else. As a matter of fact, all human action involves the possibility of failure and success as one of its contituents. The fact that things can go in one way or in another is an essential ingredient of our lives. There are many other aspects of our lives, too, but the fact of possible worlds is certainly one that is experienced as a constituent. We, as commonsense people, perceive, understand and explain our surroundings, and one principal moment in that process of interpretation is *problem-solving* and the construction of possible worlds. The tools of interpretation are *models*, structured internal representations of environments (Shweder 1991, Kamppinen 1997).

Since rationality is shared by human beings, its explanatory power is not enough to account for differences in thought and action. The burden of explanation is shifted onto meaning-systems, or models, which are processed in thought and action. In comparative religion, the *religious models* are in focus.

The concept of model has numerous uses and it must be clarified first. We can distinguish between the following notions: generic model, cognitive or mental model, cultural or folk model, and religious model.

Model in its generic sense designates any structured *object M* that is partly similar with another *object O*, and in virtue of this similarity *M* can represent *O*. A model can be abstract (for example, a mathematical model), or concrete (so-called model object). This generic concept of model is widely used in science, technology, the humanities and the social sciences. The generic models are not usually thought to reside in anyone's head in particular; they are objective constructs or concrete objects (Bunge 1973).

Cognitive or mental models are psychological entities. These models are in the minds or brains of individuals. One crucial issue with respect to cognitive models is whether they are the experienced structures or subconscious mechanisms. The prevailing view in cognitivism is that cognitive models are not identical with experienced structures, but rather are the mechanisms that produce them.

Cultural or folk models are social entities. They are not the property of any single individual, but come to existence, change, affect other things, and die in social contexts where there are several individuals participating. Theories of cultural models are based on the position that individuals do not act in a void, but negotiate shared realities.

Religious models form a subset of cultural models. Their hallmark is that they refer to superhuman powers or agents. Religious models will be examined more closely below.

Models and theories are closely related. Although in standard philosophy of science models are parts of theories, or backed by theories, both notions designate conceptual systems.

The commonsense view of reality can be seen as a grand model or theory of reality. It is comparable to scientific theories, even though it does not go as deep into reality as they do. Yet, Common Sense is a theory: it describes, systematizes, and explains phenomena. Common Sense includes several subtheories. These describe distinct regions of reality. We have commonsense theories of physical objects, of persons, of man — environment interactions, of men's cognitive abilities, and of their basic needs.

3) The commonsense notion of rationality

Anthropological and historical disciplines (including comparative religion) have been strongly influenced by so-called folk psychological or commonsense views of rationality. Folk psychology involves a reflective component: whenever we ascribe beliefs and desires to other persons, we assume that they resemble ourselves. Our folk methods of belief ascription are holistic in the sense explicated by Gilbert Ryle (1949).

The commonsense view of rationality holds that (i) only intentional systems can be rational and (ii) there are three brands of rationality: cognitive, evaluative, and practical. Intentional systems are systems capable of beliefs, desires and action. We think of ourselves as the primary models of intentional systems and rationality. In our contemporary surroundings there are numerous representational systems but we are happy in ascribing beliefs only to our kind. The ascription of beliefs and desires is a normative action. In ascribing the belief 'that p' to another person (or system) we are actually assuming that it is the state in which I would be if I had asserted 'that p' (Stich 1983). Therefore only those systems which are isomorphic enough to us, qualify for rationality. The ascription of beliefs and desires is holistic and Rylean throughout (Ryle 1949).[3]

The basic units of intentional systems are beliefs, desires and actions, and the respective inferential rules, or codes of rationality. Nicholas Rescher (1988) has distinguished three varietes of rationality: epistemic, practical, and evaluative. Epistemic rationality is a property of beliefs, practical rationality pertains to action, and evaluative rationality characterizes desires.

The commonsense view of *epistemic rationality* is that, in general, we should accept true statements and reject false ones. There are three strategies serving this purpose: direct perception, generalization by induction, and deductive inference from true premises. The norm of epistemic rationality can be suppressed in particular contexts, if other resources like time, interest, and the prospective applications of knowledge are taken into account. *Practical rationality* is a set of rules for choosing the optimal means in the pursuit of certain goals. The dominant rule of practical rationality is the maximization of expected utility. This hard core view of practical rationality is accepted both in commonsense and professional decision making, the only difference being that they have different views of relevant utilities. *Evaluative rationality* concerns the goals and values themselves — what kinds of things are worth pursuing, what are the ultimate values, goals valuable in themselves.

The hallmark of a commonsense theory of rationality is that the varieties of rationality are tightly interconnected. Practical rationality or action needs epistemically and evaluatively sound beliefs and desires in order to function, and the boundary conditions for epistemic rationality are determined by ultimate values and evaluative rationality.

4) *Religion and rationality*

Religion appears to question the assumption of rationality: religious beliefs concerning the furniture of the world, or religious methods of justification by means of faith or mystical experience have been cited as the paragons of irrationality. Yet they should and can be incorporated into the cognitivist paradigm. Supernatural entities are still entities, and faith as a foundation of belief is still a foundation of belief. One particularly important role in the interpretation of religious thought and action is played by religious models, especially ontological and functional models such as those found already in William James's account of religious experience. Another important source of interpretation in making sense of religious phenomena is naïve physics or commonsense ontology, as already pointed out by Emile Durkheim.

Religious models

Common sense is, in Robin Horton's terminology, a kind of first-level theory. Empirical correlations of the type 'whenever A occurs, B occurs' constitute its theoretical part. Explanatory theories that would highlight the imperceptible mechanisms responsible for observed correlations are required. Horton has labelled these theories 'second-level theories' (1982). They are recruited for answering the questions that remain without solutions on the level of commonsense. Religious models are second-level explanatory models; they can fulfil the task of answering the questions that stem from the first level. Commonsense is happy with its world of physical objects, persons, and causal networks.

The explanatory character of religious models has two aspects: cognitive and conceptual. The cognitive aspect means that religious models provide explanations for individuals who utilize them. The conceptual side means that religious models have conceptual characteristics that qualify them for the task of explaining. That is, they concern the general aspects of reality, they posit nomic mechanisms, and they are not relative to any specific space-time locations.

In short, the hallmark of religious models is that they involve hierophanies, ontological commitments to the sacred. The term 'hierophany' was widely used by Mircea Eliade (e.g. 1959). The notions of 'ontological commitment' and 'sacred' require clarification. The ontological commitment of any propositional belief can be identified by its truth conditions, that is, what must exist if the belief is true. For example, the belief 'a vagabond spirit frightened her' commits itself to the existence of at least one spirit, which was, furthermore, capable of frightening her. In the same way, the belief that 'three crows just flew by', commits itself to the existence of three crows. The rationale behind this strategy of tracing ontological commitments is to accept beliefs at their face value. In this cognitivism differs radically from so-called symbolic interpretation of 'exotic' beliefs, which assumes that the people under study never really believe what they claim to believe (Beattie 1964).

The notion 'sacred' is connected to the concepts of the supernatural, unexplained, unexplainable, unperceivable, and unscientific. 'Sacred' is geared to our ideas of understanding and explanation. 'Sacred' is something that is not intelligible within the commonsense view of the world. Two clarifications: first of all, the phenomena may well be intelligible against some other epistemic background, another set of cultural models. The identification of the category 'sacred' is, therefore, culture-bound. Secondly, the given background knowledge that is normally used is our Western, scientific, materialistic world view. I think that there is no escape from this. At least the primary identification of the sacred is made from the viewpoint of our 'best knowledge' of the natural, profane world. This does not mean that we are automatically drawn into scientific realism or, worse, scientism. Rather, in comparative religion we are interested in identifying the religious models, and in understanding the sets of cultural models in relation to which they are intelligible.

Hierophanies involve supernatural mechanisms which are referred to in the pertinent explanations. It is worth making a distinction between supernatural explanations and their explananda. The phenomena may be found as a complex causal chain where a single supernatural cause transforms its effects into supernatural ones. The supernatural cause and its alleged effect are easily treated as one thing. Supernatural mechanisms are beyond the reach of unaided perception. Assumptions concerning their existence and dynamics must be inferred from experience and general models. In other words, religious models are theoretical models.

A Jamesian view of religious models: building a religious robot

Religious belief systems and institutions are cultural means of problem solving par excellence. Religious problem solving involves religious models, that is, models that posit supernatural entities. These entities and their properties are utilized in managing the construction of reality.

Religious models enter problem solving in the definition of situations, their constituent nodes and links. That is, religious models circumscribe, among other things, the ontological and axiological furniture of the world, by answering the question of what 'there is'.

Religious models are exceptionally useful in filling in the gaps of uncertainty: no event occurs without purpose or without being linked to multiple other events. From the viewpoint of problem solving, religious models are interesting precisely because they claim to introduce certainty, determinism, goodness and evil into the human world of uncertainty, relative good and relative evil. The specific cognitive tools utilized in religious problem solving are models, or more precisely, ontological and functional models.

The ontological model imposes an entity structure upon a domain of phenomena. The functional model draws a further distinction and divides the multitude of entities into two types: theoretical and empirical. The ontological model, on the contrary, merely tells us that we are dealing with some entity. Supernatural entities are suitable subjects for ontologization, since interaction with them is more feasible if they are construed as bounded entities. The primary experience of control for humans, both onto- and phylogenetically, is the control of clearly bounded concrete things that move according to a clear-cut, billiard-ball sort of causality.

According to William James, there is in religious experience a specific reality-feeling that imposes the entity structure upon a domain of phenomena:

It is as if there were in the human consciousness a sense of reality, a feeling of objective presence, a perception of what we may call 'something there', more deep and more general than any of the special and particular 'senses' by which the current psychology supposes existent realities to be originally revealed. (James 1960, 73, emphasis removed)

James gives examples of such encounters with the 'something there'. In a story told by a friend, the ontological characteristics of this 'something' are nicely described: 'I felt something come into the room and stay close to my bed. It remained only a minute or two' (James 1960, 74, emphasis removed).

On this occasion the 'something' is experienced as entering the room and remaining there a couple of minutes. In another encounter, only its presence is felt; its comings and goings go unnoticed. There is an ontological model derivable from the text. The model is constituted by three properties: The 'something' in question (1) can enter a space, (2) can stay there for a determinate period of time, and (3) can be in a particular place.

The ontological model endows experienced objects with reality. As the previous example shows, objects of religious models are not devoid of properties even when only ontologized. They are equipped with what we may call their constituent properties, in virtue of which they can be there at all. *Being there implies being in some particular way rather than in another.*

The study of religious problem solving, especially the search for ontological models, has an interesting parallel in Artificial Intelligence. There is a field of study known as 'naïve physics', the theory of salient, commonsense properties of the physical world. The need for naïve physics is usually introduced by the so-called Salad Bar Problem (Smith 1995). It goes as follows: supposing we have to build a robot that can make choices at a salad bar, what kind of algorithm or theory should it be programmed in order to deal with tomatoes, lettuce, fellow salad eaters, and blue cheese dressing? The theory should enable it to differentiate between the causal properties of solid objects like tomatoes, and liquids like blue cheese dressing. In order to survive in the salad bar, the robot should also be able to differentiate between a human being and a piece of lettuce. To apply a fork to a human being would bring about consequences that would be drastically different from the consequences brought about when applying a fork to a piece of lettuce! Moreover, the robot should know what it means for some entity to be inside some other entity — canned soft drinks can be manipulated quite differently from those that are without closed containers. The theory behind the robot's programme, however, cannot be the standard, scientific physics, since it would be too complicated. Therefore it must be naïve physics, a systematized commonsense theory of reality (Hobbs & Moore 1985).

Let us imagine a religious robot. What kind of theory should it have in order to manage in the world of supranormal entities? To begin with, it should share our naïve physics of the material world. That is, that there are pots, pans, persons, rocks and all that. But in addition it should have a sort of naïve physics of supranormal entities. This religious naïve physics would inform the robot concerning the comings and goings, the presence and absence, the location, size, and the causal effects of the supernatural entities.

The functional model transforms the objects cognized into a network of nodes and links that makes up the 'something there'. A functional model draws a distinction between theoretical and empirical entities, the former being those whose existence or non-existence is not proved nor disproved by the facts of immediate sense-experience, and the latter being those to which one can give a sensible content.

    Theoretical and empirical entities together form a system of links which gives each entity a specific functional role in the network. Different entities have different roles, since to be a 'different entity' is to possess a different set of links. Empirical entities, for example, have perceptual roles, whereas the role of theoretical entities is to systematize other entities.

    Religious experience operates with both types of entities. James writes that religions are filled with concrete objects which can be sensed and which can therefore provoke religious sentiments. He continues: 'But in addition to these ideas of the more concrete religious objects, religion is full of abstract objects which prove to have an equal power'. (1960, 70) These abstract objects are theoretical entities. There are two basic types of relations between empirical and theoretical entities. On the one hand, theoretical entities are used to explain empirical entities, to systematize the sense-experience. This aspect is called 'top-down explanation'. James emphasizes this role of abstract ideas:

The whole universe of concrete objects, as we know them, swims ... in a wider and higher universe of abstract ideas, that lend it its significance... Such ideas... form the background for all our facts, the fountain-head of all the possibilities we conceive of. They give its "nature", as we call it to, every special thing. Everything we know is "what" it is by sharing in the nature of one of these abstractions. We can never look directly at them, for they are bodiless and featureless and footless. (1960, 72)

Treating theoretical entities in such a manner ontologizes them: 'We turn towards them and from them, we seek them, hold them, hate them, bless them, just as if they were so many concrete things' (James 1960, 72).

    Empirical entities are used to give an account of what the imperceptible theoretical entities are like. This 'bottom-up explanation' has its rationale: the human cognitive system is basically a vehicle of organic intelligence that is tied to its perceptible environment. This environment is expected to have tangible existence, to provide shelter and nourishment. The primacy of the perceptual environment leaves little room for theoretical entities that are totally separated from sense-experience and basic psycho-biological needs.

    To sum up, the functional model structures a domain of phenomena by imposing distinctions between theoretical (imperceptible) and empirical (perceptible) entities. The former is used to systematize the latter, while the latter is used to give a partial account of the meaning of the former.

    James' own religion is pragmatic. According to Pragmatism, beliefs are first and foremost rules for action. This often-heard thesis of pragmatism is usually interpreted as saying that the cognitive, experienced nuances of mental phenomena are not relevant at all. But James' conception of the practical consequences of a thought is quite broad:

> To attain perfect clearness in our thoughts of an object, we need then only consider what sensations, immediate or remote, we are conceivably to expect from it, and what conduct we must prepare in case the object should be true. Our conception of these practical consequences is for us the whole of our conception of the object (1960, 427).

This is a straightforward application of the functional model: theoretical entities are given functional accounts on the basis of how they affect the human experience.

The model of God in James' theory is therefore a functional model. Only those properties of God matter that are of pragmatic consequence. For Pragmatism, the metaphysical properties of God do not matter, only its moral properties. Examples of metaphysical properties include 'simplicity', 'immateriality', and 'necessariness', whereas 'holiness', 'omnipotence', and 'omniscience' are moral properties. 'Pragmatically, the most important attribute of God is his punitive justice' (James 1960, 430). The moral properties affect human lives since their consequences must be taken into account in human conduct. The theoretical entity 'God' is characterized by its practical consequences and therefore even its moral properties are ontologically committing. God must have some definitive properties in order to be able to act in certain ways. Consequently, *homo religiosus* must possess a naïve physics of the supernatural entities with whom he or she interacts.

Durkheim on naïve physics and rationality

That religious communities have a shared commonsense ontology or naïve physics is one of the less well-known theses of Emile Durkheim:

> If men did not agree upon these essential ideas at every moment, if they did not have the same conception of time, space, cause, number, etc., all contact between their minds would be impossible, and with that, all life together. (1965, 30)

There is a correspondence between the reality and its commonsense representation, that is, the commonsense ontology which describes some parts of the world as they are. As Durkheim observed:

> From the fact that the ideas of time, space, class, cause or personality are

constructed out of social elements, it is not necessary to conclude that they are devoid of all objective value. (1965, 31-32)

In assessing Tylor's animism, Durkheim outlines a naïve physics for the soul. The following passage indicates quite clearly how Durkheim analysed the commonsense ontological aspects of religious thought and action. Most prominently, such analysis renders the religious phenomenon intelligible by means of showing that it is rational:

Of course, this double [the soul] reproduces all the essential traits of the perceptible being which serves it as external covering; but at the same time it is distinguished from this by many characteristics. It is more active, since it can cover vast distances in an instant. It is more malleable and plastic; for, to leave the body, it must pass out by its apertures, especially the mouth and nose. It is represented as made of matter, undoubtedly, but of a matter much more subtile and etherial than any which we know empirically. (1965, 67)

In defining religion, Durkheim makes an interesting note about 'savage' rationality; how, as a matter of fact, exotic explanations are quite straightforwardly rational from the native point of view:

But, as matter of fact, these explanations which surprise us so much, appear to the primitive man as the simplest in the world. He does not regard them as a sort of ultima ratio to which the intellect resigns itself only in despair of others, but rather as the most obvious manner of representing and understanding what he sees about him. (1965, 40)

Rationality is linked with a naïve physics of religious entities. In Durkheim's scheme, the religious ideas of force, boundary, etc. were primary, and other related ideas came later. Religious forces, equipped with consciousness, are not irrational as such:

the idea of physical forces is very probably derived from that of religious forces... Even the fact that religious forces are frequently conceived under the form of spiritual beings or conscious wills, is no proof of their irrationality. (1965, 40)

Since religious forces act lawfully from the native viewpoint, they are not miracles for them. Religious forces are predictable and instrumentally rational; there are no miracles involved: 'That is why the miraculous interventions which the ancients attributed to their gods were not to their eyes miracles in the modern acceptation of the term'. (Durkheim 1965, 41) Durkheim provides a detailed, even if implicit, argument concerning rationality when he discusses the argument of animism. Durkheim argues that animism, or the hypothesis of the double, is not motivated well enough. If it were an automatic response to dream experiences, it should be the most obvious for the intellect. Primitives are rational and they choose the most economic explanations. On the assumption of rationality, the hypothesis of the double is not convincing:

> But if this hypothesis of a double is to be able to impose itself upon men with a sort of necessity, it should be the only one possible, or at least, the most economical one. Now, as a matter of fact, there are more simple ones which, it would seem, might have occurred to the mind just as naturally. (Durkheim 1965, 73)

To paraphrase it in the form of an explicit argument:

a)   People (we and the savages) are rational.
b)   Rationality involves the idea that of two explanations (which have equal explanatory power) we should choose the more economic one.
c)   Animism is more complex than other explanations.
d)   Therefore, animism could not have prevailed as Tylor argues.

Religious models exist mainly in order to explain things, to make things intelligible. This claim has been the hallmark of the so-called intellectualist or cognitivist school in comparative religion (Horton 1970, 1982; Lawson and McCauley 1990). It is quite surprising to find the same claim in Durkheim's text:

> For religious conceptions have as their object, before everything else, to express and explain, not that which is exceptional and abnormal in things, but, on the contrary, that which is constant and regular. (1965, 43)

Another claim of the cognitivist school is that the core of religion is a belief system, because behaviour and other cultural artifacts have to be defined in terms of beliefs. This claim is also found in Durkheim:

> Religious phenomena are naturally arranged in two fundamental categories: beliefs and rites. The first are states of opinion, and consist in representations; the second are determined modes of action. Between these two classes of facts there is all the difference which separates thought from action.

> The rites can be defined and distinguished from other human practices, moral practices, for example, only by the special nature of their object. A moral rule prescribes certain manners of acting to us, just as a rite does, but which are

addressed to a different class of objects. So it is the object of the rite which must be characterized, if we are to characterize the rite itself. Now it is in the beliefs that the special nature of this object is expressed. It is possible to define the rite only after we have defined the belief. (1965, 51)

5) *'I am right, you are wrong'*

Although a broad view of rationality allows us to understand and systematize religious phenomena, it does not follow that religious statements are true by the same token. We should remain able to claim that even though we are open to other methods and constraints of problem solving, *our* views and methods are the most optimal of those that we know.

The cognitive approach in comparative religion, which utilizes the notions of rationality, religious model, and problem solving, does help us in making sense of our object of research: religious phenomena. This much is quite unproblematic. But a further, reflective step brings forth the twofold presence of rationality in comparative religion, which was already referred to above: How should we assess the rationality of our objects of study in comparison with our own rationality? The problem is radicalized when we encounter different realities, for example, realities populated with supernatural entities. If we are to take the informants' views literally, and if we are to interpret them as 'charitably' as possible, then what we end up with is sometimes problematic, sometimes disturbing.

Emile Durkheim, whose ideas on rationality were discussed above, provides us with a standard starting point. Namely, to characterize religion in terms of the supernatural requires that there be a lawful natural order of things, a scientifically described reality, against which the supernatural is defined:

In order to say that certain things are supernatural, it is necessary to have the sentiment that a natural order of things exists, that is to say, that the phenomena of the universe are bound together by necessary relations, called laws. (1965, 41)

Durkheim makes numerous remarks about the relationship between common sense, science and religion, and it is not at all clear how to interpret them. First of all he claims that primitive religion gives us a wrong picture of the world: 'But the conception of the universe given us by religion, especially in its early forms, is too greatly mutilated to lead to temporarily useful practices' (1965, 98). Contradictions with experience would have swept religion away if its original task would have been to provide knowledge of how things actually work:

failures, being infinitely more frequent than successes, would have quickly shown them that they were following a false route, and religion, shaken at every instant by these repeated contradictions, would not have been able to survive. (1965, 98)

Errors survive in history, especially if they are practically true or successful; they do not need to give any exact theoretical picture of the world. Some commonsense knowledge is like this: 'In this category are a large number of the maxims of popular wisdom' (Durkheim 1965, 99). This view is in contradiction with the view expressed in *Primitive Classification* (1963), where Durkheim and Mauss claimed that religious systems provide first and foremost a theoretical understanding of the world. Here Durkheim has moved into the position that they were false to begin with and have survived solely because errors, in general, may survive. In yet another place Durkheim proposes that institutions must be geared into the nature of things, otherwise they would not exist: 'If it [an institution] were not founded in the nature of things, it would have encountered in the facts a resistance over which it could never have triumphed'. (1965, 14)

Thus we have a puzzle: on the one hand, religious systems seem to be false accounts of what there is; on the other hand, they accord with the real mechanisms of the world in some sense. The solution is simple: on the one hand, the manifest picture of the world provided by religious systems is wrong, that is, the native believer is wrong in explaining a rite or a myth; on the other hand, the religious system survives because it does not contradict the reality too radically.

These two aspects of religious systems are not enough to provide a positive reason for their existence. The fact that they exist, allows us to conclude that they must have some minimum accordance with the real mechanims of nature 'out there'. Yet we must turn to the positive reasons of existence in order to give a more profound explanation of religious phenomena. Durkheim has no doubts about the existence of such true, effective reasons:

The most barbarous and the most fantastic rites and the strangest myths translate some human need, some aspect of life, either individual or social. The reasons with which the faithful justify them may be, and generally are, erroneous; but the true reasons do not cease to exist, and it is the duty of science to discover them. (1965, 14-15)

The Durkheimian stance has been criticized on the basis that we have no grounds for claiming that 'we are right and they are wrong'. The anti-positivist or extreme relativistic view proposes that there is no way to assess and grade different methods of problem solving, since we live in different forms of life, which all are self-contained and on the same level (Winch 1958). However, Nicholas Rescher (1988) has argued that there is a way of finding the difference, and that the scientists and scholars who conduct research cannot just choose to drop scientific rationality and pick up some other rationality which has been identified by using the tools of scientific rationality in the first place. The use of scientific rationality in the first place commits us to the position that it is an optimal set of methods. Why would we have chosen it in the first place if this was not the case? (For a full argument, see Kamppinen and Revonsuo 1993).

Conclusion

Are there any further contributions that may be extracted from the cognitivist framework? The debate about rationality and relativism has been conducted very much in terms of two warring camps: the natural science oriented positivism, and social scientific relativism. The first tends to construe human beings in terms of causes, and the second in terms of reasons devoid of any causal powers — to put it bluntly, people are either mindless brains or brainless minds (Karlsson and Kamppinen 1995). Cognitivism appears to provide the golden mean, where causally effective reasons are possible, and where there are links between the different levels of reality: the biological, cognitive, and cultural. Why should we opt for the golden mean? Because it is a rational thing to do.

Notes

1. The specific contributions of William James and Émile Durkheim will be dealt with in due course below.
2. The ideal type of rationality can be destilled either from the common sense view of human behaviour, or from the various scientific disciplines dealing with persons. Daniel C. Dennett's (1987) theory of intentional systems is an example of what should be included in an ideal type of rationality. The key elements are optimality, coherence, and survival: Rational beliefs, desires and actions are optimal in regard to the rest of beliefs, desires and actions of the systems. Coherence is a specific case of optimality — beliefs and the propositional commitments of desires and actions should not imply logical incoherences. Survival of the system — its persistence in the real world — indicates that it has calibrated its beliefs and desires in a somewhat right way. Stronger types of rationality would involve such virtues as the transitive preferences and maximizations of expected utilities.

3. Holism in the ascription of beliefs and desires means that beliefs and desires are ascribed as bundles: for example, when we ascribe a belief to Peter that there is a river in front of him, we expect him to have related cognitive states as well – that he sees or hears its presence, that he will slow down, that he beliefs that there is something in front of him, and so on. The ascription of desires and plans of action would require further assumptions about Peter's basic desires, feelings and ultimate goals.

Holism pervades all belief and desire ascription. It only gets more complicated as we move from the concrete beliefs about rivers into abstract or exotic beliefs.

Rationality, Social Science and Religion

Roger Trigg

Content and Context

The study of religion, like any other intellectual discipline nowadays, is under attack as involving merely one perspective amongst many. Its rational basis is questioned; it can be viewed as just one more social phenomenon. Yet, paradoxically, the study of religion itself often wishes to treat religion as a mere social fact to be studied, and is dismissive of any theological agenda. The problem is why a study of religion can claim to have an insight into what is the case at the level of the reality of religious practice, without taking seriously the possibility that religious believers themselves could conceivably have any insight into what is the case concerning any divine reality. Why should scholarly interpretation claim a superior knowledge to that claimed by participants in a religion? How can claims to truth be allowed at one level but not at another? Yet if the notion of claims to truth is dismissed altogether, that can be as destructive of scholarship as of religion.

The very idea of truth is, of course, much contested. It is tempting to tie it closely to the activities of science and to the possibility of verification through scientific method. That was the positivist agenda, and it had the major disadvantage that it tended to change the subject from what is true to how we can find it out (Trigg 1989; 1993). The focus was thus changed from reality (at whatever level) to human capabilities. A realist theory of truth (Alston 1996) is far preferable in that the link between truth and an objective world is thereby maintained. What is believed and its putative connection with reality thus becomes of more significance than the fact that it is believed or who believes it. Linked with this, though not necessarily implied by it, would also be a metaphysical realism that insists that objective reality is always independent of our conceptions of it (Trigg 1989). That is necessary for a proper understanding of science (Trigg 1993), and it could also be argued that it is essential for any understanding of religion. Even atheism is a realist position, making claims about the character of reality.

The positivist view of the logical deduction of theories from neutral data has been much criticized in recent years. The influence of hard-line empiricism lingers on in many unexpected places and in ways that are not always predictable. Since, however, the work of Thomas Kuhn gained prominence, it has been generally accepted that even science is at least to some extent a social product, related to particular times and places, and to be understood in context. There have been many attacks on the idea that science discovers uncontroversial facts on which theory can then be based. The history of science shows how interpretation can enter in at every level. What is to count as a fact, and which facts are relevant, are typical questions that cannot be addressed without presuppositions arising from one's theory. The very notion of uninterpreted data, to which we can appeal to help us to decide between theories, has to be discarded. Theories not only help us to interpret data and to determine what we are to treat as real, but are themselves adopted for many reasons, not all of them related to the nature of the phenomena being investigated. Science, it is claimed, is itself a social and cultural construction, and claims to scientific objectivity must be suspect. The so-called 'strong programme' in the sociology of knowledge has a lasting influence in its reduction of the idea of truth to what is held true by a society (Bloor 1976). Some even talk of 'post-modern science', a science bereft of the certain foundations claimed for it by positivism. For instance one writer says (Rouse 1991, 158):

The idea that there is a 'natural world' for natural science to be about, entirely distinct from the ways human beings as knowers and agents interact with it, must be abandoned.

The result of this rooting of scientific theory in social context has been a concentration not on what people ought to believe, or the rational grounds of belief, but rather on the fact of their belief as demonstrated in their practices. Science has thus to lose its preeminence as the sole exemplar of rationality and even as the holder of monopoly rights on truth. As a result, the social causes and context of scientific belief have seemed to many practitioners of the sociology of science to be more relevant than what the belief purports to be about (Trigg 1993, 155ff.). This process has mixed effects. It means that the arrogance of positivism has to be discarded. Social science need no longer feel that it has to mimic the physical sciences in amassing hard measurable data and deducing theories from them. Humans need no longer be seen as merely complicated physical objects. The emphasis turns to the social and communal background of those who hold the beliefs, whether they are about electrons or human activities.

This can mean at the extreme that the sociology of knowledge becomes imperialistic and imagines that all explanations of belief are fundamentally sociological in character. Scientific theories are then no longer about 'the world' at all. Their construction is the effect of their social background. Their meaning can only be grasped in context, and they reflect that rather than describing an independent world. The proponents of different theories are then bound, as Kuhn suggests (1962,102), to live in different worlds. There is no way that they can be understood as being about objective reality. Sociologists of science put much effort into explaining how the process of construction occurs. They will for instance enter a laboratory and examine the practices there in the same spirit as a social anthropologist will go and live with a remote tribe in the hope of understanding its life (Trigg 1993, 151ff). In each case, the aim will be to place the people being studied in their social context, so as to understand how the participants view their practices.

The emphasis on social context, on the fact of belief rather than on what belief is about, makes the purpose of science very problematic. The world recedes, and the idea of truth becomes a social construct. No one, even in principle, it seems, can gain contact with reality whatever that may be. The 'sociological turn', i.e., the transmuting of epistemology into sociology (Trigg 1993, ch.7), makes it unclear why people are doing what they are doing. Physical science cannot then be said to be searching for truth, building our knowledge, or uncovering the nature of reality. None of the categories can be grasped without being related to persons. The issue will be whose view of truth, whose knowledge or whose picture of reality is being employed. Then, we are told by sociologists of knowledge, sociological explanations will be produced as to why this or that group would adopt such views. Truth becomes what is held true, and reality what is conceived as real. No one can attain a God's-eye view from which to give an authoritative ruling on what is true or real. We are all caught up with particular perspectives and operate with our own presuppositions. The minute this is admitted, it is claimed, the emphasis moves from *what* is believed to *who* believes it, from *content* to *context*.

Yet if what people say is merely a reflection of the interests of a particular social background and of sectional interests, they need not be taken seriously. There will be no reason for me to change my mind if I think differently. If I fully understand your motives for saying something, it will be an accident if you hit on the truth. Indeed the concept of truth will be reduced to what a particular person or group holds true. This raises the issue of reflexivity which haunts the sociology of science, as it must haunt anyone who assumes that talk of reality can be translated into talk of what is believed. The 'sociological turn' invites the response that sociologists themselves are as much involved in interesting practices as anyone they wish to study. No doubt sectional interests motivate sociologists as much as anyone else. Other sociologists can presumably study them. The *sociology* of the sociology of science beckons, and we seem to be involved in an infinite regress. This is inevitable if no one can ever say anything without the focus immediately being moved from what is said to the social context in which such a claim makes sense. The subject is always being changed. When the content of belief is subordinated to the fact of belief, no one can ever assess, let alone discuss, the question of the truth of what is held.

The very idea of a rationality that can be detached from its context, so that people can have reasons for belief, is demolished. Reasons come to be what people hold to be reasons. There is no possibility of assessing them, or of distinguishing the good from the bad. That would require a clear distinction between subject and object of belief, between the person or group studying and the object studied. Placing beliefs in their context may seem harmless, and even desirable. When, however, this means that they can only be related to their surroundings, and when this applies in turn to the beliefs about their relation to context, the result is that no proposition can be rationally assessed. We are always forced to look at extraneous influences and presuppositions which go to form someone's frame of reference. What counts as a good or bad reason for belief is always made relative to the group in which the belief gains currency. 'Truth' becomes a sociological question. It cannot be distinguished from what people happen to count as true, and, because there will always be disagreement, truth becomes relative to places and times.

The consequence, however, is that any aspiration to a common base for belief has to be discarded. We cannot then, it seems, have beliefs about the same objects when we disagree. The 'object' cannot be meaningfully detached from the belief. The result is to ensure that we are all, collectively and individually, imprisoned in a world of our own construction. People who talk of 'societies' or 'groups' or 'theories' may see the construction of truth as a collective matter. Certainly the influence of the later Wittgenstein has ensured that emphasis is placed on the public, shared nature of concepts (Trigg 1991). Indeed language is regarded as of central importance. Just as there are many different languages, there will, it is assumed, be different systems of belief or ways of life. Wittgenstein, however, (1953, 242) made 'agreement in judgments' of central importance in giving a basis for a shared form of life. Since it is clear that agreement is never absolute, the question must arise how much apparently insoluble agreement can be allowed within one group before it is recognized that there are two groups. It is striking that followers of Wittgenstein can refer to religion, Christianity or Catholicism equally as embracing forms of life (Trigg 1973,72). Since even Roman Catholics betray differences of emphasis, not to say outright doctrinal disagreement, the question remains as to how far this process should go. If agreement is made the yardstick, the danger is that in the end we are each liable to find ourselves in a form of life comprising one person. This is not surprising since if we continually stress the fact of belief rather than what the belief is about, divergence of belief becomes crucial. Yet this in turn produces problems about mutual understanding and translation. If I live in my world and you in yours (or we each belong to communities that construct different ones), how can I ever hope to understand you, or vice versa?

We are thus brought to the issue of the incommensurability of theories. Indeed it may appear possible that the social realities constructed by different cultures may be so different that they deserve to be called 'different worlds'. This has been a constant theme since the work of Kuhn pointed out that, after a 'paradigm shift' in scientific theory, even scientists could find themselves in different worlds. For example, Kuhn says of a transition from one theory to another:

Though most of the same signs are used before and after a revolution — e.g. force, mass, element, compound, cell — the ways in which some of them attach to nature has somehow changed. Successive theories are thus, we say, incommensurable. (1970, 266)

Kuhn apparently still wants to talk of 'nature' but the notion becomes meaningless if whatever is said about it is firmly embedded within a particular theory, and different views of its constituents cannot even be compared. The world envisaged is simply the reflection of our theory, and may well be seen in this way as a result of psychological or sociological pressures. Once more, the fact of belief, and its context, gains priority over its content.

Subject and Object

The world, however, cannot be an intra-theoretical notion. The distinction of subject and object is of critical importance. Without a realist conception of what there is, as existing independently of our conceptions of it, we are left simply with 'reality-for-us' (Trigg 1989, ch.1). It will vary according to who we are. The nature of reality becomes a reflection of our beliefs about it rather than their target and justification. It is made dependent on human capabilities and limitations so that what we can know has everything to do with us and nothing to do with reality. It is certainly true that how we relate to the world depends on our location in space and time and on our abilities. Social conditions, too, play their part in enabling us to gain knowledge or in constraining our quest for it. Nevertheless that there is a world to discover is not a result of belief. That it has a determinate nature (determinate enough to allow the evolution of humans) is not itself a matter of social construction. If we think that everything is the reflection of belief and conceptual scheme, we become like people looking down into a well and imagining someone is looking up at them. In fact, all they see is their own reflection. Similarly science becomes merely a reflection of our capabilities and limitations.

In every form of intellectual endeavour, beliefs and what they purport to be about, have to be distinguished. Otherwise beliefs could never be mistaken, since those who differ from us will be understood as simply having beliefs about different objects. Without a clear logical break between subject and object, changing views about the same object cannot be distinguished from the introduction of fresh beliefs about new objects. In the development of quantum mechanics, for example, it could be said that at each stage 'electron' meant something different rather than that accepted theory about the nature of the electron had progressed. Without some such distinction, we do not just find translation between theories problematic. The whole structure of human rationality begins to crumble. The distinction between our current beliefs and what they are about underpins all forms of intellectual activity.

Unless we can to some extent stand back from the social influences that impinge on us, rational discussion with those who disagree becomes impossible. If my beliefs only gain their meaning from their overall context, prising them apart from that context will simply deprive them of such meaning that they possess. The more that 'holistic' views of meaning are canvassed, the more we become imprisoned within a theory or set of assumptions. The very idea of a rational detached examination is being challenged (Trigg 1989, ch. 4). There seems to be no middle way between commitment to a theory or an inability to understand its full meaning. Kuhnian views of science impel many to this conclusion in science, but similar modes of argument can be applied to religion. The same issue is also raised when social anthropology has to confront the problem of understanding alien societies (Trigg, 1985, ch. 4). When the views of the later Wittgenstein about 'meaning as use' are applied to religious language, we seem to be left with the choice of using such language as participants in a religious form of life, or of failing to understand it. The believer, and the unbeliever, or indeed the scholar, then no longer can be held to contradict each other. There is then no basis for any rational assessment of belief, since they cannot be understood to be referring to the same objective world. The mere fact that it is held is enough. We are forced back into a relativism which maintains that while a belief may be true for the person holding it, insofar as it is believed, no further question of truth can arise. It cannot be true for those who reject it and indeed they cannot know what they are rejecting. Atheism understood as outright denial of religious belief becomes logically impossible. This kind of relativism has been termed 'conceptual relativism' in that the very meaning of the concepts applied becomes relative to those embracing them (Trigg, 1973, ch.6).

Attacks on the possibility of realism, of the intelligibility of there being an objective state of affairs logically independent of whatever we may happen to think about it, come from a variety of quarters in modern thought. Post-modernists emphasize how the varying interpretation of texts means that there is no one way in which the text should be understood. There is no such thing as *the* meaning. This can be generalized into the post-Nietzschean view that everything depends on one's perspective and that all is interpretation. It is significant that Nietzsche himself was intent on demolishing the distinction between subject and object (Nietzsche 1968, 480). The disparagement of rationality that this involves is closely linked to a repudiation of truth as such.

Without the possibility of truth, without the ability to aim at reality as a target, it becomes unclear what the purpose of the physical sciences is. If science is merely Western science, the kind of thing that people happen to believe at a particular location and epoch, we may, it seems, become aware of the fact of our belief but have no possible grounds for it. Why should we go on believing? Yet the situation is even more desperate. When we reflect on our predicament, we are in effect standing back from ourselves and seeing ourselves as objects of belief. Our beliefs are second order ones about our first order beliefs. The minute we accept that we have to concentrate on the fact of belief rather than its context, we are doing what has already been claimed to be impossible. We are examining our beliefs in a spirit of rational detachment, and recognizing the belief as a 'fact'. Yet on our own assumptions all we are doing is producing another set of beliefs, which by definition cannot be about anything beyond themselves, not even other beliefs. We cannot, it seems, escape the distinction between what is the case and the fact of belief. As soon as we reduce the one to the other, we are still treating the fact of belief as something objective, which can be discussed.

All of this becomes of pressing importance when we do not just consider reflection on our own beliefs but when we wish to study other people's, as in the study of religion. Any refusal to accept a distinction between the object of our study and the fact of our study will raise considerable difficulties. What we study will be made into the construction of our own theorizing. Instead of finding out something, we are in other words making it up. That is what the contrast between construction and discovery amounts to. Whatever we say is more of a reflection of our predicament than a statement about someone else's. Yet, in fact, once the split between the subject and object of belief is discarded, not only science becomes impossible since it is no longer about anything. The sociology of science also becomes impossible, since it too depends on the assumption that scientific beliefs can somehow be studied. At each level, social science, like the physical sciences, demands an 'object' to study. If other peoples' beliefs cannot be viewed as they are, and will always be merely an intellectual construction by ourselves, social science crumbles. The threat of a regress is often invoked as a warning, but in fact the *sociology* of the sociology of science becomes impossible for the same reason that the sociology of science itself is ruled out. We cannot then just take beliefs and examine them without accepting that our interpretation, our theories or our concepts construct what we purport to study. All possible knowledge is bound within a particular context. This merely undermines the whole idea of knowledge.

This constructionist position has affected religious studies so that comparison of apparent similarities and differences between religions is alleged to be the product of 'the scholar's mind for the scholar's own intellectual reasons' (J.Z. Smith 1990, 51). Comparison, we are told 'does not necessarily tell us how things 'are' ', but rather merely how they might be conceived or 'redescribed'. We are told the 'comparison provides the means by which we 'revision' phenomena as our data to solve our theoretical problems.' In other words, students of religion are engaged in an exercise which reflects their needs and purposes and apparently has little to do with what they are studying. Indeed, the very idea of there being an object of study slips away. When everything is constructed, there is by definition nothing to discover, nothing by which our judgments could be seen to be true or false. The idea of reality is banished or at the very least put in inverted commas. There is nothing real, only our judgments of what is real, and they have their source, apparently, in aims and purposes that may have little to do with any alleged similarities or differences within the sphere of religion. Everything is rooted in history, so Jonathan Z. Smith can say (1990, 109) that 'the claimed ahistorical character of myth is a product of the scholar's gaze and not of some native worldview.' Yet scholars, for their part, will be rooted in an evolving history and so their judgments are bound to their own context. At each level, both what is being studied and the act of studying can only be set on this view against their context and understood accordingly. Jonathan Z. Smith may not intend to be putting forward an explicitly sceptical view, or to be claiming that everything is socially constructed. The point, however, is that any strong emphasis on the fact of historicity inevitably ends up by being an attack on the possibility of rationality. No one can then ever be sufficiently detached from their circumstances to reason about any reality. All they see and study is a mere reflection of their own presuppositions. What happens to be the case, inevitably drops out of account, in favour of historically situated judgments. The dangers of relativism draw near (Trigg 1993, 219). Yet the view that there is no reality but that what we take to be reality is constituted in some ways by our judgments, is still implicitly appealing to the fact or reality of those judgments.

Nothing can be asserted without the idea that truth is being asserted (Trigg 1973, 150ff). The previous sentence is, of course, no exception to this rule, but since its aim is to claim truth, any self-reference is hardly destructive. Language itself depends on the possibility of distinguishing what is the case from what is not. The very idea of assertion as opposed to denial depends on this. It does not matter what I say, if there is no difference between something being so or not. There is no way I can be mistaken, since there is nothing in virtue of which I can be wrong. Meaningful language and babbling must be put on a par. Language must presuppose the possibility of truth and the pursuit of any intellectual study presupposes that there are ways of being wrong. If I cannot be wrong, I cannot be right either.

The practice of any social science has to depend on the basic distinction between, say, a set of people holding particular beliefs or their not doing so. If it is purely in the business of construction, anything goes. The same goes for the very science which some sociologists wish to investigate. Physicists, too, are concerned with something beyond their own processes of belief formation. No explanation of the conduct of physics can leave out of account the fact that the point of physics is to uncover the workings of the physical world. Assuming anything else undercuts the possibility of rational assessment of theories and evidence.

The Importance of Truth

When we come to the academic study of religion, the same constraints of rationality apply. Any religion has to take a stand on the nature of reality and the place of humans in it. It involves beliefs about what is the case as well as about human life. Some, like Wittgenstein, stress the role it plays in people's lives. Others, influenced by positivism, may be tempted to treat religion as a mere matter of subjective commitment. We are then forced back to concentrating on the fact of belief rather than its content. Sociologists and others may want to restrict themselves to the social setting of religion. Religious institutions and their workings are clearly an appropriate object of study, as is the history of their development. The sociology of science can be very enlightening about the workings of scientific institutions and the way in which knowledge can be socially accepted and disseminated. Similarly the sociology of religion can show many of the functions of a religious organization, its dynamics and its interactions with a wider society.

All this is made possible by the assumption that we can distance ourselves from an object of study sufficiently to examine it dispassionately. Physicists are not likely to be personally involved with the physical objects they wish to study, but students of religion cannot escape having certain views about the religion they are studying. In physical science the separation of subject and object seems easier than in the social sciences, although quantum mechanics provides plenty of arguments about interpretation in this area. We are however all members of society and cannot step outside it in the way that physicist or chemist can often be separate from the physical system under scrutiny. Science has often seemed to require by definition impartiality, neutrality and objectivity in the scientist. The question is how far these scientific virtues are possible in the study of religion.

These virtues are, however, typically properties of people and not the object of study. What so much social theory has tended to do is to break down any distinction between the two. Once positivism is jettisoned there seems no prospect of any access to neutral data. The desirability of total neutrality is, anyway, questionable. It is more important to have a correct theory than to be a neutral umpire refusing to be committed to any. In the same way, being objective is surely linked to the nature of the object of study. Scientists should not be side-tracked by external factors or what they would like to be the case. That would make them less likely to obtain knowledge of the reality they are studying. Impartiality also demands a willingness not to be swayed by prejudice, but again the purpose of science should not be such as to encourage impartiality to truth. In other words, the more the nature of science or social science is investigated, the more is it clear that rational detachment and criticism does not require any coyness about the question of truth. At whatever level of intellectual enquiry we are participating, it must be obvious that we are concerned with what *is* the case. Rationality and the possibility of truth cannot be divorced. Students of religion pursue the truth about their object of study as much as any physicist or sociologist of science. As in any intellectual discipline, inquiry and the pursuit of truth in that sphere are inseparable. Without the possibility of the latter, the former is pointless.

How far does this affect the study of religion in all its forms? Such study must certainly presuppose that truth is at stake in the sense that it cannot say anything with impunity. Not everything is equally valid. Just as the study of science cannot lose sight of the fact that science is itself a rational activity, so the study of religion raises the question in acute form whether religion itself involves a rational appeal to truth, and whether it is mistaken or not in what it says. It is surely characteristic of any religion that it is in some sense believed to be true by its adherents. Some accounts deny this and choose to interpret belief as expressive or symbolic (Trigg 1985, 91ff.). An advantage of this approach is that if a set of beliefs are not to be understood as claiming anything, we can concentrate on the nature of the believer. Such beliefs will, *ex hypothesi*, tell us a lot about the people holding them and nothing at all about the reality they confront. For instance, rituals connected with the harvesting of crops may express gratitude that all is safely gathered in, or symbolize a sense of dependence on the rhythms of nature. Provided we do not start wondering *who* or *what* is the recipient of such gratitude, we may settle for an account of the role such behaviour plays in the life of the community and of the individual. We may interpret the beliefs so that they appear to be mere attitudes, even emotions, without any apparent rational role. This, though, must entail that they are not directed at anything at all since the minute we accept that the attitudes being expressed are attitudes to 'the world' or 'nature' or 'God', the question has to be raised how each of these is conceived.

No religion, in fact, can escape making claims of some kind, although clearly some religions have a more consciously worked out intellectual basis than others. If we are told a system of belief is symbolic, the question must be faced as to what it symbolizes and whether the symbols are appropriate. Religions are never just constituted by people holding beliefs. The beliefs are about something. This conclusion is often resisted even by those who wish to emphasize the worth of studying them. It may seem as if religions as social facts cannot be approached without a view being taken up as to their truth or falsity. Yet this would invalidate the study of religion. It would become something else, whether apologetics or an explicit attack on religion. It is hardly surprising that many studying religion in a scientific spirit become impatient with issues about truth. They feel quite rightly that they could be side-tracked into specific theological problems. Studies of religion do not imply participation in religion or adoption of its assumptions.

Comparative religion would then be impossible, because no one could be committed to several religions at once. No one wants to become immediately involved in disputes between religions. Can anything be said about religion without this happening?

A comparison with science shows that this fear is erroneous. It is possible to talk about the conduct of science without coming to any conclusion about the truth of particular scientific theories. What however is essential is to realise that their primary purpose is their claim to truth. Relativist views which reduce all belief to the fact of belief are not merely internally inconsistent in simultaneously accepting and rejecting the notion of a fact. They also do fundamental harm to the role of science, and forget that its fundamental purpose is the pursuit of knowledge. Similarly it is possible and desirable to talk of religion in a scientific spirit (understood as being detached and critical). Its effects on human behaviour can be seen and its role in society assessed. This does not, however exhaust the nature of religion or even deal with its most important aspects. The sociology of science can imagine that it can 'explain' science, but in so doing it removes the possibility of science itself explaining anything else, since it becomes a mere epiphenomenon of local social arrangements. Any treatment of religion that does the same to religion also fails ultimately to get to grips with its real nature. Any human phenomenon is complex and variegated and the study of religion can throw much light on this. Yet once it is recognized that it makes claims itself, it has to be seen in a wider context. There are limits to what can be usefully said about religion, as with the study of science, without getting to grips with the particular claims of particular religions. A sociologist of science may be able to make illuminating comments about what made the development of quantum mechanics possible at a particular time. Economic questions and issues about the availability of technology help to provide some of the background. In the end, however, the most important feature about quantum theory is that it is a theory about the nature of sub-atomic reality. There are arguments about its interpretation and about the scientists' relationship with what they are measuring, but that proves the point.

We may well accept that there are different ways of interpreting religious claims about the nature of apparently supernatural reality and our relationship with it. Nevertheless they are at the heart of all religion. Comparative religion may draw attention to differences between types of claims, but a great disservice is done to all religion if it is forgotten that truth is at stake. It is not a question of adjudicating between claims but of recognizing that at the basis of every religion there must be some propositional belief which may or may not be true. The kind of neutrality which plays down the role of such claims distorts religion as much as any view of physical science does when it sees it as a mere social activity.

There are profound differences between religion and science, not least the fact that the former seems to make demands on the way human life is lived. Nevertheless they are both concerned with the nature of reality. There are some who so wish to espouse the 'integrity of science' that they are unwilling to accept this. They cannot accept that religion has a distinctive subject-matter and would play down the importance of this for believers. They would pursue a policy of methodological positivism which is reluctant to envisage even the possibility of any transcendent reality beyond the reach of human science. In a sense this is quite right, since the attribution to any god of the causation of particular processes would stop science in its tracks. What science does not look for, it will not find. As a methodology, this can contribute to the development of science. It is much more dubious as metaphysics. Reality should not be arbitrarily confined to what is accessible to human science. Modern physics, whether in quantum theory, chaos theory or elsewhere, can provide many examples of aspects of physical reality which are in principle beyond our reach. A physicalism or naturalism which makes science, and perhaps merely present-day science, the arbiter of what exists, is pursuing a dangerous course. It is making reality once again depend on human judgments and not the other way round.

This kind of naturalism based on the preeminence of science also extends to the study of religion. One writer (Drees, 1995, 268) who admits that his naturalism is itself a 'metaphysical position' claims: 'Religions are phenomena within reality. Thus they can be studied just like other phenomena.' Yet, if they are held to be merely human phenomena, humanly produced and perhaps just projections of human concerns, they may be made more accessible to study. Any idea, however, that religions may succeed in reflecting some transcendent reality has been ruled out. It may be tempting for any study of religion to restrict the nature of religion to whatever lies within its grasp. It is important, however, to recognize that far from taking religion at its own evaluation or even remaining neutral, this view has emphatically concluded that religious aspirations to the transcendent are at best irrelevant and at worst fraudulent. It has taken a specific stand on the nature of religion and one, moreover which could hardly be accepted by most religious believers. Concentration on the fact of belief will distort the belief. From most people's perspective the most important feature of any belief they happen to hold is not that they hold it, but that it aims at truth.

It has often been recognized that, in the field of religious studies, there is a tension between the view of the 'insider' and that of the 'outsider'. Indeed, one result of the view of the later Wittgenstein, that the meaning of concepts lay in their public and social use, was that participants in religious 'language-games' had a monopoly of understanding. Those who were not employing such concepts in their way of life were by definition excluded from understanding them. This gave priority to the insider, but some views of religious studies do the reverse. Again the origins lie in a philosophical position, this time naturalism. Don Wiebe, for instance resists the view that religious believers should somehow dictate the terms under which the discipline of religious studies is to be conducted. He says:

According to the 'insiders' no proper understanding of religions is possible unless religio-theological categories are somehow incorporated into the methodological framework employed by the student of religion. The 'outsider' on the other hand sees such a methodological injunction as putting in jeopardy the very existence of an academic study of religion. (1993, 11)

This perhaps presents too stark an alternative in that an appreciation of the insider's point of view does not preclude an outsider's analysis. Wiebe, however, believes that religious studies is a scientific discipline attempting like other sciences to give explanations and, like many scientists, he yearns for complete, rather than partial explanations. He writes: 'To restrict the study of religion to pure description precludes what seems to be of the essence of science, namely, explanation and theory' (1994a, 121). It will thus not be enough to show what people believe to be true. If the student of religion is engaged in a truly scientific enterprise, it seems to be necessary to show why such things are believed in the first place. Wiebe would not allow the autonomy of religion so that religion can only be seen in its own terms. However he assumes that the converse must then be the case and religion's own understanding can be put completely on one side. Yet the comparison with the sociology of science immediately demonstrates what a dangerous form of reasoning this is. Once the claims of other people are reduced to the mere fact that they claim them, the same procedure can be invoked again at the next level, so that the explanations are themselves deemed to be in need of explanation.

Wiebe would block this move by assuming a priority for a so-called scientific approach over religious views. In other words, lurking in the background is an old-fashioned positivism which refuses to accept that any religion can be making any meaningful claim to truth. Wiebe himself distinguishes very firmly between the 'mythopoeic' nature of religious thinking and the scientific approach. He says of the former that 'it is a mode of thought that is not rational or cognitive, in the sense that western science is rational and cognitive' (1993, 40). This certainly nails his colours to the mast and in effect aligns him with the crude verificationism of A.J. Ayer in *Language, Truth and Logic* (1946). Since the latter view cannot account for the theoretical entities of modern physics, it scarcely commands confidence. Yet such an aggressive worship of science also carries further dangers since it is by no means clear what can count as science. Wiebe, despite his naturalism, is ready to allow scientific status to the study of religion. That is the point of his argument. It is, however, one thing to demand rational and critical detachment from beliefs so that they are not taken at face value. No doubt a phenomenological approach to religion could be accused of being too ready to settle for mere description. The very act of comparison between religions, and an examination of their social role, would demonstrate that more must be involved. Yet the assumption that religion is not a matter of reason, but that the 'scientific' examination of religion is, must be questioned.

The limitation of reasoning to one mode of activity, namely the physical sciences, has been soundly criticized by many post-positivist philosophers from the later Wittgenstein on. Yet if it is so limited, the point is that it is experimental science, understood in the narrowest way, which is being held up as an example. Such a view is normally coupled with a reductionist position, holding that everything can ultimately be translated into physical terms. Yet this itself challenges the very possibility of social science as a separate enterprise. Indeed there have been plenty with Wiebe's view of the importance of science who have denied that social sciences are sciences. Either they can be translated into the language of physics or they are saying nothing. This though would raise terrible difficulties for religious studies since they would be left without any proper sphere. Physicalism and naturalism undermine all social science. If the theories of the practitioners of religious studies are to claim their own validity, we must be allowed to break out of the strait-jacket of a narrow scientism glorifying the physical sciences.

The Concept of Truth and the Study of Religion

All intellectual endeavour depends on a distinction between subject and object. The study of religion is no different. It requires us to reflect on what we are studying. There is often a concentration on the fact of belief and its effects. What is happening is that the very distinction between subject and object which makes the study of religion possible, is being deemed inappropriate in religion. Institutional and social facts become easier to deal with than abstract beliefs. The latter can get reduced to the former. Yet if the study of religion is to be consistent, it should be willing not only to lay claim to rationality itself, but should also accept that those who are the object of their study may have an equal claim to rationality in the formation and sustaining of their beliefs. Rationality is not the prerogative of the scientist.

At each level, the subject and the object of belief must be carefully distinguished. Religious believers are also subjects with beliefs that at least purport to be about reality. How far such beliefs succeed in referring to reality is another issue and one that students of religion may not feel it is within their remit to tackle. It cannot, however be simply brushed aside as unimportant. Whilst a methodological agnosticism may seem appropriate on the part of investigators, that should not deter them from understanding that the perceived truth of a religion lies at the heart of its importance for a believer. One consequence of the stress on the importance of beliefs about truth in religion is to allow the possibility that some religious beliefs could actually be true, that, for instance, divine reality has actually been revealed in some instances (Alston 1991). If that were the case, no further explanation would be necessary. This is precisely what many students of religion do not wish to allow, for the simple reason that their own attempts at explanation would be much more circumscribed. There always remains less to explain when someone believes what is true than if they fall into error. This is why the so-called 'strong programme' in the sociology of knowledge was eager to insist that similar modes of explanation be available for all beliefs (Bloor 1976). Without the discounting of truth, causal explanation of a traditional scientific kind cannot get a grip since rationality is its own explanation. If someone believes something which is true, and believes it because of its truth, there seems little point in wanting a stronger explanation. The best of all reasons for believing something is because it is objectively true. We do not want elaborate causal explanations as to why someone sees the need to take an umbrella when it is raining. They clearly (and correctly) believe that it is raining. It is only neurotic behaviour which seems to cry out for attention. Once, therefore, religious studies go on from the description and comparison of belief to forms of causal explanation, the tacit assumption has been made that the content of the beliefs is irrelevant.

In fact, the urge to give an external explanation for religious belief all too often comes from the view that such belief is in fact false. It should not be explained in terms of the direct intervention in this world of a transcendent God, which is what most theists would believe. Benson Saler makes it clear that the whole anthropological enterprise tends to proceed on that assumption. He says:

Few anthropologists appear to subscribe to the theory that humanity has religion because it was originally given or established by God. Rather, most account religion to be a variable, cultural creation. (1993, 7)

The point to be made is not that anthropologists are necessarily wrong in their assumptions. It seems that they have, however, without argument, taken it for granted that those they are studying are unlikely to have valid religious grounds for their beliefs. This might, if it were the case, limit the scope for scientific explanation. By ruling out the possibility, however, and seeing religion as inevitably a human creation, we see a characteristic switch from content of belief to fact of belief. The nuances of what is accepted as true are regarded as irrelevant. Yet if the same treatment were meted out to the beliefs of the anthropologists themselves in a sociological exercise, their own claims to truth (and hence to our attention) would immediately disappear. It may be that religion is a special case in the range of human belief (perhaps because it allegedly refers to a transcendent reality), but that would need considerable argument. Certainly, too, as Saler indicates, the mere fact of religious difference is an important element in the situation. Scientific, even anthropological theories, can — and do — vary, though, without pretensions to truth being inevitably dismissed. Indeed, disagreement in science has sometimes been thought to be an important element in the ability of scientists to winnow out the true from the false.

We must be wary of discounting claims as to the nature of reality made by religion, through an eagerness to give thorough explanations. Such global ambitions can easily be self-defeating. The question must always be asked why the people under investigation cannot continue, say, to make claims to truth (in their case, perhaps concerning a supernatural reality), while the investigators can make assertions about what is true at the level of reality they are studying. In the case of religion, the missing ingredient may be a reductionist positivism which threatens the autonomy of any social science as much as that of religion.

As has already been conceded, beliefs may be held at very different intellectual levels. Some may be held totally uncritically, others after they have been winnowed through a prolonged process of reasoning. Some contemporary Christianity, for example, with its sophisticated philosophy and metaphysics, is clearly very different from apparently unreflective religious practices. However, whatever their overtly rational basis, the claims that any religion makes about reality must be its defining feature. That is what the ordinary believer assumes, and a 'scholarly' analysis that denies this must rest on something more than the assumptions of an old-fashioned positivism. Neutrality towards religious claims may be necessary at one level in studying religion, but it must be recognized that they comprise the heart of a religion. Students of religion should not confuse their own necessary detachment from issues of the truth of a particular religion, with the erroneous judgment that claims to truth are unimportant for those who profess a religion. They should, further, not be too ready to assume that there could be no possible rational justification for the beliefs. In religious studies, two dangers await. In the desire to be 'scientific' the practitioners of the discipline may be drawn to a naturalist assumption that the only reality is that accessible to contemporary science. All truth is scientific truth. Such a position makes any social science a questionable enterprise since it tends to give priority to physics and looks to the reduction of every science to the most basic one. Yet without a firm retention of the idea of different levels of explanation and understanding, social science, not to mention religious studies, is likely to disappear (the controversial attempt in recent years of some forms of sociobiology to 'take over' social science is an example of this process). Another danger is that in revulsion from such a narrow scientism, the continuing emphasis on the fact of belief leads us into the view that claims to truth, in whatever area, can be ignored. It is sometimes even implied that it is true that there is no such thing as truth. Whatever the underlying incoherence of asserting such a position, the stress on the social construction of all belief (even presumably the belief that beliefs are socially constructed) is widespread. We seem caught between a narrow scientism and a nihilistic relativism. It is therefore imperative that in every field and at every level the distinction between the subject and the object of belief is upheld. Why people have the beliefs they do can never totally remove the further question of the validity of these beliefs. This is true in any religion and it is also true in the study of religion. What the practitioners of the latter must be careful to avoid is a willingness to claim truth for themselves but fail to recognize that the same urge to truth forms the basis for much religion. Whether truth is actually achieved in either sphere is another issue.

Social Facts, Metaphysics and Rationality in the Study of Religion as a Human Science

Jeppe Sinding Jensen

Descriptions and analyses of 'things religious' require the use of categories and concepts which are, semantically speaking, non-realist and devoid of any 'essence'. Religion, magic, society, dendrolatry, and incubation oracles are *not* natural kinds; they are conceptual constructions and analytical devices whereby the world of human action is divided and translated into comparable and understandable categories. All concepts in the study of religion are concepts imagined, invented and employed. As in any other study of socio-cultural realms such concepts are constructions, but they are socially and ideologically real — and some are better constructions than others.[1] Thus, we must be able to distinguish between different classes of meaning and discourse, because although religions, cultures, science and theories in and of it all are, without exception, social facts, there are none the less profound differences as to their status. How can we differentiate between facts and the purely fictional? What are the ontological differences between market economy, class struggle, French cuisine and Santa Claus? Aren't they all 'just' social facts and thus constructions? As nominalists may we not call anything whatever we want? Where are the constraints? What are the rules and what is rational?[2]

We must consider some of the ramifications of these problems. In the following I shall attempt to define rationality in the cultural sciences and in the study of religion in a search of possible criteria of demarcation.

Religious facts are social facts. Representations, ideas, actions, and institutions that are part of religious systems are social realities, and it is only by treating religion in a 'social fact' perspective that the study of religion becomes at all possible. The alternatives are irrational or subjectivist intuitions on which no scientific intersubjective discourse can rely. If I am thus reducing the religious to the social, what then are the possibilities of reducing 'social facts'? In my opinion a reduction of the religious to the social is methodologically meaningful, whereas a reduction of the social to the neurological, e.g., does not seem to hold much promise for a study of religion. A reduction of the social (as meaningful) would equal a reduction of the intentional and this does not seem to work.[3]

Like language, concepts as social facts may only be 'transmitted' from one mind to the other *because they are public phenomena*. Likewise, it is difficult to imagine social facts that may not be expressed in language, simply because they are linguistically constituted in the first place. I shall therefore presume that, whatever else we may conclude about social facts and collective representations, they are, in some sense, language-like. There is not really anything like a 'private social fact'. Consequently, we may study social facts *'in themselves'* as symbolic and meaningful entities. The hermeneutics involved are not restricted to understandings of the interpretations of actors; social facts may be interpreted on their own in their ideological dimension as discourse. The social and cultural sciences must be 'realist' in the sense that they not only have empirical subject matters but also general theoretical objects — on the reflections of which they constitute what counts as empirical matter in the first place. Positivist social science is on the wane, but this does not imply that the object of social inquiry dissolves. The 'reality' of social facts can be upheld insofar as the semantic character of things social warrants their public availability.[4] Our notion of religion as a social fact defines it as publicly available and accessible; it is as communicative and semantic as language. Social facts could thus be considered from perspectives analogous to those of non-referential semantic holism.[5]

Theories as social facts

Social facts are studied through theories that are also social facts, in a way similar to language, which may only be studied in and through language. Social categories are public because they are semantic, this goes for scholarly theories as well. A non-public theory that cannot be expressed in language is an absurdity. We must accept an idea of science as a cultural system which moves between interpretation and explanation, between theory and practice. Then again, there are those who hold that such forms of scholarship are not science, because they are 'strongly incomplete', non-predictive and not explanatory in the conventional causal sense.[6]

These are some of the considerations we shall have to meet to validate scientific discourse on the socio-cultural in general, and to fulfil the specific requirements of a rational and disciplined study of religion — a field of human activity often considered in Western scholarship to be a prime example of irrationality. When, however, religion is seen not as an object in the physical world, nor as a psychological entity located in individual minds, but as an instance of Karl Popper's (1979) 'third world'[7] of objective contents of thought in accordance with our notions of the public availability of the semantic and the social, then other perspectives and avenues become possible.

All we can say is that studies of religion as well as the theories backing them are social facts. Then, there are two major attitudes to this state of affairs and its consequences. One view, quite fashionable, holds that since theories, and all that comes with them, are socially or historically contingent, then objectivity and rationality are impossible, unobtainable, and irrelevant. The other position, which I shall defend, argues, contrarily, that precisely *because* theories are social facts, then they are both *intersubjective and controllable* and therefore amenable to scientific scrutiny as well as theoretical reflection. Ivan Strenski states:

Theories are social and historical facts just as much as they are *loci* of arguments. As such, theories ought to be studied historically and socially just as much as we study them for their cogency (1993,9) and:

I have tried to treat theories as 'social facts', and thus to see how the intention of their authors in making them and the environment of discourse which made them possible, may be seen to interact and produce the theories as we know them. I have shown that the authors of theories created them in contingent ways, and that they changed their minds often quite radically. There is more to understanding a theory than understanding how it hangs together (or not) logically; that 'more' comes into focus when we see that theories are themselves social facts with their histories and real location in human society. (Strenski 1989, 210)

We must accept at full value the theoretical consequences of theories being social facts, namely the requirement of incessant critical self-reflection. If myths think themselves in men, then theories being external, discursive and coercive 'facts' are responsible for the way we think, and like good shamans we should learn to control the spirits that possess us. This is where deconstructive reflection is an advance in the human and social sciences. However, deconstructionism often seems to slide into scepticist relativism where the social and historical character of theories and scientific inquiry is thought to jeopardize the very idea and possibility of science and rationality. We shall have to demonstrate that although theories of religion are social facts they are not merely bound to the accidental, to common sense, or to folk-theories.

Science as social fact: the critique

It is a common relativist view that science reflects values and interests of a particular time and mode of thought, so that the concepts and logics involved do not possess 'timeless validity'.[8] Along with a general 'interpretive turn' such views have left us with the impression that the social and human sciences are radically subjective enterprises.[9]

In a radical relativist approach, the fact of cultural construction becomes not the result of analysis but a premise from which all discourse is derived. Roger Trigg criticizes this 'sociological turn' in epistemology:

In this situation, falsity becomes mere deviation from a social norm, and ontology has to be discarded... Reason is thus left with little role, embedded in social practices and used to re-assert their prejudices... The very distinction between an object and its representation is abolished. (1993, 152)

Obviously, such 'social epistemologies' would in the end blur the distinction between religion and the study of it. When the 'subjectivity thesis' is matched with empathetic hermeneutics the end results become either individual confessions or collective solipsisms such as 'cultural heritage management'. Autochthonous interpretations are then privileged and unassailable, a curious mixture of contructionism ('how others view us') and essentialism ('how we view ourselves'). Political and ethical concerns override methodological ones and the study of religion becomes an impossibility, because not only would generalizations have no validity, but descriptions and interpretations would only be deemed valid insofar as they correspond to 'indigenous' epistemologies. The study of Inuit or Maori religion, of Islam, Judaism and any other religious tradition is then reserved for insiders along with their views of how to conduct it.[10] The irony of the situation is that all these varieties of relativism are in fact guided by concepts of objectivity — however unreflected, what we might call 'privileged objectivity', that is, truths that are accessible only through a cultural or social membership. In a large measure these problems stem from the failure to see that values in science are of more than one kind. Values are *also* social facts, but it does not mean that all values are of the same kind; there are differences in principle between scientific judgments and characterizations on the one hand and moral and political appraisals on the other.[11] Thus, the morally normative views, however much they influence the *practice* of science, belong principally and analytically to another sphere, and therefore it is *possible to distinguish between them*. Relativists continue to react as if positivism was the *only* possible constraint on subjectivism. And in this respect they appear as positivists in disguise — maintaining a view of the world as constituted of brute facts and subjectivities only.[12]

We acknowledge the fact that the social world of meaning is a human construction and we also accept that any higher-order level of knowledge and representation, including science, cannot be but a construction. A few examples: Émile Benveniste noted in one of his founding essays in linguistics that the reality of an object is inseparable from the methods given for its decription (1966, 119).[13] Anthropological representations of cultures are social facts and results of human practices in history (e.g. Rabinow 1986). Quite a number of interpretations of religions appear as alternative world-constructions or theologies reflecting more the interests of the researchers than the those of their 'objects'.[14] It would, however, be erroneous to conclude that the idea of 'social facts' which from the outset was introduced to emphasize the empirical character of the social realm should lead to the conclusion that logical extensions of the concept to cover also theories and scientific practices would land us in a field of subjectivities. My point is that these subjective views are also reflective of social facts, and that they are therefore amenable to analysis and scholarly judgment — subjectivity is objectlike because subjectivities are only discursively available in semantic and social form. Quine's pronouncement that knowledge of physical objects is only available to us as 'cultural posits' does not mean that science is just one more 'belief system' or 'religion' — that is to read Quine the wrong way round.[15] As things stand, the study of religion is, more than any other study, in need of adequate ideas concerning the forms of rationality that can underwrite it. However, the disorderliness of the present condition should not be a cause for despair, only for increased reflection and a recognition that the study of religion can be pluralistic and yet controlled. In fact, this is the situation confronting all forms of science on questions of pluralism and objectivity.[16]

Metaphysics and rationality in the human sciences

What, then, are the possibilities of rational justifications of practices in the human sciences? The study of religion is the study of created worlds and of metaphysical ontologies. To many a scholar or philosopher of science it would seem no less than mysterious to conduct rational inquiries into such a field. Contrariwise, I argue that such inquiry is perfectly possible and in no way mysterious. In a certain sense, the study of religion is *even less mysterious* than the study of the physical world. Religion is directly accessible because it is itself a semantic phenomenon (although the reality of the ontologies it refers to lies outside the scope of inquiry). Religion simply is what people say and do in certain ways in certain situations. It is plain social reality. So, if we can defend rationality in the social sciences there will be solutions to our theoretical conundrums, without, however, imagining the study of religion becoming anything that resembles the traditional picture of 'hard' science.[17]

I am firmly convinced that the question of metaphysics in the study of religion, contrary to a common assumption, need not worry us. For one, the purported truth claims of religious systems are beyond scientific inquiry, all we can say about them is that, as they are *talked about*, they are social and semantic facts. The visions of mystics are not (yet) amenable to photographic reproduction but the discursive representations of them are subject to public availability. Second, as *we know* it, metaphysics in religious discourse are no different from metaphysics in any other kind of discourse; religion is no privileged symbolic realm, its semantics does not have any special ontological status.[18] If we are to understand *anything at all about religion* there seems to be no better option than Donald Davidson's theory of semantics, because it rests on metaphysical premises that make sense in the study of religion:

> it caters to truth, meaning, the possibility of understanding and (radical) interpretation. It explains how humans can understand each other across time and space and it explains why religious semantics are extensions of semantics in general, and how they can be meaningful without reference. No special metaphysics is needed; religious beliefs are semantically speaking *just beliefs*, and that is all. (Penner 1995, 247)[19]

Thus, religion does not demand privileged procedures for its analysis, there is no such thing as a 'religious method'. In the following, I shall consider religion to be part and parcel of socio-cultural reality and the study of it in no more need of privileged methods or singular forms of rationality than other human and social sciences, and common to all enquirers. But what are they?

Rationality in the practice of science

Rationality is not in things in 'themselves', it is a human attribute: when the last human disappears so does rationality. 'The human ability to reason must be the starting-point for all our thinking. Once we try to deny it, or explain it away, we merely use the very ability we attack' (Trigg 1993, 230). In the same vein, Harold Brown proposes a new model of rationality 'consistent with the spirit of critical rationalism' (1988, 193) which includes historical and social dimensions, but is not relativist. As Brown notes:

various groups of theologians who belong to different religions may all be engaged in a fully rational endeavor, and the same may hold for, say, Azande witch doctors. But while this possibility does follow from our model of rationality, it does not have quite the pernicious significance that some will see there... to claim that a belief is rational is not the same as claiming that it is true, and while rational acceptance of a claim depends on assessing evidence, some forms of evidence provide a stronger warrant for belief than other forms of evidence. Thus while questions of denominational theology may be capable of a rational solution, it does not follow that we have no basis at all for choosing between, say, a scientific and a theological world-view at those points at which the two views conflict... Note also that I have not returned to the relativist position...according to which every social group is automatically rational. On that view, rational behavior is rule-following behavior and any group following socially accepted rules is *ipso facto* rational according to their own standards.... In other words, we must not confuse the thesis that what is rational to believe, or do, is relative to a particular situation, with the thesis that rationality is relative. (ibid. 194-5)[20]

There is no instant rationality:

In the course of our search for truth we will rationally accept claims that will later be rejected, and rationally reject claims that will later be accepted, but a surer and more efficient method does not seem to be available. (227)[21]

Permit me, here, to return to Ernest Nagel's classic ideas concerning the relations between the social and the natural sciences[22] where he convincingly demonstrates that rationality in social science *is* possible and that it does not rely on 'sui generis' forms of logic. Studies of the velocity of molecules and psychological states of actors in social interaction are obviously different, but:

despite these differences, the crucial point is that the logical canons employed by responsible social scientists in assessing the objective evidence for imputation of psychological states do not appear to differ essentially (though they may often be applied less rigorously) from the canons employed for analogous purposes by responsible students in other areas of inquiry. (1961, 484)[23]

Similarly, on the claim that the student of human affairs proceeds by way of understanding, *Verstehen*, Nagel, argues:

His ability to enter into relations of empathy with the human actors in some social process may indeed be heuristically important in his efforts to *invent* suitable hypotheses which will explain the process. Nevertheless, his empathetic iden-tification with those individuals does not, by itself, constitute *knowledge*. The fact that he achieves such identification does not annul the need for objective evidence, assessed in accordance with logical principles that are common to all controlled enquiries, to support his imputation of subjective states to those human agents. (484-85)

The ultimate question is to what extent historical reasoning as based on induction by analogy can be judged as warranted, 'an objective sense in which some judgements of what is 'reasonable' are better than others, *even if we cannot give a general criterion'* (Putnam 1987, 74).[24] There is no such thing as *the* scientific method: 'The hope for a formal method, capable of being isolated from our judgements about the nature of the world, seems to have been frustrated' (ibid., 75). This is not giving in to a total relativism, neither in the natural, the social nor any other sciences, or other matters of concern to humans, the view:

does not require us to give up our pluralism or our fallibilism: one does not have to believe in a unique *best* moral version, or a unique *best* causal version, or a unique *best* mathematical version; what we have are *better and worse* versions, and that *is* objectivity. (ibid., 77)

Thus, our moral, scientific, etc. images are nothing but human, and precisely for that reason can they be altered, rejected, combined and perhaps even advanced. 'Doing science' is in itself reflective of values. Therefore, value judgements do not only belong to the 'lesser sciences', nor do they represent a detrimental condition that corrupts our scholarly enterprises. The so-called 'Value-oriented bias' of social inquiry *need not* in itself present obstacles to establishing facts and satisfactory explanations. This also goes for the selection of problems of investigation:

there is no difference between any of the sciences with respect to the fact that the interests of the scientist determine what he selects for investigation. But this fact, by itself, represents no obstacle to the succesful pursuit of objectively controlled inquiry in any branch of study. (Nagel 1961, 486-87)

Similar conclusions can be reached concerning the problem of the influence of the researcher's own standards, which may in principle be minimized and overcome 'through the self-corrective mechanisms of science as a social enterprise' (ibid., 489). Therefore, it would be 'absurd to conclude that reliable knowledge of human affairs is unattainable merely because social inquiry is frequently value-oriented' (490). On a close parallel to the situation in the study of religion, it would be absurd to conclude that it cannot be conducted because of problems past.

Claims to the effect that value-free sciences are *in principle* impossible, that facts and values are inseparable and indistinguishable serve as epistemological backbone in current forms of relativism. However, as Nagel notes, this critique

confounds two quite different senses of the term 'value judgment': the sense in which a value judgment expresses *approval or disapproval* of either of some moral (or social ideal)... and the sense in which a value judgment expresses *an estimate* of the degree to which some commonly recognized (and more or less clearly defined) type of action, object, or institution is embodied in a given instance. (492)

Nagel applies the term 'appraising value judgments' to the former and 'characterizing value judgments' to the latter. Crucial for the distinction are two logical features: you need not, when making a characterizing value judgment, 'affirm or deny a corresponding appraising evaluation.' And, 'although characterizing judgments are necessarily entailed by many appraising judgments, making appraising judgments is not a necessary condition for making characterizing ones' (493).[25] Nagel's distinction, corresponds to my own differentiation between *moral* and *methodological* normativity. We may, as I see it, be committed to values of 'scientific probity', to objectivity and rationality which are normative and value-laden concepts in themselves. We do not, however, necessarily treat these as moral precepts (which they also are) in scientific practice, rather, they become values of methodological normativity. To be sure, there are often difficulties in the social and human sciences in distinguishing these two forms of value judgments, not least in the study of religion, where terminologies and theoretical presuppositions tend towards the vague, but these difficulties in practice 'provide no compelling reasons for the claim that an ethically neutral social science is inherently impossible' (Nagel 1961, 495).

Undoubtedly, scholarly evaluations depend on social and historical situations and conditions, a point that has been amply demonstrated in studies of the practice of science by, e.g., Thomas Kuhn, Michel Foucault, and Paul Feyerabend.[26] Commonly, insistent relativist critiques from a sociology of knowledge perspective would hold that:

1) there is a necessary and logical connection between the values of the scholar and his competence,
2) social institutions change and so do the intellectual requirements for understanding them, and
3) concepts and theories are reflective of their locus in history.

According to historical or sociological relativism the truth of a proposition depends on its genesis or its context. The crucial question is whether, says Nagel, 'the principles employed in social inquiry for assessing the intellectual products are *necessarily* determined by the social perspective of the inquirer' (500). At least some statements about human affairs must be neutral or have a validity beyond their own situation, otherwise relativist propositions would be true only for some, i.e., those asserting them, an argument that leads only to self-defeating skeptical relativism. The way out is to propose that social scientific inquiry is relative to certain conditions, but this goes for all scientific practice; historicity is not subjectivity. Nagel's conclusion on the logical structure of investigation in the social sciences is that: 'it is not in principle impossible for these disciplines to establish conclusions having the objectivity of conclusions reached in other domains of inquiry' (501).

My reintroduction of Ernst Nagel's classical (late empiricist and pre-Kuhn) work is not an attempt to promote it as a canonical standard for evalutions of scientific epistemology; that would run counter to my general conception of the role of values in relation to rationality — it is only to note that he convincingly showed how the logically structural problems besetting scholarly pursuits *outside* the natural sciences are *not in principle* different from those confronting the natural sciences. Claims about a specific, '*sui generis*' nature of social scientific inquiry based on alternative canons of logic, value-ladenness, empathy and methodological individualism do not withstand scrutiny and criticism. These 'boundary' conditions must therefore also pertain to the study of religion. It is certainly true that in the time since Nagel there have been revolutions in the philosophy of science, probably more than in science itself, and that some epistemic foundations have been shaken. Extreme logical empiricist scientism was eventually succeeded by radical relativism. Both of these orientations are detrimental to the study of religion, the one because it relegates the phenomenon to be studied to a realm of the bizarre and the other because it obscures the difference between the study and its object.

Unity in plurality: the disorder of things

The study of religion deals with complex cultural and cognitive phenomena and it therefore needs to proceed from a theoretically well-supported, balanced and pluralistic view of science, such as, e.g., the one proposed in John Dupré's 'disunity' of science theory.[27] The apparent disunity of science is, according to Dupré, an indication that the ideal of scientific unity has been lost. The 'atomistic materialist' ideal of microphysics as the mother of science and the bedrock of reductionism has been challenged and found wanting.

Various attempts at a recovery of unity must be deemed equally implausible (Dupré 1993, 221-243). The pressing problem of demarcation between science and pseudo-science seems unresolvable through a single criterion. Solutions in terms of falsification have been rejected by philosophers of science. This is, in my view and also in Dupré's, unfortunate, because we are left without a universal methodological criterion of science or a clear solution to the question of 'genuine scientific merit' (223). Since Thomas Kuhn's work:

there has been an increasing tendency to downplay the role of *all* systematic, reason-driven factors in the explanation of scientific change and to focus increasingly on broader ideological, political, and other extrascientific factors. (Dupré 1993, 233)

In certain areas we may even question the idea of 'evolutionary epistemology': the idea of a gradual approach to truth through accumulation of empirical knowledge and theoretical refinement; the study of religion is one field which comes to mind here. Dupré discusses (239 ff.) possible criteria for a demarcation of science, e.g., coherent relations between theory and empirical data, that science is cooperative and cumulative, and that genuine sciences should seek general laws and principles. The conclusions, however, are that although some of these demands may be fulfilled by some of those activities we consider scientific, it is impossible to obtain comprehensive correlations that cover all these activities. Various sciences exhibit such pluriform characteristics that we may at most apply a 'family resemblance' classification: 'there can be nothing unique about science, because there is nothing common to the various domains of science' (263). Dupré then suggests a 'pluralistic epistemology' or 'promiscuous realism'. The immediate impression is one of ardent relativism or epistemological anarchy but his intention is 'to try to sort the scientific sheep from the goats' (263) without resorting to an outdated positivist philosophy; the question of realism need not, as a philosophical position, depend upon reductions to physics. Dupré's 'promiscuous realism', may well be of assistance to the study of religion,[28] because it is pluralist without lapsing into relativist obscurantism.

The characteristics of 'pluralistic epistemology' are, I think, better understood by direct quotes from Dupré:

Science, construed simply as the set of knowledge-claiming practices that are accorded that title, is a mixed bag. The role of theory, evidence, and institutional norms will vary greatly from one area of science to the next. My suggestion that science should be seen as a family resemblance concept seems to imply not merely that no strong version of scientific unity of the kind advocated by classical reductionists can be sustained, but that there can be no possible answer to the demarcation problem. (242)

Dupré admits that his thesis excludes a simple criterion of demarcation; nevertheless, it would be fatal if we had no principles for assessing the superiority of some claims over others, e.g., evolutionary theory, based on empirical research and theoretical criticism versus creationism, based 'on oracular interpretations of an ancient book of often unknown or dubious provenance' (243). Permit me to quote his proposals for a normative epistemological standard at some length:

I suggest that we try to replace the kind of epistemology that unites pure descriptivism and scientistic apologetics with something more like a virtue epistemology. There are many possible and actual such virtues: sensitivity to empirical fact, plausible background assumptions, coherence with other things we know, exposure to criticism from the widest variety of sources, and no doubt others. Some of the things we call 'science' have many such virtues, others very few...But the approach I advocate also implies that a solution to the second problem [of demarcation] is unlikely to be forthcoming. Many plausible epistemic virtues will be exemplified as much by practices not traditionally included within science as by paradigmatic scientific disciplines. Many works of philosophy or literary criticism, even, will be more closely connected to empirical fact, coherent with other things we know, and exposed to criticism from different sources than large parts of, say, macro-economics or theoretical ecology. In general, I can imagine no reason why a ranking of projects of inquiry in terms of a plausible set of epistemic virtues (let alone epistemic and social virtues) would end up with most of the traditional sciences gathered at the top. No sharp distinction between science and lesser forms of knowledge production can survive this reconception of epistemic merit. It might fairly be said, if paradoxically, that with the disunity of science comes a kind of unity of knowledge. (242-3).[29]

What can be said to count as knowledge was discussed above in relation to semantics and I, as a consequence, consider the demarcation problem to be in some sense solved — at least in the study of religion because it rules out claims based on religious intuitions. From the 'wider' concept of science, a view accrues that the study of religion is just as 'scientific' as any other project of inquiry or knowledge-gathering without emulating popular and outdated, scientistic conceptions of science. Not all that looks, or used to look like science, is science.[30]

In the latter part of this century the image of science has changed drastically. Not only have the natural sciences been 'epistemologized', deprived of the idea that they have unlimited and unmediated access to the mathematical order of the universe itself, it is also true that the *'Geisteswissenschaften'* hold fewer *'Geister'* these days: the arts and humanities have been increasingly desubjectivized. Human sciences, on the other hand, have become more 'objective' in the sense that they presuppose, e.g., cultural, linguistic or semiotic systems, through which those human affairs they study are mediated — subjects and collectivities become bearers of meanings that are, as we have learnt, cognitively testable.

A 'no problem' thesis for the study of religion

I suggest that we think of the study of religion as just one such 'knowledge-gathering practice' that complies with the same ontological and rational premises as all other practices of science. This suggestion is in accordance with a pluralist view of the sciences, which despite their variations and variability, are activities whose execution depend on a range of 'epistemic virtues'.[31] Against relativist critiques we are (still) able to say that there are no principled grounds for considering 'objectivity' (as an ideal) to be less relevant in the study of religion than in any other study of human affairs and that our studies do not *per se* rely on logical canons or forms of rationality different from those of other fields of science. Scholars of religion are as liable to fall into holes they don't see, as are astro-physicists, ophtalmologists and anyone else. All rational science must resort to unambiguous language, the semantics of which being composed of everyday language with specific domain extensions like 'quarks' or 'dendrolatry'. On the semantic side, the study of religion may suffer from the same problems as all other disciplines, but it may also retain the virtues as well.

I shall give my reasons for propounding a 'no problem' thesis: if scientific rationality is a problem in the study of religion, it is historically and accidentally so and not by any inherent necessity. Consequently, rationality holds the same position in the study of religion as anywhere else. The 'no problem' thesis maintains:

1) that there is *no special problem* for the study of religion, and
2) there are accountable reasons why rationality is not to be considered as much a problem as we may have thought.

Some of the earlier history (study) of religions does fall into the category of the 'less rational', so we may say that the 'cumulative and cooperative' aspects of the project of science, insofar as the study of religion has been concerned, must, by necessity, be manifested in re- and deconstructions; but such activities are *also* cumulative knowledge-gathering. What may seem to be a weakness in the study of religions as opposed to many 'stronger' programmes could finally turn out to be an example of many virtues. Rationality, as we have seen, is no longer a state of affairs resulting from the operations of formal procedures or pre-theoretical empiricist veracity. Rationality comes out as a set of criteria for 'reasonableness' along with the reflective understanding of our standards as human images that can be right or wrong. This is not relativism. It is, on the contrary, as much realism, as we can get — because we *simply have to be reasonable*.[32] Nor is this 'voodoo epistemology'. It is what makes communication at all possible.[33] Remember the premises of semantics: signs mean something (however they manage to do so...) and display holistic semantic intra-corrigibility, which (literally) makes interpretation possible. Some things are certainly hard to understand, but that doesn't mean that nothing can be understood. When, hermeneutically speaking, some amount of *Verstehen* is unavoidable in the inductive analogies on which studies of human affairs rely, it does not follow that we are stranded in a field of mere subjectivities. If strict formal procedures of verification and falsification cannot be upheld in the study of religion, it is so only because the same conditions apply to any other field of 'knowledge-gathering'.

On the other hand, the idea of unambiguousness as one of the main characteristics of rationality is characteristically off-set by the nature of the codes of religious communication and semantics. We may say that ambiguity is part of the religious code itself. Semantic 'aberrations' such as concepts of the Trinity, Nirvana, gods appearing as sweet potatoes or the symbolism in Ndembu Isoma rituals, all tell us that we are concerned with utterances that are meaningful despite their lack of reference to the 'real' world. But then again, we concluded above that nothing is true simply by virtue of referring to the 'real world': the furniture of the universe comes with no names and there is nothing in the 'real world' that corresponds to a sentence.

When religious semantics differ from 'everyday' semantics, it is not because they are 'alternative conceptual schemes' with *sui generis meanings*, but because they are extensions of ordinary semantics which are transposed and become meaningful in religious discourse, precisely by their ambiguous, inverted, and counter-intuitive character. They are not 'irrational' or meaningless just because they do not 'hook up' to the real world. Still, in all their code and domain switching, religious semantics and religious discourse do disregard certain fundamental, logical and rational principles of human communication — that is how they are disclosed as religious in the first place.

Ironic, then, is our knowledge that religion and religious discourse have been the warrants of all cultural semantics the world has seen — at least until very recently. Here is another reason why a rational, comparative and general study of religion contains questions of a most intriguing and fascinating character. And not only for scholars of religion.

Notes

1. None have, to my knowledge, put it as clearly as Jonathan Z. Smith in the Introduction to *Imagining Religion* (1982): 'Religion is solely the creation of the scholar's study. It is created for the scholar's analytic purposes by his imaginative acts of comparison and generalization. Religion has no independent existence apart from the academy' (xi). The very complex philosophical accounts concerning in- and extensions of concepts I leave aside here.

2. See e.g, on the 'end of epistemology' Paul Rabinow's (1986) discussion of the consequences for anthropology of the positions of Richard Rorty, Ian Hacking and Michel Foucault.

3. Cf. Putnam's arguments (1987, 13f) against the possibility of a reduction of the intentional, which are all the more convincing because he formerly held the reductionist views he now counters. I disregard 'cognitive' studies here because they are, in this connection, not really reductive in that they cannot be 'about religion' without incorporating religious conceptual schemes — with semantic properties. See Malley (1994) on 'eliminative materialism' and 'emergent properties' in the study of religion. I regard certain motivations behind current cognitive studies on religion to stem from the same source as mine in this essay: the concern to situate and legitimate the study of religion within the confines of scientific practice and discourse. Hence, my lack of attention does not indicate any denigration.

4. Cf. also Claude Lévi-Strauss in his introduction to Mauss (1987, 37): 'Like language, the social *is* an autonomous reality (the same one moreover); symbols are more real than what they symbolize...'. Saussure never directly quoted Durkheim's idea of the social fact, but the influence is there: 'le langage est un fait social' (1973, 21), cf. Holdcroft (1991, 27). On social facts, and Durkheim's 'social realism', e.g.: Hollis (1994, 100ff), Lukes (1988), Parkin (1992, 18f), and Alexander (1990).

5. Penner (1995) is a commendable introduction to (Donald Davidson's) holist semantics in a study of religions perspective. See also Lawson and McCauley (1990) and Fodor and LePore (1992) for overviews.

6. An 'incomplete discipline' is, in philosophy of science parlance, one that depends on variables and theories from outside the discipline. This of course, and more so in my version, makes the study of religion an *extremely incomplete* discipline, which, in my opinion however, is its strength.

7. Popper made an interesting note on the history of this concept in a bibliographical note (from 1978) in the revised 1979 edition (152): the distinction between thought in the objective and the subjective sense can be traced back to Heinrich Gomperz in 1908, then, in 1918, Gottlob Frege used the term 'Das dritte Reich' (later an

unpopular term). Note this term also in G. van der Leeuw's 'Epilegomena', quoting the psychologist E. Spranger: 'Das Reich des Sinnes ist ein drittes Reich, dass über der blossen Subjektivität, wie über der blossen Objektivität liegt.' (1933, 636). Of course, the in- and extensions of the concept have been transformed since then.

8. My recycling of Ernst Nagel's (1961, 488ff) succinct critiques of historical relativism shows how little even relativisms have changed (!). In this context I conceive of relativism broadly, therefore no specific references.

9. This is an impression not to be substantiated here, but see e.g. Gellner (1992) for probably the most acerbic critique around.

10. These observations relate to both the crisis of conscience in anthropology and of identity in the study of religion, see e.g. Lawson and McCauley (1993). On ideas of privileged access to cultural (re-)constructions see relevant examples and critiques in Hanson (1989). In the study of Islam these ideas — as an antidote to 'Orientalism' — are prevalent; an example is Davies (1988) who advocates anthropological studies of Islam cast in Islamic idiom only. Also, note that an increasing number of publications on religion are concerned with 'dialogues' etc...

11. In a sophisticated analysis of value-orientation in social science, Ernst Nagel argued the possibility of objectivity in the study of human affairs (1961, 485). The division between 'characterizing' and 'appraising' value judgments is Nagel's (491ff and below). It largely corresponds to my own proposed distinction between methodological and moral normativity.

12. Trigg (1993, 153) formulates it thus: 'The shadow of positivism still lies over us if we assume that the only alternative to having empirical foundations firmly laid is for scientific reason to be displaced by power struggles and other forms of social 'negotiation'.' Larry Laudan (1996) convincingly demonstrates how (relativist etc.) post-positivism in fact relies upon positivist epistemological regimes and appears as 'positivism's flip side'.

13. Originally: 'on a reconnu que le langage devait être décrit comme une structure formelle, mais que cette description exigeait au préalable l'établissement de procédures et des critères adéquats, et qu'en somme la réalité de l'objet n'était pas séparable de la méthode propre à le définir.'

14. Cf. Clifford Geertz' formulation (1968, 22): 'From one point of view, the whole history of the comparative study of religion...can be looked at as but a circuitous, even devious, approach to a rational analysis of our own situation, an evaluation of our own religious traditions while seeming to evaluate only those of exotic others.'

15. Don Wiebe argues against the conflation of the two in his contribution in this volume. The issue here also refers to the intellectualist-symbolist controversy, i.e., on Robin Horton's views of religion; see Buchowski (1995) and in this volume, for a succinct overview.

16. Cf. Putnam's conclusion on the question of objectivity and conceptual relativity (1988, 113): 'What is factual and what is conventional is a matter of degree. We cannot say, 'These and these elements of the world are raw facts, the rest is the result of convention.' This is not a relativist view since '...to say that truth is objective (with a small 'o') is just to say that it is a property of truth that whether a sentence is true is logically independent of whether a majority of members of

the culture *believe* it to be true. And this is not a solution to the grand metaphysical question of Realism or Idealism, but simply a feature of our notion of truth' (109).

17. Although I do not agree on the consequences, I think there is much to the pragmatism espoused by Richard Rorty in his 'Science as Solidarity' (1987); for instance, his view (46) that human and social sciences need not be judged by the standards of natural sciences concerning prediction and control. It should be remembered that many of Rorty's claims are elements in a philosophical dispute over the relations between philosophy and science.

18. Cf. my generalized semiotic notion of religion (Jensen 1993).

19. A benefit of Davidson's theory is the possibility of explaining both (the failure of) relativism and how universality in a theory of meaning can be achieved without recourse to foundationalism or reductions to 'brain-states'.

20. I have quoted here Brown's views at considerable length because of their clarity, coherence and relevance. Brown makes a strong case and his discussions of current concepts of rationality are commendable reading. Cf. also Nozick's highly instructive arguments (1993).

21. Brown's final note runs thus: 'rationality is a tool for attempting to understand the world we live in and for deciding how we ought to act, and the fact that this tool is far from ideal does not undercut the point that it is the main tool we have. To put the point another way: we seek truth, and it would be most valuable if we had it, but the demand that we only believe true claims, is a demand we are not capable of fulfilling. To require that we only accept those claims which are rationally grounded, is to demand something that is within our grasp' (1988, 228). Such is the starting point for the study of religion.

22. My 'return' to Nagel should only be taken to indicate that I find much sound reasoning in his work that could (still) benefit the study of religion, not that I ultimately align myself with his ideal views of science. See e.g. Putnam (1987, 66ff) for a critique of Nagel's idea of 'immature' disciplines — the study of religion would have been one of them.

23. In a critique of relativism in cultural anthropology Melford Spiro expresses similar viewpoints, here concerning scientific explanation:'...the contention that the scientific conception of cause is restricted to material conditions is hardly self-evident... For by the most rigorous conception of cause — any antecedent condition in the absence of which some stipulated consequent condition would not occur — purposes, motives, intentions and the like, for all their being nonmaterial, are no less causal than hormonal secretions and subsistence techniques' (1992a, 137-38).

24. Putnam here quotes Nelson Goodman's argument that a purely formal criterion for distinguishing 'good' from 'bad' analogies is 'ruled out'.

25. In the study of religion this distinction undermines the view that one is neces-sarily promoting, e.g., a theologically normative view of religion simply by using the term 'religion' in a characterizing way, *even if* your characterizations are estimated against, say, a common Roman Catholic view of religion as an institution.

26. The patient reader may now want to know my reasons for not elaborating on these scholars who figure so prominently in contemporary debates instead of discussing Nagel's late-positivistic 'unity of science' ideals? Simply because the problems that Nagel dealt with are still with us, and it is a gross, but *very* frequent mistake to consider Kuhn, Foucault and Feyerabend to be high-spirited relativists: Kuhn is a realist, Foucault's critiques deal with historical 'positivities' and Feyerabend's 'anything goes' concerns methodological rules only.

27. The title of Dupré's work seems squarely to oppose my previous discussions based on commonalities among sciences, but relevant problems of scientific epistemology are presently much better explained by a theory of disunity than they were by the former positivist ideal of unity. I have found it useful to confront the two.

28. 'Certainly I can see no possible reason why commitment to many overlapping kinds of things should threaten the reality of any of them. A certain entity might be a real whale, a real mammal, a real top predator in the food chain, and even a real fish' (262). I included this last sentence to stress that 'promiscuous realism' does not include the entities of religious ontologies.

29. Dupré's terminology follows Anglo-American usage and therefore differs from mine; I freely rely on a French conception where 'sciences humaines' cover the humanities. One reason for doing so is my firm conviction, that the 'epistemic virtues' *must be the same*, although variously distributed, hence the extensive reference to Ernst Nagel.

30. To take but one example of scientistic strategies for recognition which has also been influential in the so-called scientific study of religion, i.e., sociology and psychology of religion: 'That this aspect of scientism — perhaps we should call it 'mathematicism' — is a sociologically significant contributor to scientific prestige seems hard to dispute. It is again perhaps best illustrated by the pre-eminent influence of economics, with its characteristic appeal to abstruse mathematical models of little empirical worth, among the social sciences' (Dupré 1993, 223). The public seems to confer a special ontological status to numbers, but I deplore the fact that I have found it hard (in the academy) to converse with colleagues from other fields. Some consider it improbable that we can be scientific non-quantitatively: the arts and humanities is for them akin to edifying entertainment.

31. Returning to Dupré's moderated anti-essentialist view of science: 'While I am reluctant to advocate the extreme tolerance of Paul Feyerabend... I have stronger prejudices against astrology, theology, and even alchemy — I would certainly reject the dogmatic monotheism of much contemporary philosophy of science... I would like to suggest that rather than seeking a criterion of scientificity, we should attempt to develop a catalogue of epistemic virtues. Some of these will flow naturally from the philosophical tradition: empirical accountability, consistency with common sense and other well-grounded scientific beliefs, and perhaps the more aesthetic virtues such as elegance and simplicity' (1993, 10-11).

32. Putnam concludes his discussion on 'being reasonable' by asserting: 'The fact is that we have an *underived*, a *primitive* obligation of some kind to be reasonable, not a 'moral obligation' or an 'ethical obligation', to be sure, but nevertheless a very real obligation to be reasonable' (1987, 84).

33. Along with Putnam's and Davidson's views referred to here, there are similar conclusions to be found in Jürgen Habermas' ideas of 'universal pragmatics' as the basis of meaningful communication (1979, 1-68).

Rationaltity and Evidence:
The Study of Religion as a Taxonomy of Human Natural History

Gary Lease

Prologue

In a recent and quite unique confession, physicist Alan Sokal admitted to having tweaked the noses of theoretical humanists (i.e. various stripes of deconstructionists, 'deep' readers, critical analysts, narratologists, and the like). Using the time-honoured tools of both irony and tom-foolery, Sokal concocted a mish-mash of contemporary humanistic jargon and bizarre natural science claims to propose that at long last science had been able to prove that external reality does not exist. The joke, of course, lay primarily in the fact that a leading American journal of cultural studies accepted and printed this artful parody (Sokal 1996).

More to the point is Sokal's justification for having tricked the humanist world of scholarship: his persuasion that 'nonsense and sloppy thinking' have led to a widely shared denial of the 'existence of objective reality', or at the very least of its relevance. To put it baldly, for Sokal 'facts and evidence do matter' (1996, 63). And not just for the natural sciences, I must add. Theorizing, particularly in the humanities, is rapidly gaining at best a silly, at worst a sullied reputation. Witness the judgment of one of America's more wide-ranging and cogent critics of science and culture:

The displacement of the idea that facts and evidence matter by the idea that everything boils down to subjective interests and perspectives is — second only to American political campaigns — the most prominent and pernicious manifestation of anti-intellectualism in our time. (Laudan 1990, x)

This is serious business: the results matter. Reality, however conceived and manipulated, must be dealt with. While deconstruction, that hegemonic expression of postmodernist literary theory now found in virtually every nook and cranny of the humanist world, rightly emphasizes that the stories, myths and paradigms people make up about reality cannot be ignored in our quest to understand human past and future, it is equally vital to pursue our attempts to make the source of those constructs intelligible. Reality, nature, world: these cannot be dismissed (Lease 1995a). In other words, nothing is off-limits to the probe of reason, that critical faculty of the human species that allows coherent, persuasive, and thus shared understandings of both humans and the reality in which they cooperate.

A proposed manifesto

What has this to do, however, with the study of religions, those paragons of supposed transrational, non-rational or irrational experiences, knowledges and exercises? If religions are indeed purely cultural constructions, does that mean that it is impossible to identify a single global religious system, either universal in all its main elements or differentiated into self — and other — traditions? Or is it possible that religions do in fact participate in a broad-ly-based framework of objective reality, adapting from historical moment to historical moment, from situation to situation, from culture to culture the understanding and presentation of such an entity called 'religion'?[1] Against those who strive to remove or restrict rational investigation of so-called religious manifestations and phenomena, and above all from the task of identifying what counts as religion (and what does not count as religion!), I want to propose here that reason and reality have everything to do with the study of religions. Assuming that we all 'know' about religion because we 'all' intuitively participate in it, is a gross example of the old logical mistake of begging the question (*pace* Otto and above all Eliade).

A physicist colleague at the University of California in Santa Cruz, expert in quantum mechanics and the cosmological niceties associated with the increasingly disciplinized focus on the universe's first three minutes, claims that he can speak as authoritatively as anyone else about the 'god' prior to those first three minutes, since everyone participates in religion and therefore 'knows' about it. Indeed, he goes on to offer a 'sort of theoretical theology, a spiritual analogue of theoretical physics'. As he and his folk-singer wife probe the connections between contemporary quantum cosmology and the kabbalah, they find that 'the search for scientific truth can be a form of guidance. It is as divine as any other' (Primack/Abrams 1995, 69; 73).

This search is fueled by the persuasion that 'modern cosmology is closing in on the real story of what happened at the beginning of the universe' (Cole 1996, 38). Science, to many of its current practitioners, has the 'flavour of a religious calling, complete with moral codes, perseverance in the face of adversity, and passion for total commitment' (Cole 1996, 39). Primack is convinced that 'new theories of the universe's origins may be the wellspring for the 21st century's creation myths' (Primack/Abrams 1995, 66).

On the other side of the coin, however, my physicist colleague and his fellow scientists would howl in righteous indignation if I, as a scholar of religions, were to offer a lecture on quantum mechanics: where, afterall, is my specialized, and above all official training in that difficult area? A rejoinder that we all participate immediately in the world of physics, receives a snort in rebuff. To put things candidly: while experience of, and participation in *reality* may suffice for existential integrity, they do not automatically allow that *reality* to be made intelligible. Study of reality that may lead to understanding does not spring fully armed from the head of experience, but rather comes slowly and with great difficulty from the workshop of reason.

Reason and evidence: A prolegomenon

Rationality, the exercise of human reason, turns on the notion of evidence. By what criteria, by what canons of judgment do we allow some understandings to count as reliable and accurate representations, even assessment of reality, and others not? The key elements in the establishment of evidence are few but vital:

1) We assemble observations, we analyse and sift them, and we subject those observations to judgment. In other words, from our observations we form concepts and recount experiences. These, in turn, constitute our evidential data.

2) The greatly feared divide between the observed (reality) and the observer (human reason) is not bridged by identifying the two, but rather through relationships between observers (human intersubjectivity). To put it another way, data can only begin the transformation into evidence when it is shared, or better, sharable. Key therefore to evidence is the access of the data to others, in principle to any other human one might encounter. At the very least, this access to sharing concepts and experiences must be acknowledged, even if it is not realized in every instance.

3) In order for the data of evidence aborning to gain such access, it must be expressible or articulable. A common mode of sharing must be devised (e.g. language, experiment, experience) that will allow others access. Such modes of sharing are neither genetic or a-priori, nor are they esoteric. Fundamentally these avenues of access are open to anyone who invests the time and hard work to learn them; they are neither automatic, as many contemporary advertisements for language acquisition would have it, nor are they a 'right' bestowed merely by asking for them.

4) Finally, data achieve the shift to evidential status when they are claimed as real. A basic choice or judgment is made, on the basis of mutually accepted criteria that transcend the uniqueness of any one individual experience or perception.

The goal of such an evidential process as I have proposed here is to create the basis for making reality intelligible. Can, in other words, the vast array of relationships and experiences with other beings that is the world, be adequately and accurately represented in conceptual terms? Can, furthermore, such concepts be used to design a web or pattern of relationships between humans and all others, such that one might claim a link to reality? Put another way, the goal of the rational establishment of evidence is the logic or pattern of relationships that allows the drawing of conclusions, the reaching of judgments.

To make this even more clear, let me forcefully declare that the goals of evidence are not to replicate experience; not to validate as real this or that particular experience or claim; not to establish, in other words, exclusive norms or systems governing reality absolutely.

While Sokal is quite right when he claims that 'there is a real world; its properties are not merely social constructions; facts and evidence do matter' (1996, 63), it is equally true that reality is never fully accessed, and evidence about that reality is not dogma. Rationality is the road to shared intelligibility, but it is never complete and never final.

The non-rational, on the other hand, represents ultimately a tyranny of the esoteric or individual over the rationally shared. In such a scheme, the unique is praised precisely for its lack of access for others, and though unshared is proclaimed to be universal in its extent. As a result, experiences and concepts based on hidden, or inaccessible, 'revelatory' events are turned into evidences upon which claims are based; in turn, demands follow that such claims must be incorporated by all others.

The hallmarks of the non-rational pursuit of reality are, therefore, that the foundational experiences and resulting claims are unchanging because unchangeable; are unadaptable because unshifting; are these things and more because they are identified with 'real' reality, i.e. with the transcendent or another, deeper, truer reality, different from the reality of world and other, as the noted American mythologist and Jungian disciple, Joseph Campbell, spent a lifetime proclaiming: 'The way to become human is to learn to recognize the lineaments of God in all of the wonderful modulations of the face of man' (Campbell 1968, 389-90, also 385-6; also Eliade 1975, 92; 192-3; Otto 1969, 112-3). There is no recourse from such claims because there is no rational sharing of evidences; the only moral categories are those of loyalty and betrayal; the only judgments to be made those of acceptance or rejection. Listen to one description that stands for so many others:

And that God, that Hebrew God — you can't escape Him! What's shocking is not His monstrous features — plenty of gods are monstrous, it seems almost to have been a prerequisite — but that there's no recourse from Him. No power beyond His. The most monstrous feature of God, my friends, is the totalitarianism. This vengeful, seething God, this punishment-ordaining bastard, is ultimate. (Roth 1995, 278)[2]

Ultimate claims are precisely that: claims that are demands, and thus judgments bereft of evidential support. Non-rational conduct must not only ignore, it must deny evidence. How best, then, to achieve the intelligibility of reality that is at the base of shared understanding? I propose that reason works most effectively through the assembly of evidences that are gleaned from 'natural' histories of observed phenomena, of claims, and, therefore, of reality. A 'natural' history takes as its starting point Newman's pithy summation: 'In a higher world it is otherwise, but here below to live is to change, and to be perfect is to have changed often' (Newman 1960, 63). The constant, kaleidoscopic shifting of identity, be it of the individual organism or its creations, be it of society or its institutions, is the bedrock of change. Sustaining identity becomes the most vital, and yet the most artificial task facing humans in their many cultures. A so-called natural history seeks to trace emergence, or primal identity; development, or mature identity; and dissolution, or death of identity (Bateson 1972, 448-66; La Barre 1970, 1). There, of course, is the rub: a natural history takes not only origin and development seriously, but above all the death or disappearance of the phenomenon or organism under study. As a widely-read astronomer recently and very soberly concluded:

Can humanity, in principle, survive forever? Possibly. But we shall see that immortality does not come easily and may yet prove to be impossible. The universe itself is subject to physical laws that impose upon it a cycle of its own: birth, evolution, and — perhaps — death. Our own fate is entangled inextricably with the fate of the stars. (Davies 1994, 7)

And religion is not excepted.[3] Such 'natural' histories have four basic components that permit them to establish collections of evidences:

1) they always attempt to trace the origins or sources of observed phenomena. Since no reality in which we actually live, as opposed to

imagine, lies outside of change, the 'pedigree' of reality is vital to understanding it at any given stage. The notion of 'where' an observed reality has emerged from is essential to making it available to others; origin allows any observed reality to avoid the trap of uniqueness that leads to non-rational denial. The story of Christian origins, for example, now threatens to become a datum of independent ethnographic interest: since the nineteenth century so much attention has been paid to the location, sources and dynamics of this particular religion's emergence, that it threatens to overwhelm other aspects of its history altogether.

2) they always attempt to trace the development or patterns of change in an observed reality over time. The 'history' of reality is essential to making it intelligible. The reality observed and to be made intelligible does not have to be the way it is; its history tells us how, and with what connections, it arrived to confront us. Reality is contingent, and so is our understanding of it, and history is the medium by which we master that fundamental fact (Gould 1989, 51). Recall Newman's trenchant criticism of Protestantism: 'To be deep in history is to cease to be a Protestant' (Newman 1960, 35). Without, in other words, a coherent account of the process of change that lies between the narrated emergence and the present point of observation, establishment of identity becomes difficult if not impossible.

3) they always attempt to trace the death or demise of reality. All evidence that can be shared points to the utter impermanency of reality: 'As the breath of oxen in winter', or so has it the Zulu warrior recorded by Allan Quatermain (Haggard 1928, 665). It is in death that origins and history reach their union and intelligibility becomes possible. It is finally the acknowledgement of identity's impermanence that completes a natural history. Death is not the wages of sin, but rather the consequence of having lived.

4) they always attempt to trace origins, history and death in a taxonomy that in labelling the moments and dynamics of observed reality pursues the establishment of meaning: a taxonomy creates identity, the key element of intelligibility. Peter Berger once defined religion as the 'audacious attempt to conceive of the entire universe as being humanly significant', or, as I would put it, to make reality intelligible (1969, 28).

Since, however, identity is impermanent, creation of a taxonomy bears witness to the inability of identity, in this case of religions, to survive in an effective and meaningful manner: thus the primary categories of 'dead' and 'living' religions! Taxonomic identity, then, becomes the key to intelligibility, and therefore the chief motor of rational evidence. As a consequence, the study of reality results in intelligent taxonomies that can be shared in principle with any other human being. The establishment of taxonomies of religions that can be shared with anyone is thus the goal of a 'natural' history of religions, not the exclusivist testimony of believers to their faith nor the effort of the survivalist to sustain a never changing identity.

Taxonomies of religions

But what kind of taxonomies for religions do we find? In contrast to sober and careful attempts, all too seldom found (Smith 1993), they are often circular paths, conmen's avenues, flim-flam of the crassest sort. We run the gamut: from classical languages, where first it is 'religare', telling us that religion has to do with a 're-binding' of humanity to the divine from which it was unbound; then it is 'relegare' or 'relegere', pointing to a 're-reading' (the 'gathering' of words into sentences), or a double-reading of the conventional in order to reach the depths that lie beyond the obvious (La Barre 1970, 8-9); to the 'sacred' of Otto and Eliade, complete with awe and fear; to the sweetness of the mystical moment, though neither classical figures such as Teresa of Avila or of Lisieux, nor more modern spiritual gurus such as Thomas Merton or Baba Ram Das, can show or share that experience, but rather must bemoan the fact that there are those of us deprived. You think that I may exaggerate? Let me show you a contemporary professor and scholar of religion:

I don't see 'religion' as an abstract character but a finger pointing towards a distant star, one that burns right there in the heart of every desiring human being. It's not the external form or the 'constructed complexity' but the motive power of a valid interior life fully conscious of its connectedness and mutuality in living authentically. You might call it 'religion' or 'spirituality' but the labels are far less significant than the experience. I wonder how many persons are in the study of religion that actually end up there because beneath the flow of ideas and interesting discourse there is an aspiration (even a distant hope) that the heart of the Infinite is, after all, not so inaccessible nor so conditioned as to invalidate profound and deep personal transformations? (Zos 1995)

If these claims are meant to be taken seriously, then I would propose that we give them justice. Let us dare to produce a genuinely generic taxonomy of religion for a real generic human being, a human being who results from observation of reality and shared evidences mutually agreed upon. If so, then I might envisage an authentic science of religion that:

1) never comes to closure on what constitutes its 'object'. In other words, the so-called object of 'religion' would always be shifting, would always be contingent, would never be final. Just like our other rational objects.

2) would be forced to weigh its evidences as also always shifting, both in force and in substance. In other words, the ethical, moral, ritual, and intellectual choices that adherents of a particular religion consider to be demanded by their beliefs, or demanded by 'religion' in general would constantly be changing, would never be absolute. Just like our other rational evidence assemblages.

3) would not posit the 'reality' or validity of any religion's claims or persuasions (beliefs) as the object of study and intelligibility, but rather the origins, the history, and the death of such claims and their resulting functions. Just like our other rational natural histories.

4) would recognize therefore that desire and need are not identical. In other words, a genuine science of religion would acknowledge that a choice of reality does not constitute hegemony over all of reality or over others. As a result, the shell-game of transcendence, now almost a self-evident piece of equipment in every student's toolkit, would be recognized for what it is: the carnival barker's come-on designed to turn every desire into a need, rather than deriving needs from hard-won and shared evidences. Just like our other non-rational slips.

5) would make clear that 'bearing witness', or giving testimony to evidentially-based choices or claims of the real is not the task of rational study leading to intelligibility. Such a study is not an act of belief, which always remains singular. Just like our other studies of reality.

What might such a taxonomy look like in practice? Let Philip Roth show us once again, using the Hebrew god as his example:

God's jerking off alarms you? Well, gods are alarming, girls. It's a god who commands you to cut off your foreskin. It's a god who commands you to leave your mother and father and go off into the wilderness. It's a god who sends you into slavery. It's a god who destroys — it's the spirit of a god that comes down to destroy — and yet it's a god who gives life. What in all of creation is as nasty and strong as this god who gives life? The God of the Torah embodies the world in all its horror. And in all its truth. You've got to hand it to the Jews. Truly rare and admirable candor. What other people's national myth reveals their God's atrocious conduct and their own? Just read the Bible, it's all there, the backsliding, idolatrous, butchering Jews and the schizophrenia of these ancient gods. What is the archetypal Bible story? A story of betrayal. Of treachery. It's just one deception after another. And whose is the greatest voice in the Bible? Isaiah. The mad desire to obliterate all!

The mad desire to save all! The greatest voice in the Bible is the voice of somebody who has lost his mind! ... Mind if I have a Pepsi? (Roth 1995, 278)

We need, I conclude with Roth, a new taxonomical language for the study of religion. We need a language that deals with reality, with evidences and with the rational, not with the esoteric and the unique. We need a taxonomy stripped of the categories of transcendence, of divinity, of the supernatural and the superhuman. We need an approach as direct and unadorned as Roth's fiction. We need a taxonomical scheme that places emphasis on the rational establishment of sharable evidence and not on the confession of singular, personal, hidden experiences; on the function of those confessions and those categories rather than on their truth or validity; on the power and the consequence of those persuasions and beliefs rather than on their imposition or acceptance.

In other words, as Jonathan Z. Smith has recently made so clear, we need — desperately need — a rational study of religion (Smith 1990, 143; also Lease 1995b, 16-19). A 'manifesto' traditionally has a positive, sometimes even strident character. It not only makes public the goals we seek, but also the motives and desires which underpin them. A manifesto therefore strives to achieve action and change: it is neither epithet nor eulogy. In this spirit, then, and in asking for a return to the rational in the study of religion, I am also calling upon us to purge our language and our thought of the sacred. The genuine study of religion demands nothing more, but above all nothing less.

Notes:

1. For the former possibility, see my essay (Lease 1994). For the latter, see, as leading examples, Rudolph Otto and Mircea Eliade.
2. See also Lease 1995b, 137-187, where such demands are turned into a political programme.
3. For example, see John Hinnels' *A Handbook of Living Religions*, 1997, implying, quite obviously, that there are dead religions against which the living are measured.

Rationalism and Relativity in History of Religions Research

Luther H. Martin

Historians of religion, in their enthusiasm to establish disciplinary autonomy, have distanced themselves from ordinary historiographical practice. As Mircea Eliade asserted programmatically in his 1951 study of shamanism, for example: 'the *history* of religions is not always the *historiography* of religions' (Eliade 1964, xvi). Although Eliade acknowledged that 'historical conditions are extremely important in a religious phenomenon (for every human datum is in the last analysis a historical datum)' (Eliade 1954, xiv), he argues a few pages later that 'in the [*now really?*] last analysis' religious life is 'ahistorical' (Eliade 1964, xix; for a discussion of Eliade's view of history, see Allen 1988). Eliade's ahistorical 'phenomenological attitude' (Eliade 1964, xv) echoes Joachim Wach's observation that 'phenomenology knows nothing of any historical 'development' of religion', a theoretical dictum subsequently cited approvingly by both van der Leeuw and Pettazoni (Wach 1924, 82; van der Leeuw 1938, 688; Pettazoni 1967, 217). Unless, however, the realities of religions be confessed as the manifest consequence of some transcendental 'essence', they remain — as Eliade concluded in his initial 'last analysis' — historical data, subject, thereby, to ordinary historical inquiry (Martin 1991, 120; Martin 1994a, 335). Consequently, the history of religions as an academic enterprise is, or should be, a species of general historiography and its historiographical explanations must be pursued without recourse to any *deus ex machina* (following Carr 1961, 96). As is the case with general historiography, the proper objects of the history of religions are *res gestae*, 'human doings in the past', and not theological claims to hierophanous *gestae dei* that are properly the subject matter of *Heilsgeschichte* (Collingwood 1956, 9).

The more interesting issue, however, is not what should be the clear distinction between historiographical objects as *res gestae* and *gestae dei* but the distinction, first made by Hegel, between *res gestae* and the *historia rerum gestarum*, 'the narration of human doings' — between, in other words, an objective and a subjective view of history (Hegel 1956 [1861], 60), rationalistic and relativistic views of history well illustrated in the theoretical differences between nineteenth-century historicism and a new, twentieth-century historicism. Whereas the old historicism emphasized an assessment of the historical data which, when sufficient and sufficiently sorted out, were understood to speak more or less for themselves, the new emphasizes the exigencies of culture, politics, and prejudice in the construction of historical narratives, often at the expense of the data.

Historicism old and new

In his recent review of *Not Out of Africa*, Mary Lefkowitz's challenge to the Afrocentrism occasioned by the first volume of Martin Bernal's *Black Athena* (1987), Glen Bowersock writes that:

truth in the writing of history has come under fire repeatedly in recent years in relativist interpretations that have sometimes turned history into little more than rhetoric. The result has been a kind of collegial standoff in which anyone's views, no matter how bizarre, might be accepted as one possible way of looking at things. (1996, 7)

While an inevitability of historiographical hermeneutics is acknowledged by all historians, the posing of innovative questions generated by new theoretical formations should not abrogate the positivity of data by which the historiographical enterprise is constrained. This is the position most forthrightly set forth in the famous nineteenth-century historicist mandate to reconstruct the past *'wie es eigentlich gewesen'* (von Ranke 1885, v-viii). This historicist dictum, intended to suggest that historiography properly made descriptive rather than the prescriptive or normative judgements associated with philosophy, was reshaped by the ascendency of the scientific ideal during this century into the positivistic goals often attributed a more narrow 'science' of history. This objective view of historiography, which held that the past might be definitively known, contributed to the establishment of history as an academic discipline late in the century.

As a descriptive enterprise, nineteenth-century historicism stood in opposition to any metaphysical absolute of philosophy or to any transcendental norm of religion which holds human existence to be more than its circumstances. It attempted, consequently, to dissociate itself from the validity of theory, whether from the Enlightenment theory of natural law, from any universal construct of values held to be applicable to the diversity of human societies — whether taken to be of divine or human origination, or from generalizable political norms. However, readily available records of political achievement, collected in state archives that had recently been established with the emergence of European nationalism in this century, influenced a comprehensive view of human history along similar lines. This theoretical conviction concerning the relationship between political power and the shape of history came to dominate German historiography (Iggers 1983, 4).

The historicist focus on archival texts was formative in shaping a philologically grounded historicism of religion. These historians of religion, and biblical scholars especially, were concerned not only to establish the most accurate record of religious expressions but to locate their texts and subsequent commentaries in the appropriate historical contexts. Whereas the historical-critical investigation of biblical texts and the restriction of their meaning to their historical context challenged the transcendental authority traditionally attributed them, this work was nevertheless continued, albeit within the contraints of a politics of religious orthodoxy.

On the other hand, those historians of religion who had embraced the historicist concern with value-neutral description departed from the historical-critical method of liberal biblical scholars to argue that a historically contingent or situated view of religious phenomena could not explain their 'essence', an assumed religious reality that they supposed religions really to manifest. They considered this specifically 'religious' meaning to belong to a transhistorical nature of the human spirit that is best discovered by comparative and ahistorical study. These 'phenomenographists' of religion joined conservative biblical theologians in rejecting historicism, along with social scientific research, as a reduction of revealed, or essential, religion to human construction.

During the final third of the twentieth century, a loose coalition of historical and anthropological scholarship emerged in France and the United States that has been termed the 'new historicism'.[1] This new movement shares with nineteenth-century historicism the fundamental premise that all human events and expressions are historically and socially constituted. However, in contrast to the historicists' Enlightenment faith in reason to direct and, thus, to comprehend history, the new historicists represent the Romantic view of the autonomy of history in which reason itself is understood to be a historical construct. Reason itself, located in the process upon which it reflects, is, in this view, deemed meaningful and valid only in its setting. Whereas, the historicists refused to acknowledge their own historical contingency (Iggers 1983, 17), the new historicists view all historical knowledge as relative to the standpoint of the historian.

Although historicism had understood human ideas and ideals to be historically constituted and had rejected idealist abstraction for an emphasis upon situated fact, its view that a politically shaped history was the key to knowledge tended to be all-encompassing. In contrast to the lingering Enlightenment ideal of universal human values implied in this totalizing project of the old historicism, the new historicism emphasizes a local politics of value — including especially that of the historian. Historiography cannot, in the view of the new historicists, imply social or political neutrality.

The focus on the political orientation of the historian by the new historicist emphasizes, in contrast to the historicist assumption of a past contingent with the present through some specified law of political change, the situated character of the past as 'other' to the present. The new historicists have become allied thereby with those anthropologists who are concerned with issues of the validity and propriety of Western categories in the study of other cultures (Silk 1987; Darnton 1984, XIII, 3-7). In the words of Robert Darnton:

this anthropological mode of history begins from the premise that individual expression takes place within a general idiom, that we learn to classify sensations and make sense of things by thinking within a framework provided by our culture. (1984, 6)

However, documentations of historically constructed distributions of power by these historians have all too often resulted in their insights being subjected to their own ideological, and often idiosyncratic, assertions of power, especially by their post-modernist representatives, especially in the contemporary study of religion in North America (a point already discussed by Carr 1961, 29-32).

With the social scientists, the new historicists also understand human acts and expressions to be embedded in any, and all, cultural manifestions. The distinction between the literary texts that so preoccupied the historicists and the nondiscursive practices and cultural materials observed by anthropological fieldworkers are thereby dissolved. In contrast to the political and diplomatic concerns that dominated the work of the old historicism, the new historicism is concerned more with social and cultural histories, than with the politics of everyday life.

The theoretical feature the new historicism shares with the old is its reliance upon the explanatory value of culture; for the cultural role of the historian in the case of the new historicism, for the cultural character of the historical event in the case of the old. Neither accounts, however, for culture itself, apparently ceding this task to the anthropologists who, alas, embrace this same strategy of contextual explanation (McCauley and Lawson 1996). As a consequence, the past for historicists, old and new, remains subject to the orientations of its interpreters, both of whom share a theory of history as politically shaped — the one emphasizing objective configurations of power, the other its subjective conformations. The central issue in historiography remains, in other words, one of theoretical orientation. In the words of a country song performed by Aaron Tippin: 'You've got to stand for something or you'll fall for anything.'

Historical generalization and theory

The goal of even the most positivistic of historians is never certainty about the past but, rather, decisions about probability in the face of historical possibility (see Bloch 1953, 124). Consequently, the historian of religion must concede, for example, the possibility of von Däniken's scientistic reading of Genesis as a report about the human race being the consequence of 'an act of deliberate "breeding" by unknown beings from outer space' (von Däniken 1969, 61). Nevertheless, this same historian of religion must conclude, based upon available data, that this interpretation is most improbable. The basis for this conclusion, however, is not solely what we know of historical-critical details about the Hebrew text, more data, in other words, for the incessant and inexhaustible mills of possibility. Rather, this conclusion is also based on generalizations informed by such data. As E. H. Carr has concluded:'those who reject generalization and insist that history is concerned exclusively with the unique are, logically enough, those who deny that anything can be learned from history. (1961, 84)

If, however, historical generalizations about the data are not to remain mere speculation, they must be controlled by a clearly announced theoretical project subject to critical debate. I have previously referred to the significance of historiographical theory in connection with research on the religious formations of the Mediterranean world consequent upon the conquests of Alexander the Great (Martin 1983). A review of these observations in the present context might prove instructive.

In his 'Introduction' to Franz Cumont's pioneering study of *Oriental Religions in Roman Paganism*, Grant Showerman spoke of the 'religious chaos in which the ancient world was struggling before the reign of Constantine' (Cumont 1956 [1911], vii-viii). Showerman's view reflected the prevailing generalization about this period which had been articulated by George Grote in the 'Preface' to his monumental twelve-volume *History of Greece*, the first volume of which was published in 1846. Grote wrote that, following the reign of Alexander the Great:

the political action of Greece becomes cramped and degraded, — no longer interesting to the reader, or operative on the destinies of the future world...; as a whole, the period, between 300 BC and the absorption of Greece by the Romans, is of no interest in itself, and is only so far of value as it helps to understand the preceding centuries (1854 [1846], x).

His judgement concerning the historical insignificance of the time between the death of Alexander the Great and the final incorporation of Alexander's former empire into Rome by Augustus represented the conventional view of Western history since the Romans, who modelled their own history upon that of the Greeks and, as Cumont recognized, was supported subsequently by 'conviction[s] of European leadership'(Cumont 1956, 8).

Coincidentally, biblical historians considered the period prior to the reign of Augustus — and the claimed birth of Jesus in this reign (Luke 2:1) — as a period in decline, especially of its 'pagan' religions, and, similar to Grote's general judgement about the period, of value only as a backdrop for their theologically informed construction of a new Christian era. The nineteenth-century acknowledgement of the period after Alexander was, in other words, but the grudging recognition of a 'decadent' extension to Greek political history and a prelude to Roman, a period characterized by cultural and religious decline that was reversed by the advent of Christianity.

Grote's view takes on particular theoretical interest, however, since ten years earlier, in 1836, J. G. Droysen had published the first of his three-volume history on precisely that period so cavalierly dismissed by Grote. I know of no evidence that Grote, who had begun his own work as early as 1823, knew Droysen's work (Sandys 1908, 438), though it is tempting to see in Grote's statement his response to Droysen's new historical hypothesis, encapsulated in the opening line of his first volume: '*Der Name Alexander bezeichnet das Ende einer Weltepoche, das Anfang einer neuen*' (Droysen, 1980 [1836-43], I: 3).

Like other nineteenth-century historical generalizations, Droysen's new historical period was defined in political terms. These politically shaped generalizations about the character of history became associated further with the idealization of the hero, apparent in the literature of the age as in its historiography. This romantic 'great man view of history', given formulation in Thomas Carlyle's view of history as 'the biography of great men' and by Hegel's idealization of heroic 'world-historical' individuals (Carlyle 1993 [1840], 26; Hegel 1956 [1861], 29-30), asserted the causal efficacy of exceptional individuals in initiating or altering the course of historical events. It is not surprising, therefore, that the period of time between two such exemplary political leaders as Alexander 'the Great' and Octavian 'Augustus', both romanticized in antiquity as in modernity, became recognized just in the nineteenth century as the initiators of successive historical periods. Thus, following the more influential second edition of Droysen's *Geschichte* in 1877 (Austin 1981, 7), historians increasingly recognized a Hellenistic period as extending from Alexander's Greco-Macedonian empire until the last of the 'Macedonian' monarchs, Cleopatra of Egypt, was vanquished by Augustus in 31 BC and the final Western remnant of Alexander's empire incorporated into that of Rome the following year. For Droysen, this period was 'not a disjointed, chaotic monstrosity in the development of humankind' (Droysen 1980 [1836-43], 3: 10), but rather a period of new and constructive beginnings. In the words of one commentator, Droysen's *Geschichte des Hellenismus*, 'fundamentally altered the way in which historians viewed late Greek history' (Southard 1995, 11).

Although Alexander's empire had fragmented with his death, giving support to earlier generalizations about decadence and chaos during this period, his Hellenistic ideal continued to be championed by his successors and an accelerated cultural interaction, and even interdependence, ensued among the citizens of Alexander's former empire. His programme of Hellenization was resisted, however, by a number of indigenous peoples who sought to retain their traditional cultural heritage, whether passively by preserving their local language and customs, or militantly, as in the series of Egyptian anti-Hellenic revolts from as early as 245 BC or in the Jewish insurrections against the Hellenizing zeal of Seleucid rule in the second century BC. Religion especially, in whose name resistance to Hellenization was most often mounted, became currency in the Hellenized marketplace of competitive but cosmopolitanized cultural exchange. In other words, the religious history of this period had its own disposition, an integrity recognized by Cumont but which apparently still astonished Showerman.

While the non-political dimensions of culture are most certainly implicated with the political, political criteria cannot simply be assumed appropriate for the periodization of such as religious history. If a Hellenistic period of *political* history can be terminated with the consolidation of the Roman empire under Augustus, in other words, a Hellenistic period of *religious* history is best concluded with the cultural dominance realized by Christians during the fourth century AD.

Historiographical theorizing is not only about the parameters of periodicity but includes also judgements about the essential characteristics of the periods defined. When Droysen nominated his newly defined period as 'hellenistic', he also proposed its central feature. He appropriated this adjective, which does not appear in ancient Greek, from verbal and nominal forms signifying the acquisition of the Greek language and life-style by non-Greeks. Jason of Cyrene, for example, associated 'an extreme of Hellenization' with an 'increase in the adoption of foreign ways' (II Macc. 4.13). For Droysen, this adjective epitomized his Hegelian generalization about the *westöstliche Völkermischung* that occurred with Alexander's conquests (Droysen 1980 [1836-43], 1: 'Vorwort zur Zweiten Auflage'; on Droysen's Hegelianism, especially in Vol. 1 of the *Geschichte*, see Krüger in Droysen 1967, xviii). By the end of the century, historians of religion had produced their technical term for the religious implications of this Hellenistic cultural mixture: 'syncretism'.[2]

Given the profusion of religious data from the Hellenistic period, including impressive new textual discoveries, such as the Nag Hammadi codicies, or the on-going archaeological discoveries of Mithraeae, for example, historians of religion continue to remain embarrassed by their difficulty in formulating this data into any coherent view. 'Too often', in the observation of Bloch, '[historical] research wanders aimlessly with no rational decision about where it is to be applied.' Without theorical clarity, it vacilates between imposing 'stereotyped themes ... by routine' and 'being marooned upon insignificant or poorly propounded questions' (Bloch 1953, 86).

Droysen, the only German historicist formally to address historiographical theory (Iggers 1983, 104 re: Droysen 1967), was able to propose thereby the signficance of a neglected historical time, successfully challenging conventional historical periodization. Because of the new information, insights, and inferences generated by this new periodization, that represented by Grote was discarded.

These same data and deductions subsequently produced modifications to Droysen's own generalizations about the characteristic features of this period and, indeed, about the parameters of the period itself, the differentiation, for example, of religious from political history. In contrast to a politically determined period of Hellenistic history, a religious periodization includes Christian origins among those religious expressions that had populated the Mediterranean world since the end of the fourth century BC. Consequently a new set of questions about those beginnings are only now being seriously explored from a *history* of religions view (Smith 1990; Mack 1995).[3]

A modest proposal

Questions about knowledge of the past, about relativism, truth, and objectivity, have generally been neglected by historians. In a recent book, suggestively entitled *Telling the Truth About History*, the authors observe that such questions have been relegated to the esoteric domain of the philosophy of history and 'dismissively categorized as "theory"' (Appleby—Hunt—Jacob 1994, 9, 243). 'Philosophy poses the right questions', E.L. Doctorow has the antagonist of his latest novel observe, 'But it lacks the requisite diction for the answers. Only Science can find the diction for answers'(1995, 335).

Despite his observation that historiography is a work of imagination similar to that of the novelist, R.G. Collingwood (among others) has nevertheless insisted that historiography is a science in the sense that it is constrained by evidence. Reminescent of the historicist dictum, he continues that it seeks 'to construct a picture of things as they really were and of events as they really happened' (Collingwood 1956, 246). The world of past remains, in other words, like the external world queried by science, an invariant datum which, in the formation of Marc Bloch, 'nothing in the future will change'(1953, 58). Robert McCauley and E. Thomas Lawson have recently emphasized that 'progress in science', in which I would include historiography, turns:

on the proliferation of *informed* speculations. Researchers' familiarity with the facts and their considered judgment are what inform speculations. Those speculations typically take the form of inferences to the best explanation....From these origins more sophisticated theories take shape. The continuing goal is not only to formulate new theories but to formulate *better* theories on the basis of the comparative insights that ... [the data] provokes (1996, 282).

Although theoretically oriented research is being conducted in some areas of the history of religions, theoretical models for such historical research remain, for the most part, assumed and unaddressed. It might not be too presumptuous, consequently, to suggest the work of Michel Foucault as such a model.

In Foucault's view, what is most human in man is history, and Foucault understood himself as primarily a historian (Cousins-Hussain 1984, 3-6; Macey 1993, 62; Martin 1995b, 62-67). Foucault emphasized the role of power in shaping both history and historiography. His association of knowledge with power not only proposes an analytic of the constructive dynamic of socio-historical forces but is a reintroduction, as well, of the Enlightenment principle of rationality as the corrective, through comprehension, of these power relations.[4] Foucault's overriding theoretical focus on power associates his work not only with the Enlightenment but with the political concerns of both nineteenth-century historicists and postmodernist historians. Unlike the postmodernists, however, for whom he had a deep distrust (Macey 1993, 463), Foucault gives careful attention to the data, to historical positivities. The perception that Foucault was deficient of, or cavalier with, historical data is a postmodernist fancy, mindlessly repeated by those interested in appropriating his theoretical authority and by uncomprehending critics alike. To what historiographical uses Foucault employs his data is a legitimate question that can — and should — be put to any historian. Like Droysen, however, Foucault has introduced a view of history that proposes theoretically founded questions.

Foucault's historical theory of power has allowed him to pose what, I would suggest, is the central question of any historiography: 'Why are things just the way they are?' Historians of religion have been all too prepared to accept the religious insiders' answer to this question: 'revelation', that is to say, some form of incomparable uniqueness which has been generalized, under some such category as *mana* ('power'!) or 'the Sacred', as religion's *sui generis* foundation. Rather than relationships to some Power, Foucault would conceive of religion as power relationships (Chidester 1986, 1-9). Consequently, Foucault is confident that 'religion', like that of 'literature', 'philosophy' or 'history' is a 'discursive grouping' constructed out of Western cultural history (Foucault 1972, 22), a position not unlike J. Z. Smith's oft-cited observation that 'religion is solely the creation of the scholar's study' (Smith 1982, xi). Nevertheless, knowledge of this history allows us a heuristically useful category, whether other cultures have a comparable word or category for 'religion' or not.

Foucault's 'genealogical/archaeological' historiography, challenges the theoretical privileging of origins conventionally assumed by historians, for example, the authority attributed their 'founders' by various religious traditions and accepted as their own historical reference point by historians of religion. Two exceptions to this latter practice — interesting because of their doctrinal non-orthodoxy — are the suggestions of John Wansbrough (1977; 1978; Berg 1997) with respect to Islam and those of Burton Mack with respect to Christianity (1995).

I and others have written about the assumptions of 'pure' origins inherent in the notion of syncretism. Most have attempted to salvage its usage as indications of extraordinary religious interminglings to be historically described and disjoined (e.g., Pye 1994, 222), a view that still assumes perforce some unsyncretized, normative form of religion. I have suggested, by contrast, that alleged syncretisms be understood as the ordinary historical nature of religious beginnings to be investigated as case studies for the historical diachronics of religions generally (Martin 1996).

The assumption of causal origins constitutes, in the words of one commentary 'a history in which the past is read through the teleological grid of the present' (Cousins—Hussain 1984, 4). In test of this assumption, I have questioned the relevance of psychoanalytic dream theory for the understanding of dreams in antiquity, arguing that any dream meaning, including that of psychoanalytic dream theory, is culturally contingent (Martin 1994b); questioned generalizations about individualism, arguing that, whenever individualism emerged as a positive ideology in Western cultural history, it was later than the Hellenistic period and, thus, is an inappropriate category for understanding the religions of antiquity, including those Christian origins (Martin 1994c); and I have challenged regnant conventions about secrecy and the mystery religions, arguing that secrecy was primarily employed as a strategy for defining social boundaries rather than any occultation of techniques for mysteriosophical experience (Martin 1995a). In other words, as Cormac McCarthy has so aptly observed in *The Crossing*, his unsettling historical novel about life in the American south-west early in this century, *La tercera historia ... es ésta. Él existe en la historia de las historias* ('The best arbiter of history is the history of histories') (McCarthy 1994, 411).

This is not the place for a full-blown discussion of the possible implications of Foucault's works for a history of religions.[5] Rather, it is to suggest that contemporary models of history *have* been proposed which build upon careful attention to data from a clearly theoretical perspective.

I suggest that historians of religion join with other historians not only in the pursuit of serious research but in the not inconsiderable task of historiographical reflection, theorizing about the parameters of our particular domain of *res gestae* and about the defining characteristics of this domain. In doing so, we might not only make a positive contribution to the wider discussions of the academy but even make a rational contribution to the study of *contemporary* religious doings, the discussion of which has rarely employed any recognition of their historical positivity.

Notes

1. The term 'new historicism' was first coined by literary theorists. For a review of these issues in that context, see Winn 1993.
2. Paul Wendland understood 'syncretism' and 'hellenization' as virtually synonymous processes (Wendland 1912, 129; see also Moffatt 1922, 155-7).
3. Despite Hermann Gunkel's proposal for a history of religions approach to the New Testament in 1903, New Testament research has retained a theological rather than theoretical agenda; see now, however, Mack 1995. For history of religions research in the larger area of Hellenistic religions, the work of Jonathan Z. Smith is exemplary; see, for example, Smith 1990.

4. The association of knowledge and power goes back to Francis Bacon (1598). On rationality as the antedote to power, see e.g., Foucault 1971. As this principle has been most recently expressed by Alan Sokal in an exposé (1996a) of his own nonsensical satirical essay (1996): 'we [of the Left] have believed that rational thought and the fearless analysis of objective reality (both natural and social) are incisive tools for combating the mystifications promoted by the powerful...' (Sokal 1996a, 64).

5. See the suggestions by Smith 1982, 25; Chidester 1986, and Asad 1993. Although classicists are not 'historians of religion' in the professional sense, the important study by Price 1982 and those by Brown, especially 1988, must be mentioned here.

Rationality in Studying Historical Religions

Hans G. Kippenberg

Can unreasonable beliefs be rational?

Decades ago the British social anthropologist Edward Evans-Pritchard (1902-1973) studied witchcraft, oracles, and magic among the Azande. He pointed out how the Azande explained unfortunate events by witchcraft, how they consulted oracles for identifying the culprit, and how they applied magic in defence of spiritual attacks. Evans-Pritchard left no doubt that he regarded the entire system as unreasonable: 'Witches, as the Azande conceive them, clearly cannot exist' (1976,18). How did Evans-Pritchard know that witches cannot exist? How did he know that the reasons they gave are mystical and therefore invalid? Was Evans-Pritchard right or wrong in depicting Zande witchcraft as unreasonable? Agreement or disagreement with his interpretation depends on how Zande witchcraft is understood in Western terms. Evans-Pritchard was well aware of the complexities of this task. Is there anything similar to traditional witchcraft in contemporary Western culture? In a lecture on the BBC in the winter of 1950 he told listeners, that: 'I think that I gained some understanding of communist Russia by studying witchcraft among the Azande' (1951, 129). For Evans-Pritchard, witchcraft among the Azande was analogous to notions of conspiracy commonly found in twentieth-century European political history. If this instance of 'cultural translation' is correct, then Evans-Pritchard has a strong argument for labelling witchcraft among the Azande as unreasonable. How could an enlightened scholar fight against conspiracy theories in Europe if he would regard witchcraft in Africa as reasonable?

In spite of his rejection of Zande witchcraft, the British anthropologist found the belief system to be coherent. The Azande consistently put their beliefs into practice, he observed: 'Zande behaviour, though ritual, is consistent, and the reasons they give for their behaviour, though mystical, are intellectually coherent' (1976, 159). Apparently, according to Evans-Pritchard, an unreasonable belief system can nevertheless be rational. He himself felt compelled to understand its rationality: 'I, too, used to react to misfortune in the idiom of witchcraft, and it was often an effort to check this lapse into unreason' (1976, 45). He reported, that he had seen: 'only once... witchcraft on its path'. On his usual nocturnal stroll, after writing notes in his hut, he noticed a bright light passing towards the homestead of a man called Tupoi. He followed its passage until a grass screen obscured the view. Only one man of his household had a lamp that might have given off so bright a light; but he had not been out late at night. Informants told Evans-Pritchard that he had seen witchcraft. Shortly afterwards a member of Tupoi's household died (1976, 11).

Evans-Pritchard assumed that beliefs must be judged according to two different criteria: as propositions, they are either true or false regarding an observable reality; as reasons of actions, they are either consistent or inconsistent with the action. This model allows for a special case: that a belief can be false but nevertheless consistent regarding concomitant actions. In the case that a false belief is consistently turned into practice it can be called 'rational'.

In contrast to a complete rejection of false beliefs, Evans-Pritchard introduced an additional criterion. Mary Douglas explained in her fine book on Evans-Pritchard (1981, 72): 'He tried never to declare a belief or theory not supported by action'. By distinguishing between reason and rationality, Evans-Pritchard was interested in indicating the internal consistency of systems of false beliefs. Even strange assumptions can be rational, provided that observation confirms a coherent practice.

Although this approach is methodologically superior to simply rejecting unreasonable beliefs, it does create a problem of its own. Evans-Pritchard recognized this, when writing that:

Zande behaviour, though ritual, is consistent, and the reasons they give for their behaviour, though mystical, are intellectually coherent.... [The] Azande do not see that their oracles tell them nothing! Their blindness is not due to stupidity: they reason excellently in the idiom of their beliefs, but they cannot reason outside, or against, their beliefs because they have no other idiom in which to express their thoughts. (1976, 159)

Evans-Pritchard here grappled with a problem inherently connected with his approach. According to him witchcraft clearly cannot exist. But what is the reason, then, that people did not recognize their explanations as wrong? Why do people go on believing false doctrines? What are the reasons for their stubborn error? If the answer is not 'fraud', the reasons have to be specified. John Skorupski in a marvellously lucid analysis addressed the issue as 'blocks to falsifiability' (1976, 5). If the oracle gave conflicting answers, the Azande assumed that the poison which they used in their ritual had been bewitched. They are so immersed in their beliefs that they are not able to evaluate them critically.

If we are looking the wrong way through the telescope and see Evans-Pritchard, the observer, at work, we recognize a practice very common in social studies: Sound beliefs do not deserve any explanation. Sociological explanations often are applied to 'wrong' beliefs only. They are then explained by the function they perform. Evans-Pritchard's notion of 'rational' follows this practice in social studies. An observer rejects a belief as unreasonable but recognizes its practical function. The implicit assumptions of this approach came under attack when Thomas Kuhn initiated a sociological explanation of true beliefs as well.

Kuhn focused on the natural sciences and found that even the acknowledged natural laws were not derived directly from observing nature. Observation in the natural sciences requires checking certain hypotheses. If anomalies contradict an established hypothesis, a new one must be formulated, that explains the observed facts more adequately than the previous one.

Karl Popper regarded a continuing process of falsification as constitutive for science. In his essay, *Logik der Forschung*, first published in 1935, and translated into English 1959 in an extended version as *The Logic of Scientific Discovery*, he established the so called 'critical rationalism' as a powerful theory of science. All scientific notions are inventions that attempt an explanation of the natural world.

The approaches of Kuhn and Popper converged in the sixties and seventies with Ludwig Wittgenstein's idea that the world we talk about is always dependent on the language we speak. A huge questionmark was placed behind the idea that there are universal criteria of truth that could be tested by observation. The correspondence theory of truth which claimed that 'truth' consists in a correspondence between a statement and 'the way things are' lost its persuasive power. Instead, a coherence theory of truth gained influence.

In this debate in the sixties and seventies Evans-Pritchard's book became a major example. Did it not prove that claims to truth are dependent on the culture to which they belong? In his 1964 article, 'Understanding a Primitive Society', Peter Winch referred to the Azande in support of just that kind of argument. His paper, reprinted in the anthology *Rationality*, edited by Bryan Wilson (1970) — challenged the claim that 'agreement or disagreement with reality' is the same in all cultures. In support of his argument, he relied on

Ludwig Wittgenstein's dictum from the *Tractatus* that: 'The limits of my language mean the limits of my world'. The empirical world is available only through language. Reality cannot be observed as something independent of it. A distinction such as that between mystical and scientific notions is also constituted by language.

Discriminating origin from reason in the history of religions

The title of the present volume, *Rationality and the Study of Religion*, draws attention to the fact that a distinction, similar to that proposed by Evans-Pritchard, is also crucial for the study of religions. Indeed, such an approach has a long history in religious studies. It was even part and parcel of the very beginning of the discipline. David Hume introduced it in the first sentence of his treatise, *The Natural History of Religion*, written in 1757:

As every enquiry, which regards religion, is of the utmost importance, there are two questions in particular, which challenge our attention, to wit, that concerning its foundation in reason, and that concerning its origin in human nature. (1993, 134)

Hume still believed in a foundation of religion in reason, and defended in some of his writings a teleological proof for the existence of God, proceeding from observations of regularity to the conclusion that these must be the work of a Designer. The origin of the historical religions was a different matter. According to Hume:

The first ideas of religion arose not from contemplation of the works of nature, but from a concern with regard to the events of life, and from incessant hopes and fears, which actuate the human mind. (1993, 139)

While a reasonable religion would arise from recognising the marvellous design of the world, historical religions had their origin in human fears excited by frightening events. Hume, in his essay, placed all information about the history of religions in the plot of a natural history. As human beings did not know the causes of natural events, which bestowed either happiness or misery on them, they anxiously attempted to determine them. They found no better expedient than to represent them as 'intelligent voluntary agents' (1993, 152). Each natural event was supposed to be caused by one of them (1993, 139-40). By means of worshipping them, man hoped to gain some control of nature. In order to please the most powerful agent, he started focusing his worship more exclusively. And theism was born. But the powerful god was so remote from man, that man felt the necessity of powers to mediate his relation with the distant powerful supreme power. Incessantly, and necessarily, historical religions oscillate between polytheism and theism. So theism only superficially resembled the philosophical proof for the existence of God. In fact popular theism lacked a foundation in reason. But that did not mean it could not be described and explained as logical. On the contrary!

From the very beginning, the study of religions was tied to a fundamental assumption that denied reason to historical religions. This point of departure severed religious studies from theology. Most students of religion assumed that something not founded in reason could nevertheless be logical, coherent, and rational. Many of their efforts to describe and explain religions relied on that distinction. But this approach placed a new issue on the agenda of the scholar that had to be solved. How are we to understand and describe a phenomenon which lacks reason but governs human thinking and acting? No scholar describing historical religions could avoid that issue.

When facing this issue, scholars of religious studies had to turn to the philosophy of religion. Since, however, the philosophy of religion has not been allowed to form an acknowledged division of religious studies, this particular background of religious studies is often ignored or reduced to a footnote. Even scholars defending 'theory' as a necessary part of religious studies, often do not include philosophy of religion in their understanding of theory. I regard this as a major weakness of most of the recent concerns with theoretical matters. If we want to know more about the issue of rationality in the study of historical religions, we have to take a look at the philosophy of religion.

Philosophical discourses on historical religions

Since the seventeenth century, European philosophers have addressed the place of religion in human history. The modern philosophy of religions began with Thomas Hobbes (1588-1679) who addressed the terrible religious wars of the seventeenth century in Europe. He regarded these wars as a return of human beings to their natural state. Only a powerful state could prevent the permanent state of war. But even then, peace among citizens was dependent on religions since religions had developed different attitudes towards civil loyalties. By comparing paganism, Judaism and Christianity, Hobbes outlined their differences (1651). In paganism and Judaism, civil and religious loyalties coincided. Only Christianity severed the relation between the two. By doing so, Christianity deprived national wars of their religious legitimacy but it allowed instead for internal wars among those of different faiths. For that reason Christianity had been a major factor in the civil wars in Europe.

When we look at the subsequent philosophers, we easily recognize the same issue: the relation between religious and civil loyalties. It remained crucial for David Hume, Jean-Jacques Rousseau, and Immanuel Kant. Hume (1711-76) conceived the history of religions as a psychological pendulum swinging from polytheistic to monotheistic religion and back. The public morals of a civic community depended on the pendulum swing: polytheism fostered tolerance, monotheism intolerance. Not a natural state, but the natural history of religion was responsible for the quality of civil relations among the citizens (1757). Rousseau (1712-78) and Kant (1724-1804) found the culprit of civil wars and intolerance in the ecclesiastical institutions. If the interior religion of human beings, the religion of the heart, could be freed from all institutional distortions, it would be able to create secure social relations. But the state has to take part in this process and suppress religious intolerance by force. Enlightened religions are fundamental for establishing moral obligations.

In the last quarter of the eighteenth century, philosophers began to reverse the argument. That historical religions lacked the reason of Enlightenment was not a disadvantage. On the contrary! They were valuable because they had preserved worldviews profoundly different from those of the enlightened culture. Religious language in particular was held to transmit a stock of symbols expressing human feelings and emotions which were being threatened by the enlightened culture. For the sake of true humanity man deserves religious traditions. Johann Gottfried Herder (1744-1803), especially, drew attention to language as a vehicle of non-rational meanings. Friedrich Schleiermacher (1768-1834) denied any close relationship between religion and morals. To him religion was a way of experiencing the infinite in the world. Since the infinite does not exist beyond the perceptible world, man can only grasp it within history. Both Herder and Schleiermacher rejected enlightened religion. They called, instead, upon historical religions as witnesses which gave evidence about the feelings and emotions of human life independent of enlightenment claims.

With Hegel a new twist came about in the philosophy of religion. Georg Wilhelm Friedrich Hegel (1770-1831) contradicted the romantic ideal of harmony between man and nature as it was advanced by Herder and Schleiermacher. Such an ideal seemed to him to amount only to a regression into a primordial state of human existence lacking consciousness. Hegel was convinced that it was the split between man and nature which freed the human subject from the laws of nature and created the conditions for human history. Hegel traced the origin of this conception of subjectivity to religions that rejected the world. By comparing Indian religions with Christianity he made a distinction between two types of world-rejection. In India the subject could gain salvation by contemplation, thereby sinking into the absolute and becoming free from temporal individuality. By contrast, Christianity conceived the individual as an autonomous subject transcending the world of nature. Hegel regarded this as proof of the superiority of Christianity to Indian religions. Arthur Schopenhauer (1788-1860), on the other hand, reversed this argument. The Indian way of dissolving the subject was superior to Christianity since the notion of an autonomous subject was an illusion.

The philosophical discourse on historical religions established a special type of metaphysical assumptions in the paradigms of religious studies. These assumptions differed from those described by Popper and Kuhn for the natural sciences, since they did not solve puzzles of already established paradigms. They addressed the problems of a human tradition which did not conform to enlightenment requirements but nevertheless had an impact on history.

When European philosophers recognized this contradiction between reason and history, they faced the task of explaining historical religions by additional means, mainly by the functions which religions performed. First, historical religions could be interpreted as crude explanations of natural events. Second, others regarded *morals* as the place in which historical religions fulfilled useful and necessary functions. Third, some philosophers pointed to *human emotions* as an area of contribution by historical religions. Finally, some philosophers regarded *world-rejection* as a peculiar achievement of religions, since it was constitutive for human subjectivity. These four positions developed one after the other. But their relationship was not part of a process of falsification. The succession of positions had nothing to do with a superior explanation of anomalies. They were inspired by an awareness of the limitations of Enlightenment philosophy.

Imagining historical religions in an age of modernization

Jonathan Z. Smith has conceived of theory in religious studies as an issue of imagination. In a provocative statement he wrote:

there is no data for religion. Religion is solely the creation of the scholar's study. It is created for the scholar's analytic purposes by his imaginative acts of comparison and generalisation. (1982, 11)

Though I do not regard the word 'solely' as particularly appropriate, I would like to admit his point. There are categories in the scholarly apparatus of religious studies that belong to the field of imagination, to fiction. The issue of fiction has bothered historians for more than a hundred years and recently it has come up again. Hayden White has addressed this phenomenon in a couple of books (1973; 1987). No historian's work is complete with simply analyzing the sources. From the reliable data he must shape a literary representation of the facts. By doing so he crosses in a willy-nilly manner the boundary between fact and fiction.

The foundation of an academic study of religions coincided with the beginnings of modernization. Since the second half of the nineteenth century most European countries were involved in a process of rapid social change. The repercussions that this had for daily life were momentous. Instead of working for their traditional needs, people now had to produce goods for a market. Old customs ceded to private contracts and political laws. The superior knowledge of science replaced the inherited worldview. This deep change severed societies from their ties to the past. The rise of history as the master category for human culture was due to that experience. Norms and values became antiquated. And, what about 'religion'? Many educated people in Europe believed in an imminent end of all religions. Had not the scientific progress superseded the religious worldview? Historians had to come to terms with that expectation when they directed their attention to historical religions. At this point the philosophy of religion became a central issue.

When we take a closer look at the founding fathers of religious studies, we readily recognize that no classical approach to religious studies is without philosophical conceptions at its root. Friedrich Max Müller introduced the philosophical arguments of Schleiermacher into the study of the ancient Vedic sources. Genuine religion was a taste for, and sense of, the infinite. Did not the Indian sources confirm that nature was more than mechanical laws? His interpretation sought to contradict the materialist ideology of his day. Edward Burnett Tylor described religions as a kind of natural philosophy. His notion of the 'soul' functioned to explain natural events. Though, it served intellectual needs in the beginning, this legacy of the past cannot be missed even in modern society; only the concept of the soul may preserve human dignity in an age of materialism. Émile Durkheim and his school studied primitive societies with the ideas of Rousseau and Kant in mind, i.e, that religions are necessary for establishing moral obligations among men. Even individualism, so basic to the division of labour in modern society, derives from religious history and not from the Enlightenment. In this respect, Max Weber's sociology of religion referred less to Kant than to Hegel and Schopenhauer. Weber saw in world-rejection the unique chance for societies and for individuals to escape the iron law of tradition. Religions paved the way to a non-traditional modern society. At the same time they allowed individuals to free themselves from the constraint of all kinds of institutions. All these scholars dealt with religion as something still warranted in modern society.

Thus, the classical scholars in the history of religions studied religions with philosophical assumptions in mind. This interlocking of religious history and the philosophy of religion was not accidental. These scholars of religion lived in an age in which modern civilization superseded the established religions. The notion 'religion' evoked in the mind of many educated contemporaries ideas of an outdated past. The students of historical religions had to pay tribute to that understanding. One of the most common metaphors referring to that particular understanding of religion was that of 'fossil' or 'survival'. We encounter this metaphor in the writings of E.B. Tylor and many others. But in contrast to the protagonists of modernization they assumed that any 'survival' could become a revival. The religious heritage remained at least potentially present under the new social conditions. At the end of the nineteenth century, the notion 'survival' ceded to other notions, such as 'social facts' or 'worldview', thereby indicating a hidden presence of religion even in modern society. Humans in modern society remain dependent upon religions whether or not they are fully aware of that fact. So any depiction of historical religions was structurally interrelated with a diagnosis of the threats and one-sidedness of modern culture.

The founding fathers of religious studies, like all other historians, created representations of historical phenomena which appealed to the imagination of their contemporaries. Reinhart Koselleck, one of the leading scholars in the theory of history, has made an intriguing proposal for identifying categories of the historical imagination. Every historian, he pointed out, is compelled to select data. Some he regards as relevant, whilst other data is rejected as irrelevant. When narrating past events, he turns facts into experiences that may also be expected in the future. Koselleck identified two fundamental categories at work in this process: 'the realm of experience' and 'the horizon of expectation' (*Erfahrungsraum* and *Erwartungshorizont*) (1979, 349-75).

Although we encounter similar problems concerning historical approaches in the history of religions, we lack any examination of how such categories might be applied to representations of religions. Koselleck's theory of the writing of history at least gives us a hint of what to look for. Like other historians, scholars in the history of religions must deal with the fundamental questions: To what extent do religions belong definitively to the past? To what extent do they express elements valuable for the future?

In my contribution to the issue of rationality in the study of religion, I wish to point to an obvious lacuna in our reflections on methods and theories in religious studies. When the classical scholars of religions began to deal with historical religions in the modern age, they had to address the limits of Enlightenment thought. When describing historical religions they were compelled to indicate something that stands for both human experiences and expectations. For that reason they turned to the philosophy of religion. Thus, the solutions of philosophers who pointed to the pragmatic functions of religions became part and parcel of the study of historical religions.

Dissolving Rationality: the Anti-Science Phenomenon and its Implications for the Study of Religion

Donald Wiebe

Introduction

As is well known, the current status of the study of religion legitimated in our modern Western universities is the result of successful argumentation on the part of our forebears that a scientific study of religion was possible. And yet here we are assessing the issue of how a 'rational and disciplined scientific/scholarly discourse on religion' is possible,[1] which, to my mind at least, suggests that we still face fundamental problems in the field of religious studies. Now this is not an altogether new experience for our discipline, for the emancipation of the study of religion from the religio-theological framework within which that study had been undertaken until the latter part of the nineteenth century has never fully been achieved. 'The very abundance of contemporary literature about how religions and their study ought to be conceived or organized', Sam Preus rightly contends, 'amounts to evidence of an identity crisis in the field' (Preus 1987, 17). The problem with the study of religion which we are facing here, however, is not, I think, merely a continuation of that crisis of identity; it rather catapults the problem to an altogether different level of severity.

The psychological notion of a 'crisis of identity' when taken as a metaphor is appropriate in discussions of this field because although the study of religion in the academic setting had achieved a recognizable identity as an objective and scientifically legitimate enterprise, it was all the while being undermined by a conflict of loyalties and aspirations of many of its practitioners who were committed both to the scientific study of religion and to the maintenance of religious faith. The crisis now is not that of maintaining a scientific identity in the face of the extra-scientific aspirations of students of religion, but rather with the loss of identity as a scientific enterprise altogether since the very notion of science itself is now under attack. The notion that science is a special form of reason that can bring about convergence of opinion regarding states of affairs in the world and so ground our knowledge of the world and its contents is itself in dispute. The notion of science as an epistemologically privileged type of knowledge, is today criticized as a political tactic 'to exclude, silence, or otherwise disempower socially threatening or marginal groups' (Seidman 1992a, 54). Indeed, as Steven Seidman, from whom this quotation is taken, puts it, science is nothing more than 'a social practice that is part of the ongoing struggle among groups to impose and legitimate their conflicting interests.' (ibid.) Contrary to the beliefs of those who established the scientific study of religion, therefore, and of those who now support its continuation, science is not justified in terms of genuine epistemological achievements but rather only in terms of a scientistic ideology that according to Seidman cannot justify its claim 'to promote the growth of knowledge and human rationality' (Seidman 1992a, 62). The assumption of the possibility of a rational and scientific study of religion today is therefore seen to be chimerical and the original crisis of identity — caused by the conflict of scientific and religious interests in the study of religion — is consequently dissolved, (and the 'reality' of religion saved). That, I shall argue, however, is not an achievement to be applauded by those in the field, but rather a setback to be lamented and transcended.

Dissolving rationality?

The term anti-science, I think, appropriately describes the attitude expressed by Seidman. And it appears to me that one can also appropriately speak of an *anti-science movement* amongst contemporary intellectuals in our academic institutions in that many, for a variety of reasons, seem intent upon delegitimating science itself. Whether that movement has had the effect of dissolving the rationality of science, however, is far from evident as a critique of several such proposals will clearly show. Tom Sorell's *Scientism: Philosophy and the Infatuation of Science* (1991) and Mary Midgley's *Science as Salvation: A Modern Myth and Its Meaning* (1992) provide us with clear examples of general philosophical dissatisfaction with science in our society.

Sorell, it is true, attempts to distinguish science from scientism — the latter involving commitment to science as 'the most valuable part of human learning' (Sorell 1991, 7) and holding that what is not scientific is of doubtful value — but his critique of scientism as an arrogant, epistemology-centred philosophy seems also to apply to science itself. Science, that is, in its concern to know the world, and to know it objectively, is, necessarily, it appears, insensitive to the broader culture which is and must be concerned with more than matters of knowledge and academic life. To possess culture is not to possess objective, explanatory knowledge of social life, but rather a sensibility which allows one to participate meaningfully in the life of society. Knowledge about society, consequently, cannot simply be concerned with the explanation of phenomena, argues Sorell, and the social sciences, in consequence, cannot be scientific. To insist that the social sciences proceed in the manner of the natural sciences, therefore, is to be scientistic in that it rejects as insignificant the concerns of the social sciences with practical and normative questions. Sorell does not deny that the social sciences sometimes succeed in being explanatory in a way that resembles the natural sciences but he insists that they cannot simply be identified with the natural sciences without undermining society itself, which is much more than a mere accumulation of 'facts about' and 'theories of' human behaviour. 'Culture', he writes:

is not a matter of academic knowledge but of participation. And participation changes not merely your thoughts and beliefs but your perceptions and emotions. The question therefore unavoidably arises whether scientific knowledge and the habits of curiosity and experiment which engender it, are really the friends or foes of culture? Could it be that the habit of scientific explanation may take over from the habits of emotional response, or in some way undermine the picture of the world upon which our moral life is founded? (1991, 108)

Sorell insists that his critique of scientism is not an attack on science, and he worries that it may simply help those who wish to peddle an alternative science like creation-science. Nevertheless, amongst philosophers, he insists, 'the problem is not to create respect for science but to dissuade people from worshipping it' (Sorell 1991, 177). That conclusion, however, is very much open to question.

Mary Midgley, like Sorell, is concerned that her book not be seen as an attack upon science itself. Yet, like Sorell, she also sees science as an enterprise that undermines meaning in life if it makes knowledge an end unto itself for, so understood, 'it leaves unserved the general need for understanding, and whatever spiritual needs lie behind it' (1992, 2). Science understood as the method for obtaining objective knowledge of the world, therefore, is for Midgley but a cult of information which she labels scientism. True science for her is concerned with providing a world-picture that deeply concerns us and provides our lives with significance. The task of science, therefore, is to provide persons with connection to something ultimate in the world. 'Connexion itself,' she writes, 'is not a superstition that we can get rid of. It is work that must be done one way or another. To refuse that work will not stop it being done. It will only leave it to uncontrolled play of the imagination' (1992, 95). Furthermore, science as the search for information about a purely objective — and therefore for her an alien — world (i.e., Midgley's 'scientism') is not even a possibility for it is, in Midgley's opinion, merely another faith and cannot, therefore, claim a status different from that of other frameworks of meaning. The high value put on knowledge and information by those who espouse that Enlightenment view of science, she insists, is indicative of a perception of epistemology that makes it impossible to distinguish it from a social myth. 'I strongly suspect', she writes:

that, in the end, some outward-looking reverent attitude of this sort may be an unavoidable part of any serious pursuit of knowledge, and ought to figure in any explanation of its value. Mere intellectual predation — fact-swallowing — simply is not enough to power effective thought. The world that we think *about* has to be seen as important, as having value in itself, if we want to claim that there is any great value in thinking about. (1992, 71-2)

The dissatisfaction with the rationality of scientific reasoning is not, unfortunately, limited simply to philosophers seeking some justification for a form of philosophical knowledge; it is also, paradoxically I think, to be found amongst some scientists and especially social theorists. In his recent *Fin de Siècle Social Theory* (1995), Jeffrey Alexander, for example, argues that the role of reason in social theory has dissolved because there are dimensions of our social life that rationalist thought either denied or failed to thematize. The failure of the modern social sciences, he maintains, lies in its failure to see reason for the complex textual construction that it really is, and using it merely as a tool of calculation. The task of intellectuals, he insists, is not only to explain the world in a rational, universalizing fashion, but also to interpret the world — to understand the world in a way that provides meaning to, and motivation for, living. In fact, argues Alexander, it is not possible to separate the explanatory from the interpretive task in social theory. 'Twentieth-century philosophy', he writes:

began with logical positivism and the confidence that analytic thought could know the truth. It is ending with hermeneutics, a philosophy which maintains that knowing reality in a manner that separates it from us is epistemologically impossible. (1995, 78)

Alexander insists that this abandonment of positivism does not mean that social theorists have given up on science or reason, but admits that this no longer involves the pursuit of general theories of society. Although he refuses to espouse the simple contrast between 'scientific theory' and 'antitheoretical relativism' in social theorizing, he does nevertheless maintain that theoretical knowledge 'can never be anything other than the socially rooted efforts of historical agents' (1995,91). And such a notion of agency, he assumes, undermines all possibility of deriving objective, scientific laws that can depict the universe.

What Alexander rejects, then, is the notion that social scientific knowledge has a privileged epistemological status; he rejects the idea that scientific knowledge has a universality about it and that the criteria of adjudication of its theories are not culture-bound. For Alexander, therefore, there cannot be a natural science of society, for social theory is not only science but also ideology. 'Unless we recognize the interpenetration of science and ideology in social theory', he writes, 'neither element can be evaluated or clarified in a rational way' (Alexander 1995, 10).

Steven Seidman's and David G. Wagner's introduction to their recently published reader on *Postmodernism and Social Theory* (1992) concisely summarizes the implications of much postmodernist thought for the social sciences. 'Postmodernism', they write:

criticizes the modernist notion that science itself, not this or that theory or paradigm, is a privileged form of reason or the medium of truth. It disputes the scientistic claim that only scientific knowledge can be securely grounded. It takes issue with the unifying, consensus-building agenda of science. It contests the modernist idea that social theory has as its chief role the securing of conceptual grounds for social research. And postmodernism criticizes the modernist notion that science is or should be value-neutral; postmodernism underlines the practical and moral meaning of science. (1992, 6)

Seidman is wholly convinced not only that scientific rationality has its origins in Western culture but that the rationale for what counts as warrant and evidence for propositional claims in the sciences is coherent only for Western cultural traditions. In other words, science is like other institutions — a strategy to promote particular social agendas. Consequently Seidman counsels social scientists to abandon the search for general theories and proposes instead:

a shift in the role of theorists from building general theory or providing epistemic warrants for sociology to serving as moral and political analysts, narrators of stories of social development, producers of genealogies, and social critics. (Seidman 1992a, 48-49)

He continues:

I advocate a change from a discipline-centred social inquiry whose reference point is debates in specialty areas to contextualized local narratives that address public conflicts. (Seidman 1992a, 49)

The nature of the postmodernist challenge to the study of religion

As already intimated above, the postmodernist challenge to the study of religion is a far more serious challenge than was/is the crisis of identity created by those in the field who sought/seek to harmonize their religious aspirations with their commitment to the academic (scientific) study of religion. For the most part those scholars still retained a belief in the possibility of obtaining propositional knowledge of objective facts and of the possibility of explaining those facts in terms of objectively testable theories.

Postmodernism's attack on the notion of theory, however, makes such harmonization impossible because it makes of social theory an essentially contested concept and, thereby, makes the study of all human behaviour — religious behaviour included — an essentially contested enterprise. The distinction between social theory as a philosophical interpretation of society in light of politico-ethical considerations and sociological theory as an epistemologically grounded account of society is rejected out of hand. And that makes a science of society — and therefore a scientific study of religions — impossible; unless, of course, we are ready to redefine science in non-cognitivist, non-epistemic terms. And there are many who are ready to do so both in the social sciences generally and in religious studies in particular.

Although many still hold to a natural science view of the social sciences, it is readily apparent that this is fast becoming a minority position, being replaced with a notion of science as an interpretive enterprise concerned with meaning rather than with knowledge. Ernest Gellner describes the effects of this transformation of the idea of the social sciences in the field of anthropology as follows:

In the end, the operational meaning of postmodernism in anthropology seems to be something like this: a refusal (in practice, rather selective) to countenance any objective facts, any independent social structures, and their replacement by a pursuit of 'meanings', both those of the objects of inquiry and of the inquirer. There is thus a double stress on subjectivity: the world-creation by the person studied, and the text-creation by the investigator. 'Meaning' is less a tool of analysis than a conceptual intoxicant, an instrument of self-titillation. The investigator demonstrates both his initiation into the mysteries of hermeneutics, and the difficulty of the enterprise, by complex and convoluted prose, peppered with allusions to a high proportion of the authors of the World's 100 Great Books, and also to the latest favourable scribes of the Left Bank. (1992, 29-30)

Such anthropologists, he argues, are 'hostile to the idea of unique, exclusive, objective, external or transcendent truth' (1992, 24) and consequently espouse a logical permissiveness and pluralist obscurity which amounts to a rejection of theory in the study of human behaviour.

Much the same, I think, can be said of those in our field who trade the objective scientific study of religion for one of the many new alternative approaches of phenomenology, hermeneutics, ethnomethodology, critical theory, etc. This is particularly clear, for example, in Francis Schüssler Fiorenza's rather unclear attempt to reconfigure the academic study of religion in the light of the postmodernist critique of rationality and of what he calls 'the challenge of interpretive disciplines.' (1993, 35) The Enlightenment notion of an objective and explanatory study of religious phenomena, he maintains, has no justification for proceeding as it does, and he counsels the academic student of religion to eschew science and espouse the humanities as the model for his or her own undertaking. Fiorenza writes:

Programmes in the humanities study the classics not merely for their meaning, but also for their significance, not merely as sources of past cultures, but as challenges to present cultures. Classics raise truth claims that are legitimately discussed. Such contemporary university programmes have heeded Nietzsche's scorn of his age four score and forty years ago [sic?], when he chastised its claims to be historical with an objectivism that kills the historical. (1993, 36)

The objective study of religion in explaining religious phenomena, he argues, willy nilly affects religion, and therefore cannot be objective and neutral. And since it cannot be neutral, he concludes that the student of religion not only has the right to study religion as a search for meaning but rather ought to seek the meaning religion has for the totality of life. Fiorenza draws that conclusion for it allows him, it appears, to espouse both the metaphysical truth of 'religion-in-general' as well as, relativistically, the truth of each religion in its particularity. There is some indication that Fiorenza sees the logical tension implicit in his position here for he counsels the student of religion to seek a mode of knowledge that transcends the explanation-interpretation dichotomy espoused by what he calls the positivistic student of religion. On recognition of the historical, social, and personal conditioning of all knowledge, he writes, the task of the student of religion is neither to espouse a Cartesian foundationalism nor relativism but rather 'to become critically self-aware by reflecting critically [sic] on all our presuppositions and by combining explanatory as well as interpretive modes [of thought]' (1994, 8). What Fiorenza means by 'explanation', however, is never made clear — but if by 'explanation' he means the search for a natural scientific account of aspects of human behaviour, it would appear that his injunction to the student of religion is nothing short of incoherent; and if this is not what he means by his use of the notion, it is then unclear how he distinguishes it from the notion of interpretation with which he contrasts it. In the end, therefore, the operational meaning of postmodernism in the study of religion appears to be roughly what it is elsewhere — a hostility to the possibility of objective knowledge of the facts about religions and their theoretical explanation and an espousal of the notion that knowledge of religions, as of any other social phenomenon, is always local and not general in that it is necessarily linked to a particular person in a particular culture at a particular time. Thus Fiorenza rejects the nineteenth-century approach to the study of religion which achieved recognition as a scientific undertaking in quest of a general theoretical knowledge of religions and religion (Wiebe 1994b). As he puts it:

The social location within the university means that the interpretation of concrete religions takes place within a context of the interpretation of diverse religions and the taking seriously of the claims of other religions. Such a pluralistic context requires neither a generic concept of religion nor an evolutionary comparative scheme that should serve as an interpretive or normative key, as often was the case at the origin of the discipline. (1993, 37)[2]

Some responses to the challenge

It is difficult to know what would constitute a refutation of 'decontructivist, postmodernist, and relativist challenges to established notions of rationality',[3] or how the student of religion can, in a positive way, respond to the challenges of such critiques. Can one draw upon the resources of the very rationality which is under critique to ground a refutation of that critique? Would this not be asking the critics of rationality to buy into the very 'hegemony of reason' which they believe themselves to have undermined? On the other hand, if we try to do this from a postmodernist perspective, we will surely already have given up that which we wish to defend. How then can we respond to the attack on the notion of a natural science of society — of human behaviour — and, more specifically, the notion of a scientific study of religion? Before attempting to answer these questions I shall briefly review three responses to those who would dissolve reason in the study of religion.

In a recent essay on 'Postmodernism's Impact on the Study of Religion', Huston Smith argues the necessity for students of religion to respond to what he sees as wholly negative implications of the dehegemonization of reason, namely postmodernism's political reshaping of our language in a manner that makes it 'difficult to consider the *possibility* of ontological transcendence without being charged with speaking ineptly' (1990, 662). But this is not, of course, a call for the defence of a natural scientific study of religious phenomena. Indeed, on this score Smith sees the consequences of modernity — that is, modern rationality and science — as equally problematical for the student of religion because it also deprives the study of religion of the language needed to talk about God and therefore distances the student of religion from religious reality. Nevertheless, Huston Smith does defend science to some extent — a suitably chastened science that has learned from the wisdom traditions, as he puts it, how to respect talk of transcendence. Science today, he claims, is 'conspiring with the wisdom traditions to restore the hierarchical universe — which is also the hierophanous universe — to its rightful place as the generic religious posit' (1990, 665). From Smith's point of view, then, postmodern science is moving closer to the traditional religious view in regard to the ontological truth claims found in religious traditions. Unfortunately, Smith provides no argument or evidence in support of that claim, and his notion of a hybrid mode of thought which combines reason and revelation would simply return the study of religion to the religio-theological matrix from which it emerged in the last quarter of the nineteenth century.

In a paper on 'Global Perspectives on Methodology in the Study of Religion' Armin Geertz (n.d.) focused his attention on the methodological problems for the study of religion implicit in the postmodernist stance. Although he is well aware that meta-narratives about rationality and science have lost their credence in the eyes of postmodernists, he nevertheless suggests that we must retain them but, as he puts it, in an improved, non-imperialist version which allows us to remain open to 'the other' and to difference. This requires, he maintains, power-free discourse for which he thinks the notion of conversation an appropriate metaphor. Geertz then elaborates that notion of conversation in the hopes of establishing a 'revitalized humanistic study of religion', and does so by drawing heavily upon Richard Shweder's use of the concept of divergent rationalities. Geertz names such conversation 'ethnohermeneutics', and he suggests that it can supply a new logic which is neither merely emic nor merely etic but rather brings both voices into a kind of hybrid thinking — a new voice — which has a legitimacy all its own. Ethnohermeneutics according to Geertz involves combining 'the reflections of the student of a religion' with 'the reflections of the indigenous student of that religion' (n.d. 20). And he claims that with the combined efforts of the multitude of voices and perspectives engaged in a common self-critical scientific endeavour the whole product will become 'the third perspective.' It will be the practice of ethnohermeneutics, where the perspective and the result are greater than the individuals involved (n.d., 21).

It appears to me, however, that Geertz's proposal is mixing oil and water in that the person he refers to as 'the student of religion' makes general methodological assumptions but excludes 'localizing' substantive presuppositions whereas the person he refers to as 'the indigenous student of a particular tradition' is committed to 'local' substantive presuppositions. It is obvious therefore that the pursuit of scientific generalizations is simply not compatible with the recognition of the necessarily local character of all knowledge, and Geertz can only establish an ethnohermeneutics, I suggest, by perceiving the work of 'the student of a religion' and 'the indigenous student of that religion' in terms of the notion of 'reflection', making each enterprise, therefore, a hermeneutical endeavour. And that undermines the essential character of the scientific study of religion to which the field, speaking ideally, has been committed since the nineteenth century. This is not, of course, Geertz's intention: 'Even though I warmly support intercultural understanding and cooperation and actively support it politically and organizationally', he writes:

my point of departure is built on the Enlightenment principles of a critical, humanistic approach to the study of religion. I do not thereby condone or defend the gross excesses and intentions of specific scientists, nor the ideological and political measure of scientific results. Nor do I deny the hegemonic implications of the scientific project. But equally, I do not support the programmes of radical postmodern relativism, feminist theology, New Age ontology, or the extremes of political correctness in the humanistic study of religion. Most of these are the very forces, in new guises of course, from which the comparative study of religion attempted to liberate itself during the middle of the last century. Furthermore, the fact that scientists have politics and morals, does not automatically mean that science is futile or that its results have no universal salience. (n.d. 21)

In my estimation, therefore, Geertz's proposal for the employment of ethnohermeneutics in the academic study of religion is not a particularly helpful response to the methodological problems created by postmodernists; as described here, it runs counter to the Enlightenment project to which he is obviously committed. I think a more critical response to postmodernism is needed — a response that can take seriously the cognitively legitimate complaints that critics of Enlightenment reason have raised for the social sciences and improve the quality of our scientific knowledge of society rather than jettisoning it. Ernest Gellner, I suggest, best strikes the kind of tone we ought to take up in this discussion.

In his book *Postmodernism, Reason and Religion* (1992), Gellner goes on the attack against postmodernists and their claims that the search for objective, scientific knowledge is little more than a cunning trick of dominators. The postmodernist project of replacing such scientific knowledge with hermeneutic truth, he argues, provides not liberty but logical permissiveness, relativism, and pluralist obscurity; clarity, he insists, is definitely not one of the attributes of postmodernist thought. And it is especially the discussion about the human subject around which obscurity swirls and in which relativism is, so to speak, established. As Gellner sums it up:

> The pursuit of generalization, in the image of science, is excoriated as 'positivism', so 'theory' tends to become a set of pessimistic and obscure musings on the Inaccessibility of the Other and its Meanings. (1992, 23)

The impact of such an anti-science movement in anthropology, he notes, 'means in effect the abandonment of any serious attempt to give a reasonably precise, documented and testable account of anything' (1992, 29), and its effect on the study of religion, as I have already suggested above, is much the same. Indeed, the influence of postmodernism on religious studies has in large measure come by way of the intimate ties that have traditionally existed between these two fields. Further, Gellner's query as to why anthropology departments should reduplicate the work of other persons 'already employed by the university [in departments of philosophy] to explain why knowledge is impossible' is in an equal manner appropriately directed to departments of religious studies.

In looking at the issues of 'postmodernity', 'reason', and 'religion' Gellner argues, and I think correctly so, that we are presented with three radically different positions with respect to questions of religious faith — with fundamentalism, relativism, and Enlightenment rationalism which he also refers to as Enlightenment secular rationalism and rationalist fundamentalism. Fundamentalism, of course, excludes relativism in affirming a substantive and final world-transcending revelation of an extra-mental and extra-cultural universe of meaning. Relativism on the other hand does not believe in the availability of knowledge of or access to such an ontologically other realm. Rationalist fundamentalism, however, is both like and unlike fundamentalism and relativism. It has in common with fundamentalism its belief that there is objective, culture-transcending knowledge but differs from it in that it denies the availability of a final, substantive Revelation. Like relativism, rationalist fundamentalism believes no substantive affirmation to be privileged and free from critical scrutiny, but differs from it in that it does believe that knowledge beyond culture is possible. In summary, rationalist fundamentalism repudiates substantive revelations but it does, in a sense, absolutize procedural principles for obtaining knowledge.

Gellner has no doubt that these positions cannot be mixed and matched, and for him there is no doubt which to adopt. 'I am not sure', he writes, 'whether indeed we possess morality beyond culture, but I am absolutely certain that we do indeed possess knowledge beyond both culture and morality' (1992, 54) Nor is this mere assertion on Gellner's part; it rests largely upon the success achieved by science and the sciences, and the transformation science has brought to human civilization. As he points out:

we happen to live in a world in which one style of knowledge, though born of one culture, is being adopted by all of them with enormous speed, and is disrupting many of them, and is totally transforming the milieu in which men live.' (1992, 78)

The sciences, that is, achieve certain epistemic goals which we have prized. And it is a fact about our society that the existence of such transcultural and amoral knowledge is gained by virtue of Enlightenment reason, *even though* the criteria in terms of which it establishes its knowledge claims are not either formulated easily or formulated with exacting precision, and *even though* they are not capable of authoritative demonstration. Gellner also shows clearly that postmodernist relativism hardly finds more persuasive justification for the denial of this central fact of our time: he shows that the claims of the postmodernist rest upon a facile argument that runs like this:

men live through cultural meanings, cultural meanings are ultimate and self-sustaining, therefore all cultures are cognitively equal, therefore the central fact of our time could not have happened even if it did. (1992, 62-63)

According to Gellner they have wrongly assumed that only if science cannot lay claim to objective truth can one understand the 'other' and so appreciate a humanistic perspective on the world.

If Gellner's critique is on the mark, the celebration of the end of science by postmodernists is then both premature and misguided. As Philip Kitcher has recently argued in his *The Advancement of Science: Science Without Legend, Objectivity Without Illusions* (1993), even though postmodernists have raised legitimate criticisms of the Enlightenment notion of science, the Enlightenment view is nevertheless essentially right. 'Flawed people working in complex social environments, moved by all kinds of interests', he shows:

have collectively achieved a vision of parts of nature that is broadly progressive, and that rests on arguments meeting standards that have been refined and improved over the centuries. (Kitcher 1993, 390)

Such a general argument against postmodernism, however important, is not sufficient, I think, if we are adequately to defend the idea of a rational and disciplined study of society or, more specifically, the scientific study of religions. Nor will it do simply to strike out at postmodernists in an *ad hominem* fashion as does Gellner when he rejects cognitive relativism as being only an affectation 'specially attractive amongst the more naive provincials in privileged cultures' who think it possible in this fashion to atone for their privilege and come to understand others and themselves (Gellner 1992, 71). We need, that is, to be able to show that the problems facing the social sciences are not really any different from those facing the natural sciences and, as Jonathan Turner puts it, regain the vision of early social theorists who established the social sciences in the last decades of the nineteenth century (Turner 1992, 175). Their critics, Turner maintains, have not presented a very interesting or fruitful alternative to those theorists because for them social theory can be nothing more than 'a mixture of history, philosophy, social commentary, ideological advocacy, and empirical description' (Turner 1992, 176). Such a claim, however, has not gone unchallenged and even though this is not the place to argue the dispute in any detail, it will be of some benefit here to sample the nature of the debate given its central importance in the postmodernist arsenal.

In *Practical Sociology: Post-Empiricism and the Reconstruction of Theory and Application* (1995), Christopher G.A. Bryant rejects such a disparaging description of postmodernist theorizing as mere conversation or discourse; there is no need, he argues, to make sociology (and by implication the other social sciences) as discourse and as explanation mutually exclusive. Indeed, those who do so, he suggests, make sociology an impossible science because they subscribe to an impossible conception of science. The restricted notion of instrumental reason associated with these conceptions of the social sciences, he maintains, have simply failed to deliver what was expected of them. But this is not surprising, he continues, because in the social world it is simply not possible to establish scientific laws governing society and social behaviour; to attempt to do so is to overlook the radical difference between their subject matter and that of the natural sciences. He writes:

Whilst there is no prospect of objects in nature changing their behaviour in the light of what natural scientists say about them there is just such a prospect with the objects of social scientific inquiry (1995, 52).

Bryant goes on to argue, moreover, that there is a new theoretical movement that in taking this difference into account has been able to provide a more coherent and applicable understanding of sociology as a matter of story-telling and a set of discourses showing it to be less a cumulative explanatory science than a moral inquiry. Bryant still wishes to call such inquiry 'scientific' but acknowledges that it is so not by virtue of equating scientific truth with instrumental knowledge which allows the possibility of manipulating the things of which it speaks, but rather by virtue of equating it with hermeneutic knowledge:

which enables us to come to a mutual understanding with others and critical knowledge which helps us to overcome the manipulations of others in the interests of self-determination. (Bryant 1995, 121-22)

This science, he insists, at least has the possibility of practical application in ongoing discourse which the notion of sociology as a natural science does not. 'Cognitive and moral models of the universe', Bryant then writes:

have more similarities than might once have been supposed. Cognitive models cannot exclude values, and moral models which refer to qualities, connections and consequences cannot dismiss empirical adequacy. The making and accepting of truth claims, and moral claims, both involve persuading others freely to reach a consensus, or freely to accommodate differences or negotiate a compromise. (1995, 122)

This new, more workable understanding of sociology and the social sciences generally, Bryant argues, arises because of the recognition of the importance of the notion of agency and the double-hermeneutic in social matters in the work of theorists like Norbert Elias, Pierre Bordieu, Anthony Giddens, Roy Bhaskar, and Jürgen Habermas, amongst others. Agency and consciousness, it appears, make impossible the establishing of laws of social behaviour because, when they are taken seriously it becomes clear that society is an open system 'in which the constant conjunctions of events demanded by the Humean concept of causal law rarely occurs.' (Bryant 1995, 87) Nevertheless, Bryant insists that even though this requires an understanding of sociology as a set of discourses, it does not mean that it becomes an activity in which 'anything goes' (1995,162). He adamantly claims that sociology so understood 'has a contribution to make to the reflexivity of contemporary societies different from anything poets, prophets, and pundits can offer' (1995, 162), although he does not provide criteria by which such a differentiation can be determined. Moreover, he admits that repositioning sociology in this fashion will be a difficult and protracted exercise but nevertheless thinks the future of the discipline rests upon its success in doing so. In this claim, of course, Bryant is indistinguishable from those who share the original vision of sociology as a natural science but are aware that it will not be easy to show that to be the case.

David Sylvan and Barry Glassner, it is interesting to note, see the 'heroes' of the new theoretical movement in Bryant's discussion as rationalists, even though the 'new social realists', as they refer to them, attempt 'to emphasize the simultaneous importance in sociological explanation of structural and interpretive elements' (Sylvan and Glassner 1985, 6). They argue, in *A Rationalist Methodology for the Social Sciences*, that to have a social science implies holding that order characterizes the social world and that the proper task of that science is 'to bring reason to bear in specifying that order' (1985, 1). And the 'new social realists', they maintain, do this in recognizing that the surface regularities exhibited in social behaviour are but reflections of a deeper order, the discovery of which is the task of the social scientist. This is why they reject both empiricist and hermeneutical approaches to social theorizing. The social world can be as fundamentally open-ended for the rationalist as for the hermeneuticist because it is possible to accept the importance of the notions of consciousness and agency — the importance of agents' interpretations, their rule-making and rule-following — without taking this aspect of social life to be its fundamental constituent. Thus the outcome of such rationalist inquiries, Sylvan and Glassner conclude, 'would not be a set of laws of human behaviour but a set of generative structures, capable of combining to produce empirical possibilities' (1985, 95) with respect to human behaviour, and in that sense provide some explanation of them. These are the fundamental and invariant properties of the universe which according to Jonathan H. Turner ought to concern the social scientists, for they alone are genuinely subject to theoretical analysis. Thus 'while the structure of the social universe is constantly changing', he writes, 'the fundamental dynamics underlying this structure are not' (1987, 160).

Summary and conclusions

Although the foregoing discussion of the challenge of postmodernism and of some of the responses to it does not provide an 'affirmative refutation'[4] of that challenge, it does suggest several elements that will be essential to the construction of such an argument.

    The first step in refuting postmodernism, (relativism, and deconstruc-
tionism,) I suggest, is that of internal critique. As I have already noted,
postmodernists are likely to see such a critique as an indication of self-
interest and therefore as an instance of special pleading. But such an
indictment can just as easily be lodged against their critique of science and
rationality — one can, in other words, argue the constructionist character of
deconstructivism. The claim that scientific knowledge can be explained in
terms of socio-economic status and hidden ideological commitments applies
equally to those who would make these sweeping claims about science and
reason. Paul R. Gordon and Norman Levitt have to a large extent provided
that kind of analysis of postmodernism and other similar movements in their
recent book *Higher Superstition: The Academic Left and Its Quarrels With Science*
(1994). They correctly argue that the intellectual ethos of the various
postmodernist movements is indistinguishable from that of other social
movements that champion oppressed races, castes, outcastes, etc. and
justifiably complain about their shameless resort to moral one-upmanship in
their attack on 'mere instrumental reasoning'. With the postmodernists we
have then, they argue, the 'rebirth of the philosopher as comprehensive sage'
who has the assurance that he or she is capable of profound insight into
anything and everything (Gordon and Levitt 1994, 77-78).

    Gordon and Levitt also show the internal incoherence of much
postmodernist thought and point out that those who evade such
inconsistency provide us with nothing more than assertion. In the first
instance, that is, it can be shown that postmodernists appeal to the same
canons of judgment that their arguments set out to condemn. Shapin (1994;
1996) and Latour (1987), for example, base their claims on work which they,
it appears, wish us to take seriously as careful social history and precise
ethnographic analysis. And for those who do not intend that we take their
work seriously in this sense — who refuse to distinguish evidence and
argument from assertion — there is no reason to pay them attention; if
assertion requires no justification, then neither does counter-assertion.

    A second step — still in the realm of philosophical critique — is the
clarification of the notions of modern science and of scientific rationality as
a search for knowledge rather than a search for meaning or truth; its concern
is wholly with epistemic goals. That form of Enlightenment reason which
argues that all spheres of culture — science, morality, art, and religion — can
be equally moulded by reason into a harmonious framework for meaningful
existence, is indeed an unwarranted hegemonization of reason and is, therefore, rightly open to attack. But the fundamentalist rationality which
characterizes modern science is not concerned with bringing these culture-

spheres into a harmonious world-view, and is not therefore guilty of seeking some form of hegemony; and to write off epistemology as philosophically incoherent because it cannot do this, is simply silly.

A third step in the refutation of the postmodernist challenge is the provision of a careful history of the emergence of science as a peculiar sort of value in, and for, Western culture, namely the quest for knowledge for the sake of knowledge alone. That history, moreover, will have to provide a persuasive accounting of the cross-cultural success which that peculiar cultural value has had compared to all other cultural values. Such an account will, I suggest, free us from having to deal with caricatures of scientific reasoning that would commit us to accepting a radical distinction between the natural and the social sciences. Only then will we be able to free ourselves from the moral and political goals of a religio-theological or humanistic study of religions and religion, and direct our attention to the cognitive (epistemological) goals which alone characterize science.

The final aspect of the argument to which I shall advert here is that of properly analyzing recent developments in the social sciences, especially sociology. Much more fine-tuning will be necessary before we will be able to provide a reasonably persuasive analysis of the notion of agency as a natural phenomenon as explicable as any other.

Such a fully developed argument will not likely convince the hardened postmodernist, I suspect, no matter how persuasive we might find it to be. That, however, is no reason for not undertaking the task, for it may well assist many who have not as yet been taken in by the sweeping, but unsupported, claims of postmodernism and its promises of liberation for all.

Notes

1. This is the central issue for discussion formulated by Jeppe Sinding Jensen in the 'Invitation to an international conference on rationality and the study of religion' held at the University of Aarhus in June, 1996.
2. I have provided a further response to Fiorenza's argument in my essay 'On Theological Resistance to the Scientific Study of Religion: Values and the Value-Free Study of Religion', in Czlowiek i Wartości: Księga pamiątkowa poświęcona 35-leciu pracy naukowej i 40-leciu pracy nauczycielskiej Profesora Jana Szmyda. Kraków: Wydawnictwo Naukowe WSP, 1997, 131-45.
3. This is Jensen's characterization of the major problem faced by the scientific study of religion in the 'Invitation' to the Aarhus conference.
4. Jensen's phrase in the conference 'Invitation'.

Bibliography

Agassi, Joseph and Ian C. Jarvie (eds.) 1987. *Rationality: The Critical View*. Dordrecht: Nijhoff.

Albert, Hans 1995. 'Religion, Science, and the Myth of the Framework'. In I.C. Jarvie and Nathaniel Laor (eds.), *Critical Rationalism, Metaphysics and Science*. Dordrecht: Kluwer, 41-58.

Alexander, Jeffrey C. 1990. 'Introduction: Durkheimian sociology and cultural studies today'. In idem. (ed.), *Durkheimian sociology: cultural studies*, Cambridge: Cambridge U.P., 1-21.

Alexander, Jeffrey 1995. *Fin de Siécle Social Theory: Relativism, Reduction and the Problem of Reason*. London: Verso.

Allen, Douglas 1988. 'Eliade and History', *The Journal of Religion* 68, 545-65.

Alston, William 1991. *Perceiving God*. New York: Cornell U.P.

Alston, William 1996. *A Realist Conception of Truth*. New York: Cornell U.P.

Appleby, Joyce; Lynn Hunt, and Margaret Jacob, 1994. *Telling the Truth about History*. New York: Norton.

Arieti, Silvano 1974. *Interpretation of Schizophrenia* (2nd ed.). New York: Basic Books.

Aristoteles 1941. *The Basic Works of Aristotle*, Richard McKeon (ed.). New York: Random House.

Asad, Talal 1986. 'The concept of cultural translation in British social anthropology'. In Clifford and Marcus (eds.), 141-64.

Asad, Talal 1993. *Genealogies of Religion: Discipline and Reasons of Power in Christianity and Islam*. Baltimore: The Johns Hopkins U.P.

Athanasius of Alexandria 1912. *The Orations Against the Arians*. London: Griffith Farrar.

Austin, M.M. 1981. *The Hellenistic World from Alexander to the Roman Conquest*. Cambridge: Cambridge U.P.

Ayer, A.J. 1946. *Language,Truth and Logic* (2nd ed.). London: Gollancz.

Bacon, Francis 1598. *Essaies, Religious Meditations. Of Heresies*. London: Printed for Humfrey Hooper.

Barnes, Barry 1972. 'Sociological Explanation and Natural Science: A Kuhnian Reappraisal'. *Archives européenes de sociologie*, 13, 373-91.

Barnes, Barry 1974. *Scientific Knowledge and Sociological Theory*. London: Routledge.

Barnes, Barry and David Bloor 1982. 'Relativism, Rationalism and the Sociology of Knowledge'. In Hollis and Lukes (eds.), 21-47.

Barrett, T. H. 1993. 'Tominaga our contemporary'. *Journal of the Royal Asiatic Society*, Series 3, 3, 2, 245-52.

Bateson, Gregory 1972. *Steps to an Ecology of Mind*. New York: Ballantine.

Beattie, J. 1964. *Other Cultures*. London: Routledge & Kegan Paul.

Beattie, John 1970. 'On understanding ritual'. In Wilson (ed.), 240-68.

Bell, Catherine 1992. *Ritual Theory, Ritual Practice*. New York: Oxford U.P.

Benveniste, Émile 1966. *Problèmes de linguistique générale* 1, Paris: Gallimard.

Berg, Herbert (ed.) 1997. Special Issue of *Method & Theory in the Study of Religion*, 9 (on the work of John E. Wansbrough).

Berger, Peter 1969. *The Sacred Canopy*. New York: Anchor Books.

Berlin, Brent and Paul Kay 1969. *Basic Color Terms*. Berkeley: University of California Press.

Bernal, Martin 1987. *Black Athena: The Afroasiatic Roots of Classical Culture*. New Brunswick, NJ: Rutgers U.P.

Bernstein, Richard J. 1983. *Beyond Objectivism and Relativism. Science, Hermeneutics, and Praxis*. Philadelphia: University of Pennsylvania Press.

Bernstein, Richard J. 1992. *The New Constellation: The Ethical-Political Horizons of Modernity/Postmodernity*. Cambridge: MIT Press.

Bianchi, Ugo (ed.) 1994. *The Notion of 'Religion' in Comparative Research: Selected Proceedings of the XVI IAHR Congress*. Rome: 'L'Erma' di Bretschneider.

Biderman, Shlomo and Ben-Ami Scharfstein (eds.) 1989. *Rationality in Question. On Eastern and Western Views of Rationality*. Leiden: E.J.Brill.

Bigger, Charles P. 1968. *Participation: A Platonic Inquiry*. Baton Rouge: Louisiana State U.P.

Bloch, Marc 1953. *The Historians' Craft*, (trans. P. Putnam). New York: Vintage Books.

Bloor, David 1976. *Knowledge and Social Imagery*. London: Routledge.

Bowersock, Glen 1996. 'Rescuing the Greeks'. *The New York Times Book Review*, February 25, 6-7.

Brown, Donald E. 1991. *Human Universals*. New York: Mc Graw Hill.

Brown, Harold I. 1990. *Rationality*. London & New York: Routledge.

Brown, Peter 1988. *The Body and Society: Men, Women and Sexual Renunciation in Early Christianity*. New York: Columbia U.P.

Bryant, Christopher G.A. 1995. *Practical Sociology: Post-Empiricism and the Reconstruction of Theory and Application*. Cambridge: Polity Press.

Buchowski, Michal 1989. 'Ethnocentrism, eurocentrism, scientocentrism'. In J. Kmita and K. Zamiara (eds.), *Visions of Culture and the Models of Cultural Sciences*, Amsterdam-Atlanta: Rodopi, 199-214.

Buchowski, Michal 1990. *Racjonalnosc, translacja, interpretacja*. Poznan: Adam Mickiewicz U.P.

Buchowski, Michal 1993. 'Multiple orderings of Tambiah's thought'. *Philosophy of the Social Sciences* 23 (1), 84-96.

Buchowski, Michal 1994. 'Enchanted scholar or sober Man? On Ernest Gellner's rationalism'. *Philosophy of the Social Sciences*, 24 (3), 362-77.

Buchowski, Michal 1994a. 'Contextualizing the Assumption of Rationality: An Anthropological Perspective'. *Ethnologia Polona*, vol 18: 1994, 7-16.

Buchowski, Michal 1995. 'Back to Cognitive Foundationalism?' *Philosophy of the Social Sciences*, 25 (3), 384-95.

Bunge, M. 1973. *Method, Model, and Matter*. Dordrecht: Reidel Publishing Company.

Campbell, Joseph 1968 (1949). *The Hero with a Thousand Faces*. Princeton: Princeton U.P.

Carlyle, Thomas 1993 (1840). *On Heroes, Hero-Worship, and the Heroic in History*. Berkeley: University of California Press.

Carr, E.H. 1961. *What is History?* New York: Vintage Books.

Carrithers, M. 1992. *Why Human Have Cultures*. Oxford: Oxford U.P.

Cazeneuve, Jean 1972 (1963). *Lucien Lévy-Bruhl* (trans. Peter Rivière). New York: Harper and Row.

Chavannes, Edouard 1967. *Les Mémoires Historiques de Se-Ma Ts'ien*. Leiden: Brill.

Chidester, David 1986. 'Michel Foucault and the Study of Religion'. *Religious Studies Review*, 12, 1-9.

Clifford, James and George E. Marcus 1986. *Writing Culture: The Poetics and Politics of Ethnography*. Berkeley: University of California Press.

Cole, K.C. 1996. 'Scientists' Dilemma: Factoring in Faith'. *The Los Angeles Times*, 15 September 1996, 38-40.

Collingwood, Robin G. 1940. *An Essay on Metaphysics*. Oxford: Clarendon Press.

Collingwood, Robin G. 1956. *The Idea of History*. New York: Oxford U.P.

Cooper, David E. 1975. 'Alternative Logic in Primitive Thought'. *Man*, 10, 238-56.

Cousins, Mark and Athar Hussain 1984. *Michel Foucault*. New York: St. Martin's Press.

Couvreur, F. S. 1966 (1890). *Dictionnaire Classique de la Langue Chinoise*. No place indicated: Book World Company.

Cumont, Franz 1956 (1911). *The Oriental Religions in Roman Paganism* (Introd. Grant Showerman, 2nd ed). New York: Dover Publications.

Däniken, Erich von 1969. *Chariots of the Gods? Unsolved Mysteries of the Past* (trans. M. Heron). New York: G.P. Putnam's Sons.

Darnton, Robert 1984. *The Great Cat Massacre*. New York: Basic Books.

Darwin, Charles 1872. *The Expression of the Emotions in Man and Animals*. London: Murray.

Davidson, Donald 1984. *Inquiries into Truth and Interpretation*. Oxford: Clarendon Press.

Davidson, Donald 1985. 'Rational Animals'. In Ernest LePore and Brian P. McLaughlin (eds.), *Actions and Events. Perspectives on the Philosophy of Donald Davidson*. Oxford: Basil Blackwell, 473-480.

Davies, Merryl Wyn 1988. *Knowing One Another. Shaping an Islamic Anthropology*. London & New York: Mansell.

Davies, Paul 1994. *The Last Three Minutes*. New York: Basic Books.

Dennett, D.C. 1987. *The Intentional Stance*. Cambridge, MA.: MIT Press.

de Sardan, Olivier 1992. 'Occultism and the ethnographic 'I': The exoticizing of magic from Durkheim to 'postmodern' anthropology'. *Critique of Anthropology* 12 (1), 5-25.

Doctorow, E.L. 1995. *The Waterworks*. New York: Penguin.

Domarus, Ernst von 1954. 'The Specific Laws of Logic in Schizophrenia'. In J.S. Kasanin (ed.), *Language in Thought and Schizophrenia*, Berkeley: University of California Press, 101-14.

Dougherty, J. (ed.) 1985. *Directions in Cognitive Anthropology*. Urbana: University of Illinois Press.

Douglas, Mary 1981. *Edward Evans-Pritchard*. Harmondsworth: Penguin.

Drees, William B. 1996. *Religion, Science and Naturalism*. Cambridge: Cambridge U.P.

Droysen, J.G. 1967. *Outline of the Principles of History*, (trans. E.B. Andrews). New York: Howard Fertig.

Droysen, J.G. 1980 (1836-43). *Geschichte des Hellenismus*. München: Deutscher Taschenbuch.

Dupré, John 1993. *The Disorder of Things. Metaphysical Foundations of the Disunity of Science*. Cambridge, Mass. & London: Harvard U.P.

Durkheim, Émile and Marcel Mauss 1963 (1903). *Primitive Classification*. Chicago: University of Chicago Press.

Durkheim, Émile 1965 (1912). *The Elementary Forms of the Religious Life*, (transl. Joseph W. Swain). New York: The Free Press.

Durt, Hubert 1994. *Problems of Chronology and Eschatology. Four Lectures on the the Essay on Buddhism by Tominaga Nakamoto (1715-1746)*. Kyoto: Instituto Italiano di Cultura — Scuola di Studi sull' Asia Orientale.

Eagleton, Terry 1996. *The Illusions of Postmodernism*. Oxford: Blackwell Publishers.

Eliade, Mircea 1959. *The Sacred and the Profane: The Nature of Religion*. New York: Harcourt, Brace, Jovanovich.

Eliade, Mircea 1964. *Shamanism: Archaic Techniques of Ecstasy*, (trans. W.R. Trask). New York: Pantheon Books.

Elster, Jon 1983. *Sour Grapes: Studies in the Subversion of Rationality*. Cambridge: Cambridge U.P.

Evans-Pritchard, Edward E. 1951. *Social Anthropology*. London: Routledge & Kegan Paul.

Evans-Pritchard, Edward E. 1976 (1937). *Witchcraft, Oracles, and Magic among the Azande*. Abridged Edition. Oxford: Oxford U.P.

Firth, Raymond 1985. 'Degrees of intelligibility'. In Joanna Overing (ed.), *Reason and Morality*, London: Tavistock, 29-46.

Fodor, Jerry and Ernest LePore 1992. *Holism. A Shopper's Guide*. Oxford: Blackwell.

Forke, Alfred 1964. *Geschichte der alten chinesischen Philosophie*. Hamburg: de Gruyter.

Forke, Alfred 1964. *Geschichte der mittelalterlichen chinesischen Philosophie*. Hamburg: de Gruyter.

Forke, Alfred 1964. *Geschichte der neueren chinesischen Philosophie*. Hamburg: de Gruyter.

Foucault, Michel 1971. 'On Popular Justice: A Discussion of Maoists'. In Foucault 1980, 1-36.

Foucault, Michel 1972. *The Archaeology of Knowledge*, (trans. A.M.S. Smith). New York: Harper and Row.

Foucault, Michel 1980. *Power/Knowledge: Selected Interviews and Other Writings 1972-1977* (ed. C. Gordon). New York: Pantheon Books.

Franke, O. 1965. *Geschichte des chinesischen Reiches. Eine Darstellung seiner Entstehung, seines Wesens und seiner Entwicklung bis zur neuesten Zeit* (5 vols.). Berlin: de Gruyter.

Frazer, James G. 1922. *The Golden Bough*. London: Macmillan.

Geertz, Armin W. 1990. 'The study of indigenous religions in the history of religions'. In Tyloch 1990, 31-43.

Geertz, Armin W. 1992. *The Invention of Prophecy. Continuity and Meaning in Hopi Religion*. Los Angeles: University of California Press.

Geertz, Armin W. (n.d).'Global Perspectives on Methodology in the Study of Religion'. (Unpublished paper, 1995, IAHR International Congress, Mexico City).

Geertz, Clifford 1968. *Islam Observed*. New Haven: Yale U.P.

Geertz, Clifford 1984. 'Anti anti-relativism'. *American Anthropologist* 86 (2), 263-78.

Gellner, Ernest 1985. *Relativism and the Social Sciences*. Cambridge: Cambridge U.P.

Gellner, Ernest 1992. *Reason and Culture: The Historic Role of Rationality and Reason*. Oxford: Blackwell.

Gellner, Ernest 1992a. *Postmodernism, Reason and Religion*. London: Routledge.

Giddens, Anthony and Jonathan Turner (eds.) 1987. *Social Theory Today*. Stanford: Stanford U.P.

Goodman, Nelson 1978. *Ways of Worldmaking*. Hassocks, Sussex: The Harvester Press.

Gordon, Paul R. and Norman Levitt 1994. *Higher Superstition: The Academic Left and Its Quarrels With Science*. Baltimore: The Johns Hopkins U.P.

Gould, Stephen Jay 1989. *Wonderful Life. The Burgess Shale and the Nature of History*. New York: Norton.

Grote, George 1854 (1846). 'Preface' (to 1st ed.), *History of Greece* (2nd ed.). New York: Harper & Brothers.

Gunkel, Hermann 1903. *Zum religionsgeschichtlichen Verständnis des Neuen Testaments*. Göttingen: Vandenhoeck and Ruprecht; trans. by W.H. Carruth as: 'The Religio-historical Interpretation of the New Testament', *The Monist* 1903, 398-455.

Habermas, Jürgen 1973. *Theory and Practice*, (trans. J. Viertel). Boston: Beacon Press.

Habermas, Jürgen 1979. 'What Is Universal Pragmatics?'. In idem., *Communication and the Evolution of Society*, 1-68. London: Heinemann.

Hacking, Ian 1982. 'Language, truth and reason'. In Hollis and Lukes (eds.), 48-66.

Haggard, H. Rider 1928. *The Works of H. Rider Haggard*. Roslyn, New York: Black.

Hallpike, C.R. 1979. *The Foundations of Primitive Thought*. Oxford: Oxford U.P.

Hanson, F. Allan 1975. *Meaning in Culture*. London: Routledge.

Hanson, F. Allan 1979. 'Does god have a body? Truth, reality and cultural relativism'. *Man*, 14 (3), 515-29.

Hanson, F. Allan 1981. 'Anthropologie und die Rationalitätsdebatte'. In H.P. Duerr (ed.), *Der Wissenschaftler und das Irrationale*, vol.1, Frankfurt-am-Main: Sindikat, 245-72.

Hanson, F. Allan 1989. 'The Making of the Maori: Culture Invention and Its Logic'. *American Anthropologist*, 91, 890-902.

Harrison, Peter 1990. *Religion and the Religions in the English Enlightenment.* London.

Hastings, James (ed.) 1922. *The Encyclopedia of Religion and Ethics.* New York: Charles Scribner.

Hegel, G.W.F. 1956 (1861). *The Philosophy of History*, (trans. J. Sibree). New York: Dover.

Hesse, Mary 1980. *Revolutions and Reconstructions in the Philosophy of Science.* Brighton: Harvester Press.

Hinnells, John R. (ed.) 1997. *A Handbook of Living Religions.* Oxford: Blackwells.

Hobbes, Thomas 1968 (1651). *Leviathan, or the Matter, Forme, & Power of a Common-Wealth Ecclesiastical and Civill.* London.

Hobbs, J.R. and R.C. Moore (eds.) 1982. *Formal Theories of the Commonsense World.* Norwood: Ablex.

Holdcroft, David 1991. *Saussure. Sign, System, and Arbitrariness.* Cambridge: Cambridge U.P.

Holland, Dorothy and Naomi Quinn (eds.) 1987. *Cultural Models in Language and Thought.* New York: Cambridge U.P.

Hollis, Martin and Steven Lukes (eds.) 1982. *Rationality and Relativism.* Oxford: Blackwell.

Hollis, Martin 1977. *Models of Man.* Cambridge: Cambridge U.P.

Hollis, Martin 1994. *The philosophy of social science.* Cambridge: Cambridge U.P.

Horton, Robin 1967. 'African traditional thought and Western science'. *Africa* 37. Part 1, 50-71; part 2, 155-87.

Horton, Robin 1970.'African Traditional Thought and Western Science'. In B. Wilson (ed.), 131-71.

Horton, Robin 1973. 'Lévy-Bruhl, Durkheim and the Scientific Revolution'. In Horton and Finnegan (eds.), 249-305.

Horton, Robin 1982. 'Tradition and modernity revisited'. In Hollis and Lukes (eds.), 201-60.

Horton, Robin 1993. *Patterns in Thought in Africa and the West.* Cambridge: Cambridge U.P.

Horton, Robin and Ruth Finnegan (eds.) 1973. *Modes of Thought: Essays on Thinking in Western and Non-Western Societies.* London: Faber.

Hume, David 1993. *Dialogues Concerning Natural Religion* (1776); *The Natural History of Religion* (1757). Oxford: Oxford U.P.

Iggers, Georg G. 1983. *The German Conception of History* (rev. ed.). Middletown, CT: Wesleyan U.P.

Indinopulos, Thomas A. and Edward A. Yonan (eds.) 1994. *Religion and Reductionism: essays on Eliade, Segal, and the challenge of the social sciences for the Study of Religion*. Leiden: Brill.

James, William 1960 (1902). *The Varieties of Religious Experience: A Study in Human Nature*. London: Fontana Library, Collins.

Jarvie, Ian C. 1984. *Rationality and Relativism*. London: Routledge.

Jarvie, Ian C. and Joseph Agassi 1987a. 'The problem of the rationality of magic'. In Agassi and Jarvie (eds.), 365-83.

Jarvie, Ian C. and Joseph Agassi 1987b. 'Magic and rationality again'. In Agassi and Jarvie (eds.), 385-94.

Jensen, Jeppe Sinding 1993. 'What Sort of Reality is Religion?'. In Luther Martin (ed.), *Religious Transformations and Socio-Political Change*, Berlin & New York: Mouton de Gruyter, 357-79.

Justin the Martyr 1963. *Dialogue with Trypho, a Jew*. London: Lutterworth Press.

Kamppinen, Matti 1986. 'Uskonnollinen ongelmanratkaisu ja etnometodologia' [Religious problem solving and ethnomethodology]. *Suomen Antropologi* [Journal of the Finnish Anthropological Society], 2, 61-70.

Kamppinen, Matti 1988a. 'Homo Religiosus Intelligens: An Outline for a Cognitivist Theory of Religious Behaviour'. *Temenos*, 24, 29-38.

Kamppinen, Matti 1988b. 'Espíritus Incorporados: The Roles of Plants and Animals in the Amazonian Mestizo Folklore'. *Journal of Ethnobiology*, 8, 141-48.

Kamppinen, Matti 1989a.'Cognitive Systems and Cultural Models of Illness: A Study of Two Mestizo Peasant Villages of the Peruvian Amazon'. *Folklore Fellows Communications* 244. Helsinki: Academia Scientiarum Fennica.

Kamppinen, Matti 1989b. 'Dialectics of evil: Politics and Religion in an Amazonian Mestizo Community'. *Dialectical Anthropology*, 13, 143-55.

Kamppinen, Matti 1993. 'Cognitive Schemata'. In M. Kamppinen (ed.), *Consciousness, Cognitive Schemata, and Relativism: Multidisciplinary Explorations in Cognitive Science*. Dordrecht: Kluwer, 134-68.

Kamppinen, Matti 1997. *Cultural models of risk: The Multiple Meanings of Living in the World of Dangerous Possibilities*. Finland Futures Research Centre, Turku School of Economics and Business Administration. Turku: Futu Publications.

Kamppinen, Matti and A. Revonsuo 1993. 'Ultimate Relativism'. In Kamppinen (ed.), 229-42.

Karlgren, Bernard 1915-1919. *Etudes sur la Phonologie Chinoise*. Leiden: Brill.

Karlsson, H. and Matti Kamppinen 1995. 'Biological Psychiatry and

Reductionism: Empirical Findings and Philosophy'. *British Journal of Psychiatry* 167, 434-38.

Kato, Shuichi 1967. 'The life and thought of Tominaga Nakamoto (1715-46), a Tokugawa iconoclast'. *Monumenta Nippponica* 22, 1-2, 1-35.

Kearney, Michael 1984. *World View*. Novato: Chandler and Sharp.

Kenny, Michael G. 1976. 'Alternative Logic in "Primitive Thought"'. *Man*, 11 (1), 116.

Kippenberg, Hans G. and Brigitte Luchesi (eds.) 1991. *Religionswissenschaft und Kulturkritik. Beiträge zur Konferenz The History of Religions and Critique of Culture in the Days of Gerardus van der Leeuw (1890-1950)*. Marburg: Diagonal-Verlag.

Kippenberg, Hans G. and Guy G. Stroumsa (eds.) 1995. *Secrecy and Concealment: Studies in the History of Mediterranean and Near Eastern Religions*. Leiden: Brill.

Kitcher, Philip 1993. *The Advancement of Science: Science Without Legend, Objectivity Without Illusions*. New York: Oxford U.P.

Klostermaier, Klaus K. and Larry W. Hurtado (eds.) 1991. *Religious Studies: Issues, Prospects and Proposals*. Manitoba: University of Manitoba Press.

Kmita, Jerzy 1971. *Z metodologicznych problemow interpretacji humanistycznej*. Warszawa: Panstwowe Wydawnictwo Naukowe.

Kmita, Jerzy 1988. *Problems in Historical Epistemology* (trans. M. Turner). Warszawa-Dordrecht: PWN-Reidel.

Kmita, Jerzy 1991. *Essays on the Theory of Scientific Cognition* (trans. J. Holowka). Dordrecht: Kluwer.

Kmita, Jerzy 1996. 'Towards cultural relativism (with a small 'r')'. In A. Zeidler-Janiszewska (ed.), *Epistemology and History*, Rodopi: Amsterdam-Atlanta, 541-613.

Kolakowski, Leszek 1990. 'Irrationality in Politics'. Leszek Kolakowski (ed.), *Modernity on Endless Trial*, Chicago: University of Chicago Press, 192-203.

Kolp, Alan Lee 1975. *Participation: A Unifying Concept in the Theology of Athanasius*. Unpublished Ph.D. dissertation, Harvard University.

Koselleck, Reinhart 1979. *Vergangene Zukunft. Zur Semantik geschichtlicher Zeiten*. Frankfurt: Suhrkamp Verlag.

Krausz, Michael 1989. 'Introduction'. In idem (ed.) *Relativism. Interpretation and Confrontation*. Notre Dame, IN: University of Notre Dame Press, 1-11.

Krüger, Hermann 1967. 'Biographical Sketch: Johann Gustav Droysen'. In Droysen 1967.

Kuhn, Thomas S. 1962. *The Structure of Scientific Revolutions*, Chicago: University of Chicago Press.

Kuhn, Thomas S. 1970. 'Reflections on my Critics'. In I. Lakatos and A. Musgrave (eds.), *Criticism and the Growth of Knowledge*. Cambridge: Cambridge U.P., 231-78.

La Barre, Weston 1970. *The Ghost Dance*. Garden City, NY: Doubleday.

Latour, Bruno 1987. *Science in Action*. Cambridge, MA.: Harvard U.P.

Laudan, Larry 1990. *Science and Relativism*. Chicago: Chicago U.P.

Laudan, Larry 1996. *Beyond Positivism and Relativism. Theory, method and evidence*. Boulder: Westview Press.

Lawson, E. Thomas and Robert N. McCauley 1990. *Rethinking Religion: Connecting Cognition and Culture*. New York: Cambridge U.P.

Lawson, E. Thomas and Robert N. McCauley 1993. 'Crisis of Conscience, Riddle of Identity. Making Space for a Cognitive Approach to Religious Phenomena'. *Journal of the American Academy of Religion*, 61 (2), 201-23.

Lease, Gary 1994. 'The History of 'Religious' Consciousness and the Diffusion of Culture: Strategies for surviving Dissolution'. *Historical Reflections/Reflexions Historiques*, Vol. 20, No. 3, 453-79.

Lease, Gary 1995a. 'Nature under Fire'. In Lease and Soule (eds.), 3-15.

Lease, Gary 1995b. *'Odd Fellows' in the Politics of Religion. Modernism, National Socialism, and German Judaism*. Berlin/New York: Mouton de Gruyter.

Lease, Gary and Michael Soule (eds.) 1995. *Reinventing Nature? Responses to Postmodern Deconstruction*. Washington, D.C.: Island Press.

Leenhardt, Maurice 1975 (1949). 'Preface', (trans. Peter Rivière). In Lucien Lévy-Bruhl, *The Notebooks on Primitive Mentality*, xi-xxiv. New York: Harper & Row.

Lefkowitz, Mary 1996. *Not Out of Africa*. New York: Basic Books.

Lemaire, Ton 1991. 'Anthropological doubt'. In Nencel and Pels (eds.), 22-39.

Lévi-Strauss, Claude 1987 (1950). *Introduction to the Work of Marcel Mauss*. London: Routledge & Kegan Paul.

Lévy-Bruhl, Lucien 1927. *L'Ame primitive*. Paris: Alcan.

Lévy-Bruhl, Lucien 1931. *Le Surnaturel et la nature dans la mentalité primitive*. Paris: Alcan.

Lévy-Bruhl, Lucien 1935. *La Mythologie primitive*. Paris: Alcan.

Lévy-Bruhl, Lucien 1938. *L'Expérience mystique et les symboles chez les primitifs*. Paris: Alcan.

Lévy-Bruhl, Lucien 1966 (1922). *Primitive Mentality* (trans. Lilian A. Clare). Boston: Beacon Press.

Lévy-Bruhl, Lucien 1975 (1949). *The Notebooks on Primitive Mentality* (trans. Peter Rivière). New York: Harper & Row.

Lévy-Bruhl, Lucien 1985 (1910). *How Natives Think* (trans. Lilian A. Clare). Princeton: Princeton U.P.

Lewis, C. I. 1929. *Mind and the World-Order*. New York: Scribner.

Lloyd, G.E.R. 1990. *Demystifying Mentalities.* Cambridge: Cambridge U.P.

Lukasiewicz, Jan 1964. *Elements of Mathematical Logic* (2nd ed., trans. Olgierd Wojtasiewicz). New York: Macmillan.

Lukasiewicz, Jan 1974. *Selected Works* (ed. L. Borkowski, trans. Olgierd Wojtasiewicz). Amsterdam: North-Holland.

Lukes, Steven 1970. 'Some problems about rationality'. In Wilson (ed.), 194-213.

Lukes, Steven 1973. 'On the social determination of truth'. In Horton and Finnegan (eds.), 230-48.

Lukes, Steven 1982. 'Relativism in its place'. In Hollis and Lukes (eds.), 261-305.

Lukes, Steven 1988. *Émile Durkheim. His life and work: A historical and critical study.* Harmondsworth: Penguin.

Lutz, Catherine A. 1988. *Unnatural Emotions: Everyday Sentiments on a Micronesian Atoll and Their Challenge to Western Theory.* Chicago: University of Chicago Press.

Macey, David 1993. *The Lives of Michel Foucault.* New York: Pantheon Books.

MacIntyre, Alisdair 1989. 'Relativism, power, and philosophy'. In Krausz (ed.), 182-204.

Mack, Burton 1995. *Who Wrote the New Testament?* San Francisco: Harper San Francisco.

Malinowski, Bronislaw 1948. *Magic, Science and Religion, and Other Essays.* Garden City, New York: Doubleday Garden Press.

Malley, Brian 1994. 'Reduction and religion: Lessons from eliminative materialism'. *Method & Theory in the Study of Religion,* 6 (1), 5-33.

Margolis, Joseph 1986. 'Rationality and Realism'. In idem et al. (eds.) *Rationality, Relativism, and the Human Sciences.* Dordrecht: Martinus Nijhoff, 223-40.

Martin, Luther H. 1983. 'Why Cecropian Minerva?: Hellenistic Religious Syncretism as System'. *Numen,* 30, 131-45.

Martin, Luther H. 1991. 'Recent Historiography and the History of Religion'. *Method & Theory in the Study of Religion,* 3/1, 115-20.

Martin, Luther H. 1994a. 'Introduction'. *History, Historiography and the History of Religions,* special issue of *Historical Reflections/Réflexions Historiques* 20, 335-36.

Martin, Luther H. 1994b. 'Religion and Dream Theory in Late Antiquity'. In Bianchi (ed.), 369-74.

Martin, Luther H. 1994c. 'The Anti-individualistic Ideology of Hellenistic Culture'. *Numen,* 41, 117-40.

Martin, Luther H. 1995a. 'Secrecy in Hellenistic Religious Communities'. In Kippenberg and Stroumsa (eds.), 101-21.

Martin, Luther H. 1995b. 'The Discourse of (Michel Foucault's) Life'. *Method & Theory in the Study of Religion*, 7 (1), 57-69.

Martin, Luther H. 1996. 'Historicism, Syncretism and the Cognitive Alternative: A Response to Michael Pye'. *Method & Theory in the Study of Religion*, 8 (2), 215-24.

McCalla, Arthur 1994. 'When is History not History?'. *Historical Reflections / Réflexions Historiques*, 20, 3, 435-52.

McCarthy, Cormac 1994. *The Crossing*. New York: Alfred A. Knopf.

McCauley, Robert N. and E. Thomas Lawson 1996. 'Who Owns Culture?'. *Method & Theory in the Study of Religion*, 8 (3), 271-90.

McCutcheon, Russell T. 1995.' The category "Religion" in recent publications: A critical survey'. *NUMEN*, 42, 284-309.

Midgley, Mary 1992. *Science as Salvation: A Modern Myth and Its Meaning*. London: Routledge.

Moffatt, James 1922. 'Syncretism', in Hastings 1922, 155-57.

Mongin, Philippe 1991. 'Rational choice theory considered as psychology and moral philosophy'. *Philosophy of the Social Sciences*, 21 (1), 5-37.

Morris, Brian 1987. *Anthropological Studies of Religion. An Introductory Text*. Cambridge: Cambridge U.P.

Müller, Friedrich Max 1894. *Chips from a German Workshop* (New Ed.). London: Longmans, Green and Co..

Murphy, Tim 1994. 'Wesen und Erscheinung in the history of the study of religion: A post-structuralist perspective.' *Method & Theory in the Study of Religion*, 6 (2), 119-146.

Nagel, Ernest 1961. *The Structure of Science. Problems in the Logic of Scientific Explanation*. London: Routledge & Kegan Paul.

Needham, Rodney 1972. *Belief, Language, and Experience*. Chicago and Oxford: University of Chicago Press and Basil Blackwell & Mott.

Nencel, Lorraine and Peter Pels (eds.) 1991. *Constructing Knowledge: Authority and Critique in Social Science*. London: Sage.

Newman, John Henry 1960 (1845). *An Essay on the Development of Christian Doctrine*. Garden City: Image Books (Doubleday).

Nietzsche, Friedrich 1968 (1906). *The Will to Power* (trans. Kauffman and Hollingdale). New York.

Norris, Chistopher 1995. 'Culture, criticism and communal values: on the ethics of enquiry'. In Barbara Adam and Stuart Allan (eds.), *Theorizing Culture. An interdisciplinary critique after postmodernism*. London: UCL Press, 5-40.

Nozick, Robert 1993. *The Nature of Rationality*. Princeton, NJ: Princeton U.P.

Otto, Rudolf 1969 (1917). *The Idea of the Holy*. London: Oxford U.P.

Parkin, David (ed.) 1982. *Semantic Anthropology*. London: Academic Press.

Parkin, Frank 1992. *Durkheim*. Oxford: Oxford U.P.

Parmentier, Richard J. 1985. 'Semiotic Mediation: Ancestral Genealogy and Final Interpretant'. In Elizabeth Mertz and Richard J. Parmentier (eds.), *Semiotic Mediation: Sociocultural and Psychological Perspectives*. Orlando: Academic Press, 359-85.

Penner, Hans H. 1989. 'Rationality, Ritual, and Science'. In Jacob Neusner et al. (eds.), *Religion, Science and Magic*. Oxford: Oxford U.P., 11-24.

Penner, Hans H. 1989a. *Impasse and Resolution. A Critique of the Study of Religion*. New York: Peter Lang.

Penner, Hans H. 1995. 'Why does semantics matter in the study of religion?'. *Method and Theory in the Study of Religion*, 7 (3), 221-49.

Pettazzoni, Raffaele 1967. *Essays on the History of Religions* (trans. H.J. Rose). Leiden: Brill.

Piaget, Jean 1929. *The Child's Conception of the World*. London: Routledge & Kegan Paul.

Piaget, Jean 1972. *The Principles of Genetic Epistemology* (trans. Wolfe Mays). New York: Basic Books.

Piaget, Jean 1977. *The Essential Piaget* (ed. Howard F. Gruber and J. Jacques Voneche). New York: Basic Books.

Platvoet, Jan, J. Cox, and J. Olupona (eds.) 1996. *The Study of Religions in Africa. Past, Present and Prospects. Proceedings of the Regional Conference of the International Association for the History of Religions, Harare, Zimbabwe 1992*. Cambridge: Roots and Branches.

Popper, Karl R. 1966. *The Open Society and its Enemies*. London: Routledge.

Popper, Karl R. 1979. *Objective Knowledge. An Evolutionary Approach* (rev. ed.). Oxford: Clarendon Press.

Popper, Karl R. 1994. *The Myth of the Framework. In defence of science and rationality* (ed. M.A. Notturno). London and New York: Routledge.

Preus, J. Samuel 1987. *Explaining Religion: Criticism and Theory from Bodin to Freud*. New Haven: Yale U.P.

Price, S.R.F. 1982. *Rituals and Power. The Roman Imperial Cult in Asia Minor*. Cambridge: Cambridge U.P.

Primack, Joel and Nancy Abrams (1995). 'In a Beginning ... Quantum Cosmology and Kabbalah'. *Tikkun*, 10, January/February, 66-73.

Putnam, Hilary 1987. *The many faces of realism*. LaSalle, IL: Open Court.

Putnam, Hilary 1988. *Representation and Reality*. Cambridge, MA: MIT Press.

Putnam, Hilary 1990. *Realism with a Human Face* (ed. J. Conant). Cambridge, MA: Harvard U.P.

Putnam, Hilary 1994. *Words and Life* (ed. James Conant). Cambridge, MA: Harvard U.P.

Pye, Michael 1972. *Comparative Religion. An Introduction through Source Materials*. Newton Abbott: David and Charles.

Pye, Michael 1973. 'Aufklärung and religion in Europe and Japan'. *Religious Studies*, 9, 201-17.

Pye, Michael 1982. 'The study of religion as an autonomous discipline'. *Religion*, 12, 1, 67-76.

Pye, Michael 1989 (ed.). *Marburg Revisited. Institutions and Strategies in the Study of Religion*. Marburg: diagonal-Verlag.

Pye, Michael 1990. *Emerging from Meditation* (ed., trans.). London and Honolulu: Duckworth and University of Hawaii Press.

Pye, Michael 1990a. 'Philology and fieldwork in the study of Japanese religion'. In Tyloch (ed.) 1990, 147-60.

Pye, Michael 1991. 'Religious studies in Europe: structures and desiderata'. In Klostermaier and Hurtado (eds.), 39-55.

Pye, Michael 1994. 'Syncretism versus synthesis'. *Method & Theory in the Study of Religion*, 6 (2), 217-29.

Pye, Michael 1996a. 'Reflecting on the plurality of religions'. *World Faiths Encounter*, 14, 3-11. (Full text in *Marburg Journal of Religion*, 2, 1, 1997)

Pye, Michael 1996b. 'Intercultural strategies and the International Association for the History of Religions'. In Platvoet et al. (eds.) 1996.

Quine, Willard V.O. 1960. *Word and Object*. Cambridge, MA: Harvard U.P.

Rabinow, Paul 1986. 'Representations are social facts: Modernity and Post-Modernity in Anthropology'. In Clifford and Marcus (eds.), 234-60.

Ranke, Leopold von 1885. Vorrede zur ersten Ausgabe, *Geschichten der romanischen und germanischen Völker von 1494 bis 1514* (3rd ed.). Leipzig: Duncker & Humblot.

Rescher, Nicholas 1988. *Rationality: A Philosophical Inquiry into the Nature and the Rationale of Reason*. Oxford: Clarendon Press.

Rescher, Nicholas 1993. *The Validity of Values* (Vol.II of *A System of Pragmatic Idealism*). Princeton, NJ: Princeton U.P.

Rorty, Richard 1987. 'Science as Solidarity'. In J.S. Nelson (ed.), *The Rhetoric of the Human Sciences*. Madison, Wisc.: University of Wisconsin Press, 38-52. (rpd. in Rorty, 1991, 35-45).

Rorty, Richard 1991. *Objectivity, Relativism, and Truth*. Cambridge: Cambridge U.P.

Roth, Philip 1995. *Sabbath's Theater*. New York: Houghton-Mifflin.

Rouse, Joseph 1991. 'Philosophy of Science and the Persistent Narratives of Modernity'. *Studies in the History and Philosophy of Science*, 22, 141-62.

Rudolph, Kurt 1981. 'Basic positions of Religionswissenschaft'. *Religion*, 11, 2, 97-107.

Rudolph, Kurt 1992. *Geschichte und Probleme der Religionswissenschaft*. Leiden: Brill.

Ryle, Gilbert 1949. *The Concept of Mind*. Oxford: Oxford U.P.

Sajama, S. and Matti Kamppinen 1987. *A Historical Introduction to Phenomenology*. London: Croom Helm.

Saler, Benson 1993. *Conceptualizing Religion*. Leiden: Brill.

Sandys, John Edwin 1908. *A History of Classical Scholarship*. Cambridge: Cambridge U.P.

Saussure, Ferdinand de 1973 (1915). *Cours de linguistique générale*. Paris: Payot.

Schatzki, Theodore R. 1995. 'Objectivity and Rationality'. In Wolfgang Natter et al. (eds.), *Objectivity and Its Other*, New York: The Guilford Press, 137-78.

Schüssler Fiorenza, Francis 1993. 'Theology in the University'. *Bulletin of the Council of Societies for the Study of Religion*, 22, 34-9.

Schüssler Fiorenza, Francis 1994. 'A Response to Donald Wiebe'. *Bulletin of the Council of Societies for the Study of Religion*, 23, 6-10.

Seidman, Steven (ed.) 1994. *The Postmodern Turn: New Perspectives on Social Theory*. Cambridge: Cambridge U.P.

Seidman, Steven 1992. 'Postmodern Social Theory as Narrative with a Moral Intent'. In Seidman and Wagner, 47-81.

Seidman, Steven and David G. Wagner 1992. *Postmodernism and Social Theory*. Oxford: Basil Blackwell.

Shapin, Steven 1994. *A Social History of Truth: Civility and Science in Seventeenth-Century England*. Chicago: University of Chicago Press.

Sharpe, Eric 1975. *Comparative Religion. A History*. London: Duckworth.

Shweder, Richard A. 1977. 'Likeness and Likelihood in Everyday Thought: Magical Thinking in Judgments about Personality'. *Current Anthropology*, 18 (4), 637-58.

Shweder, Richard A. 1981. 'Rationality "Goes Without Saying"'. *Culture, Medicine and Psychiatry*, 5 (4), 348-58.

Shweder, Richard A. 1982. 'On Savages and Other Children'. *American Anthropologist*, 84, 354-66.

Shweder, Richard A. 1991. *Thinking Through Cultures*. New Haven: Harvard U.P.

Silk, Mark 1987. 'The Hot History Department (at Princeton University)', *New York Times Magazine*, April 19, 47-62.

Simon, H. 1957. *Models of Man: Social and Rational*. New York: Wiley & Sons.

Simon, H. 1981. *The Sciences of the Artificial* (2nd ed.). Cambridge, MA: MIT Press.

Skorupski, John 1976. *Symbol and Theory: A Philosophical Study of Theories of Religion in Social Anthropology*. Cambridge: Cambridge U.P.

Smith, B. 1995. 'Formal Ontology, Common Sense and Cognitive Science'. *International Journal of Human-Computer Studies*, 43, 641-67.

Smith, Huston 1990. 'Postmodernism's Impact on the Study of Religion'. *Journal of the American Academy of Religion*, 58, 653-70.

Smith, Jonathan Z. 1982. *Imagining Religion. From Babylon to Jonestown*. Chicago: The University of Chicago Press.

Smith, Jonathan Z. 1990. *Drudgery Divine, On the Comparison of Early Christianities and the Religions of Late Antiquity*. London: SOAS.

Smith, Jonathan Z. 1993 (1978). *Map is not Territory*. Chicago: University of Chicago Press.

Sokal, Alan 1996. 'Transgressing the Boundaries: Toward a Transformative Hermeneutics of Quantum Gravity'. *Social Text*, Summer 1996.

Sokal, Alan 1996a. 'A Physicist Experiments with Cultural Studies'. *Lingua Franca*, Vol. 6 (May/June), 62-64.

Solomon, Robert C. 1992. 'Existentialism, emotions, and the cultural limits of rationality'. *Philosophy East and West*, 42 (4), 597-621.

Sorell, Tom 1991. *Scientism: Philosophy and the Infatuation of Science*. London: Routledge.

Southard, Robert 1995. *Droysen and the Prussian School of History*. Lexington, KY: The U.P. of Kentucky.

Sperber, Dan 1985. *On Anthropological Knowledge*. Cambridge: Cambridge U.P.

Spiro, Melford E. 1984. 'Some Reflections on Cultural Determinism and Relativism with Special Reference to Emotion and Reason'. In Richard A. Shweder and Robert A. LeVine (eds.), *Culture Theory: Essays on Mind, Self, and Emotion*, Cambridge: Cambridge U.P. 323-46.

Spiro, Melford 1992. *Anthropological Other or Burmese Brother? Studies in Cultural Analysis*. New Brunswick: Transaction Publishers.

Spiro, Melford 1992a. 'Cultural Relativism and the Future of Anthropology'. In George E. Marcus (ed.), *Rereading Cultural Anthropology*. Durham and London: Duke U.P., 124-51.

Spiro, Melford (n.d.). 'On a Feminist/Constructionist View of Emotions' (ms.).

Stich, Steven 1983. *From Folk Psychology to Cognitive Science*. Cambridge, MA: MIT Press.

Stoller, Paul and C. Olkes 1987. *In Sorcery's Shadow: A Memoir of Apprentice-ship among the Songhay of Niger*. Chicago: University of Chicago Press.

Strenski, Ivan 1989. 'Theories and Social Facts: A Reply to My Critics'. *Method & Theory in the Study of Religion*, 1/2, 196-212.

Strenski, Ivan 1993. *Religion in Relation. Method, Application and Moral Location*. Columbia, SC: University of South Carolina Press.

Sylvan, David and Barry Glassner 1985. *A Rationalist Methodology for the Social Sciences*. Oxford: Basil Blackwell.

Tambiah, Stanley J. 1990. *Magic, Science, Religion, and the Scope of Rationality*. Cambridge: Cambridge U.P.

Trigg, Roger 1973. *Reason and Commitment*. Cambridge: Cambridge U.P.

Trigg, Roger 1985. *Understanding Social Science*. Oxford: Basil Blackwell.

Trigg, Roger 1989. *Reality at Risk: A Defence of Realism in Philosophy and the Sciences* (2nd ed.). London: Harvester Press (Simon and Schuster).

Trigg, Roger 1991. 'Wittgenstein and Social Science'. In A.P. Griffiths (ed.), *Wittgenstein Centenary Essays*. Cambridge: Cambridge U.P.

Trigg, Roger 1993. *Rationality and Science: Can Science Explain Everything?* Oxford: Basil Blackwell.

Tsunoda, R. 1958. *Sources of Japanese Tradition*. New York and London: Columbia University Press.

Turner, Jonathan H. 1987. 'Analytical Theorizing'. In Giddens and Turner (eds.), 156-94.

Turner, Jonathan H. 1992. 'The Promise of Positivism'. In Seidman and Wagner (eds.), 156-78.

Tyler, Stephen A. 1991. 'A Post-modern in-stance'. In Nencel and Pels (eds.), 78-94.

Tyloch, Witold (ed.) 1990. *Studies on Religions in the Context of the Social Sciences. Methodological and Theoretical Relations*. Warsaw: Polish Society for the Science of Religions.

van der Leeuw, G. 1938. *Religion in Essence and Manifestation: A Study in Phenomenology* (trans. J.E. Turner). London: George Allen & Unwin.

Wach, Joachim 1924. *Religionswissenschaft: Prolegomena zu ihrer wissenschafts-theoretischen Grundlegung*. Leipzig: J.C. Hinrichs.

Wallace, Anthony F.C. 1961. 'The Psychic Unity of Human Groups'. In Bert Kaplan (ed.), *Studying Personality Cross-Culturally*. Evanston, IL: Row, Peterson, and Co., 129-63.

Wansbrough, John E. 1977. *Quranic Studies: Sources and Methods of Scriptural Interpretation*, London Oriental Studies 31. Oxford: Oxford U.P.

Wansbrough, John E. 1978. *The Sectarian Milieu: Conduct and Composition of Islamic Salvation History*, London Oriental Studies 34. Oxford: Oxford U.P.

Wendland, Paul 1912. *Die Hellenistische-Römische Kultur* (2nd and 3rd ed.). Tübingen: J.C.B. Mohr (Paul Siebeck).

White, Hayden 1973. *Metahistory. The Historical Imagination in Nineteenth-Century Europe*. Baltimore: The John Hopkins University Press.

White, Hayden 1987. *The Content of the Form. Narrative Discourse and Historical Representation*. Baltimore: The John Hopkins University Press.

Whitehead, Alfred N. 1959 (1927). *Symbolism: Its Meaning and Effect*. (Barbour-Page lectures, University of Virginia). New York.

Wiebe, Donald 1988.' Postulations for Safeguarding Preconceptions: The Case of the Scientific Religionist'. *Religion*, 18, 11-19

Wiebe, Donald 1990. 'Disciplinary Axioms, Boundary Conditions, and the Academic Study of Religion: Comments on Pals and Dawson'. *Religion*, 20, 17-29.

Wiebe, Donald 1991. 'Phenomenology of Religion as Religio-Cultural Quest'. In Kippenberg and Luchesi (eds.), 65-86.

Wiebe, Donald 1993. *The Irony of Theology and the Nature of Religious Thought*. Montreal: McGill U.P.

Wiebe, Donald 1994a. *Beyond Legitimation: Essays on the Problem of Religious Knowledge*. London: Macmillan.

Wiebe, Donald 1994b. 'On Theology and Religious Studies: A Response to Francis Schüssler Fiorenza'. *Bulletin of the Council of Societies for the Study of Religion*, Vol. 23, 3-6.

Wiebe, Donald 1997. 'On Theological Resistance to the Scientific Study of Religion: Values and the Value-Free Study of Religion'. In Człowiek i Wartości: Księga pamiątkowa poświęcona 35-leciu pracy naukowej i 40-leciu pracy nauczycielskiej Profesora Jana Szmyda. Kraków: Wydawnictwo Naukowe WSP.

Wikan, Unni 1990. *Managing Turbulent Hearts: A Balinese Formula for Living*. Chicago: The University of Chicago Press.

Wilson, Bryan R. (ed.) 1970. *Rationality*. Oxford: Basil Blackwell.

Winch, Peter 1958. *The Idea of a Social Science and its Relation to Philosophy*. London: Routledge & Kegan Paul.

Winch, Peter 1970 (1964). 'Understanding a primitive society'. In Wilson (ed.), 78-111.

Winch, Peter 1987. *Trying to Make Sense*. Oxford: Oxford U.P.

Winn, James A. 1993. 'An Old Historian Looks at the New Historicism'. *Comparative Studies in Society and History*, 35, 859-70.

Wittgenstein, Ludwig 1953. *Philosophical Investigations* (trans. G.E.M. Anscombe). Oxford: Basil Blackwell.

Young, Allan 1981. 'When Rational Men Fall Sick: An Inquiry into Some Assumptions Made by Medical Anthropologists'. *Culture, Medicine and Psychiatry*, 5 (4), 317-35.

Zos (pseudonym) 1995. Electronic mailing, March 29. University of California at Santa Barbara, Religious Studies Forum (anderel@listserv./ucsb.edu).

About the Authors

Michal Buchowski is Associate Professor of Anthropology at Adam Mickiewicz University in Poznan. He has been a visiting scholar and lecturer at universities in England, the United States, France and Germany. His principal interests include modes of thought and rationality, belief and symbolic systems, as well as the anthropology of Central Europe's social and cultural transition. He is the author of many publications, including: *Rationality, Translation, Interpretation* (in Polish, 1990); *Magic and Ritual* (in Polish, 1993), *Reluctant Capitalists* (1997) and *The Rational Other* (1997).

Address: Institute of Ethnology and Cultural Anthropology,
             Adam Mickiewicz University
             ul. sw. Marcin 72, 61-809 Poznan, Poland
             e-mail: MBUCH%PLPUAM11@plearn.edu.pl

Jeppe Sinding Jensen was born in 1951, and is Associate Professor in the Department for the Study of Religion, University of Aarhus, Denmark. He studied Semitic philology (BA in classical Arabic) and the history of religions in Aarhus, with a dissertation on the relation between Ancient Greek and Phoenician religions. For a number of years he was Associate Professor in the section for the study of religion, Department of Philosophy, Odense University, before taking his current post where he mainly teaches Islamic studies and methodology. His research focuses on philosophy of science problems in comparative religion. He has published mainly on contemporary Islam and theoretical problems in comparative religion. He is the President of the Danish Association for the History of Religions and is on the editorial board of several scholarly publications.

Address: Department for the Study of Religion
             The Main Building, University of Aarhus
             DK-8000 Aarhus C, Denmark
             Fax (+45) 8619 7870
             e-mail: sinding@teologi.aau.dk

Matti Kamppinen was born in 1961 and is Senior Lecturer in Comparative Religion at the University of Turku, Finland. He has done anthropological fieldwork in the Peruvian Amazon and in Finland, studying the cultural models of illness and risk.   He has a number of articles and publications to his name, including 'Cognitive Systems and Cultural Models of Illness: A Study of Two Mestizo Peasant Villages of the Peruvian Amazon', 1989; 'Dialectics of evil: Politics and Religion in an Amazonian Mestizo Community', 1989; and his most recent publication, *Cultural Models of Risk: The Multiple Meanings of Living in the World of Dangerous Possibilities*, 1997.

Address: Department of Cultural Studies, University of Turku
                     FIN-20014 Turku, Finland
                     e-mail: matti.kamppinen@utu.fi

Hans G. Kippenberg studied the History of Mediterranean Religions at the Universities of Marburg, Tübingen, Göttingen, Leeds and Berlin. He gained his Dr. theol. from the University of Göttingen in 1969, and in 1975 Habilitation at the Free University of Berlin. He has held positions in Göttingen, Berlin and Groningen. In 1989 he was appointed to the new chair for Theory and History of Religions at the University of Bremen. Some of his publications include: *Garizim und Synagoge. Traditionsgeschichtliche Untersuchungen zur samaritanischen Religion der aramäischen Periode* (Berlin/New York 1971), *Religion und Klassenbildung im antiken Judäa* (Göttingen 1978, 1982 translations); *Die vorderasiatischen Erlösungsreligionen in ihrem Zusammenhang mit der antiken Stadtherrschaft* (Frankfurt 1991); *Die Entdeckung der Religionsgeschichte. Religionswissenschaft und Moderne* (Munich 1997).   Hans Kippenberg has also edited many books including: *Religionswissenschaft und Kulturkritik* (with B. Luchesi), Marburg 1991; *Concepts of Person in Religion and Thought*, Berlin/New York 1990; *Secrecy and Concealment. Studies in the History of Mediterranean and Near Eastern Religions* (with G.G. Stroumsa), Leiden 1995; and the journals, *Visible Religion* Vol. 1 to 7; and since 1989, *Numen*, International Review for the History of Religions.

Address: Universität Bremen
                     Fachbereich 9, P.O. Box 330440
                     D-28334 Bremen, Germany
                     Fax 0421/218-7491
                     e-mail: kippen@religion.uni-bremen.de

Gary Lease was born in 1940 in Hollywood, California, the son of an actor. In college he majored in philosophy, and graduate work was done at the University of Munich in theology and history. He was awarded a Dr. theol. in 1968. He has taught at several colleges and universities, and since 1973 at the University of California, Santa Cruz. Here he has been chair of the Religious Studies, Environmental Studies and the History of Consciousness Departments; Associate Chancellor and Dean of Humanities; and currently is a Professor of History of Consciousness. His work centres on the history of the ancient world, chiefly the archaeology and history of Mediterranean religions during Late Antiquity; 19th and 20th century Germany, mainly German-Judaism and National Socialism as a religious movement; and the theory of religion, primarily religion as ideology and the confusion of religion and politics. He has en extensive list of publications including,'The Origins of National Socialism: Some Fruits of Religion and Nationalism' in *Religion and Politics in the Modern World*, 1983; 'Religion, the Churches, the German "Revolution" of November 1989' in *German Politics* 1:2, 1992; 'Delusion and Illusion: False Hopes and Failed Dreams. Religion, the Churches and East Germany's 1989 "November Revolution", in *Religious Transformations & Socio-Political Change*, 1993; *"Odd Fellows" in the Politics of Religion: Modernism, National Socialism, and German Judaism*, 1995; 'Anti-Semitism in Weimar Germany: The German-Jewish View', in *German Politics and Society* 14, 1996; and 'Denunciation as a Tool of Ecclesiastical Control: The Case of Roman Catholic Modernism', in *Accusatory Practices*, 1997.

Address: Department of History of Consciousness,
                  University of California Santa Cruz,
                  Santa Cruz, California, CA 95064, USA
                  e-mail: rehbock@cats.ucsc.edu

Luther H. Martin is Professor of Religion and former chair of the department at the University of Vermont. He is the author of *Hellenistic Religions: An Introduction* (Oxford University Press, 1987) and numerous articles on the religions of the Mediterranean world in late antiquity. He has published on theory and method in the study of religion and has edited several volumes of essays in this area, including: *Religious Transformations and Socio-Political Change* (Mouton de Gruyter, 1993) and *History, Historiography and the History of Religions* (special issue of *Historical Reflections/Réflexions Historiques*, 1994).

Address: Department of Religion,
                  University of Vermont
                  481 Main Street, Burlington,Vermont, VT 5405, USA
                  e-mail: lhmartin@zoo.uvm.edu

Michael Pye was born in 1939 in England, studied Modern Languages and Theology at Cambridge (1958-61) as an Open Scholar of Clare College. He then spent five years in Japan before taking lecturing posts in Religious Studies at Lancaster and Leeds, where he was awarded a PhD. Since 1982 he has been Professor of Religious Studies at Marburg University, Germany, interleaved with a three year period as Professor of Religious Studies at Lancaster University, England. Apart from a specialist knowledge of East Asian Buddhism and contemporary Japanese religions, he is widely travelled and has interests in broad issues of religion and society in the modern world. He is currently President of the International Association for the History of Religions (1995-2000). Some selected publications include: Ernst Troeltsch: *Writings on Theology and Religion* (with Robert Morgan, Duckworth, London 1977), *Skilful Means, A Concept in Mahayana Buddhism* (Duckworth, London 1978), *Emerging from Meditation* (Duckworth, London 1990), *Macmillan Dictionary of Religion* (Macmillan, London 1993); also many articles on various aspects of the study of religion, in particular on Japanese religion.

Address: Fachgebiet Religionswissenschaft,
                  Philipps Universität Marburg
                  Liebigstrasse 37, D-35032 Marburg, Germany
                  e-mail: pye@mailer.uni-marburg.de

Benson Saler is currently a member of the anthropology faculty of Brandeis University (USA), the President of the Society for the Anthropology of Religion, and the interim Vice-President of the newly forming Anthropology of Religion Section of the American Anthropological Association. His publications include: *Conceptualizing Religion: Immanent Anthropologists, Transcendent Natives, and Unbounded Categories* (Leiden: E.J. Brill, 1993), and a co-authored work, *UFO Crash at Roswell: The Genesis of a Modern Myth* (Washington, DC: The Smithsonian Institution Press, 1997).

Address: Department of Anthropology,
                Brandeis University
                Brown 228, Waltham, Massachusetts
                MA 02254-9110, USA
                e-mail: SALER@BINAH.CC.BRANDEIS.EDU

Roger Trigg is Professor of Philosophy at the University of Warwick, England. He has written widely on issues connected with rationality and truth, particularly in connection with the philosophy of science and of social science. Among his books are *Reason and Commitment*, 1973; *Understanding Social Science*, 1985; *Reality at Risk*, (2nd ed. 1989); and *Rationality and Science: Can Science Explain Everything?*, 1993. His latest book, to be published early in 1998 by Blackwell and called *Rationality and Religion* is based on the 1997 Stanton lectures in the Philosophy of Religion, which he gave at the University of Cambridge. He was the first President of the British Society for the Philosophy of Religion, and is currently President of the Mind Association.

Address: Department of Philosophy,
                University of Warwick
                Coventry, CV4 7AL, England
                Tl. (01203) 523523, Fax (01203) 523019

Donald Wiebe was born in 1943 in Canada. He holds degrees in theology and philosophy, having completed his PhD at Lancaster University, England. After teaching at the University of Manitoba he was in 1981 appointed Professor of the Philosophy of Religion at Trinity College and the Graduate Centre for the Study of Religion (until 1994). Since 1995 he has been Dean of the Faculty of Divinity at Trinity College and in 1997 he was appointed adjunct faculty to the Institute for the History and Philosophy of Science and Technology, University of Toronto. He has served on the Executive Board of the International Association for the History of Religions (IAHR) from 1985 to 1995, and he is currently Treasurer of the Association. He is a co-founder of the North American Association for the Study of Religion (NAASR) where he has twice served as President. He has published scores of articles in journals, edited collections of essays and proceedings, and published three books: *Religion and Truth: Toward an Alternative Paradigm in the Study of Religion; The Irony of Theology and the Nature of Religious Thought; and Beyond*

Legitimation: Essays on the Problem of Religious Knowledge. He is also editor of the series *Toronto Studies in Religion,* published by Peter Lang, New York. His primary areas of research interest are philosophy of science and the social sciences, philosophy of religion, and method and theory in the study of religion.

Address: Faculty of Theology, Trinity College
                    University of Toronto
                    Toronto, Ontario, Canada M5S 1H8.
                    Fax (1) 416 978 4949
                    e-mail: dwiebe@trinity.utoronto.ca

Index of Persons

Abrams, Nancy 137, 138
Agassi, Joseph 26, 27, 31
Albert, Hans 16
Alexander, Jeffrey 170
Allen, Douglas 145
Alston, William 99, 114
Appleby, Joyce 153
Arieti, Silvano 57, 60
Aristotle 60
Asad, Talal 156
Athanasius of Alexandria 50
Austin, M.M. 151
Ayer, A.J. 113
Barnes, Barry 26, 55
Barrett, T.H. 71
Bateson, Gregory 140
Beattie, John 26, 32, 34, 88
Bell, Catherine 45
Benedict, Ruth 29
Benveniste, Émile 121
Berg, Herbert 154
Berger, Peter 81, 141
Berlin, Brent 25
Bernal, Martin 146
Bernstein, Richard 23, 28
Bhaskar, Roy 180
Bianchi, Ugo 77
Biderman, Shlomo 22
Bigger, Charles 49
Bloch, Marc 149, 152, 153
Bloor, David 26, 55, 100, 114
Bordieu, Pierre 180
Bowersock, Glen 146
Brown, Harold 122, 156
Bryant, Christopher G.A. 179-181
Buchowski, Michal 15, 132
Bunge, M. 85
Campbell, Joseph 139
Carlyle, Thomas 150

Carr E.H. 145, 148-49
Carrithers, M. 40
Cazeneuve, Jean 48, 52
Chavannes, Edouard 73
Chidester, David 154
Clifford, James 21
Cole, K.C. 137
Collingwood R.G. 32, 145, 153
Cooper, David E. 57, 61-62
Cousins, Mark 153-56
Couvreur, F.S. 73
Cumont, Franz 149, 150
Cyril of Alexandria 51
Däniken, Erich von 149
Darnton, Robert 148
Darwin, Charles 53
Davidson, Donald 22, 31, 122, 133
Davies, Merryl W. 132, 140
de Rojas, Iván Guzmán 61
de Sardan, Olivier 39
Dennett, D.C. 78, 82, 84
Domarus, Ernst von 57, 60
Dougherty, J. 78, 80
Douglas, Mary 158
Drees, William B. 111
Droysen, J.G. 150-52
Dupré, John 126-128
Durkheim,. Emile 9, 49, 78-79, 87, 92-96, 131, 164
Durt, Hubert 71, 74
Eagleton, Terry 21
Eliade, Mircea 21, 80-81, 88, 137, 139, 145
Elias, Norbert 180
Elster, John 36, 40
Evans-Pritchard, Edward E. 29, 43, 46, 157-60
Feuerbach, Ludwig 9
Feyerabend, Paul 125, 134

Finnegan, Ruth 57
Fiorenza, Francis Schüssler 173-74
Firth, Raymond 40
Forke, Alfred 74
Foucault, Michel 125, 131, 134, 153, 155
Franke, O. 74
Frazer, James 26, 29
Frege, Gottlob 131
Geertz, Armin 67, 175-76
Geertz, Clifford 132
Geertz, Armin W. 28
Gellner, Ernest 29, 30, 172-73, 177-79
Giddens, Anthony 180
Glassner, Barry 181
Goodman, Nelson 22, 133
Gordon, Paul R. 182
Gould, Stephen J. 141
Grote, George 149, 150
Gunkel, Hermann 155
Habermas, Jürgen 21, 43, 135, 180
Hacking, Ian 31, 131
Haggard, H. Rider 141
Hallpike, C.R. 57
Hanson, F. Allan 25, 31, 32, 36-38, 132
Hegel, Georg Wilhelm Friedrich 81, 145, 150, 162, 164
Herder, Johann Gottfried 162
Herskovits, Melville 29
Hesse, Mary 31
Hinnels, John 144
Hobbes, Thomas 161
Hobbs, J.R. 90
Holland, Dorothy 78, 80
Hollis, Martin 15, 22, 25, 40, 57
Horton, Robin 25, 28, 31, 32, 34, 37, 46, 48, 57, 78, 87, 94
Hume, David 160, 162
Hunt, Lynn 153
Hussain, A. 153-156
Husserl, Edmund 80
Iggers, Georg 147, 152
Indinopulos, Thomas A. 21
Jacob, Margaret 153

James, William 78-79, 87, 89, 91-92
Jarvie, Ian C. 26-28, 31
Justin, the Martyr 51
Kamppinen, Matti 80
Kant, Immanuel 162, 164
Karlgren, Bernard 75
Kato, Shuichi 69
Kay, Paul 25
Kearney, Michael 15, 25
Kippenberg Hans G. 21
Kitcher, Philip 178-79
Kmita, Jerzy 38-39
Kolakowski, Leszek 38
Kolp, Alan 50
Koselleck, Reinhard 165
Krüger, Hermann 152
Kuhn, Thomas 31, 100-1, 103-4, 125, 127, 134, 159, 163
La Barre, Weston 140, 142
Latour, Bruno 182
Laudan, Larry 11, 19, 22, 132
Lawson, E. Thomas 21, 94, 131-32, 149, 153
Leach, Edmund 29
Leenhardt, Maurice 48, 60
Leeuw, G. van der 132, 145
Lefkowitz, Mary 146
Lemaire, Ton 24
Lessing, G.E. 68
Lévi-Strauss, Claude 131
Levitt, Norman 182
Lévy-Bruhl, Lucien 45
Lewis, C.I. 32
Lloyd, G.E.R. 57
Luchesi, Brigitte 21
Luckmann, Thomas 81
Lukasiewicz, Jan 57, 61
Lukes, Steven 25, 31-32, 57
Lutz, Catherine 53
Macey, David 153
MacIntyre, Alisdair 20, 23, 31
Mack, Burton 152, 154
Malinowski, Bronislaw 19, 29, 34, 46
Malley, Brian 131

Marcus, George E. 21
Margolis, Joseph 20
McCalla, Arthur 21
McCauley, Robert 21, 94, 131-32, 149, 153
McCutcheon, Russell 21
Meinong, Alexius von 82
Midgley, Mary 168-170
Mongin, Philippe 40
Moore, 90
Morris, Brian 21
Motoori, Norinaga 73
Murphy, Tim 21
Müller, Friedrich Max 9, 164
Nagel, Ernst 123, 126
Needham, Rodney 59
Nencel, Lorraine 21
Newman, John Henry 140-41
Nietzsche, F. 105, 173
Norris, Christopher 21
Nozick, Robert 20, 23, 133
Olkes, C. 39
Otto, Rudolf 81, 137, 139
Parmentier, Richard J. 58
Pels, Peter 21
Penner, Hans H. 21-22, 122, 131
Pettazoni, Raffaele 145
Piaget, Jean 57, 62
Plato 49, 60
Platvoet, Jan 77
Popper, Karl 16, 20, 24, 27, 37, 119, 131, 159, 163
Preus, Sam 21, 167
Price, S.R.F. 156
Primack, Joel 137, 138
Putnam, Hilary 17, 23, 31, 131-32
Pye, Michael 154
Pythagoras 60
Quine, Willard Van Orman 31, 121
Quinn, Naomi 78, 80
Rabinow, Paul 121
Ranke, Leopold von 146
Reichenbach, Hans 61
Rescher, Nicholas 22, 86

Riviére, Peter 60
Rorty, Richard 31, 36, 38-39, 131, 133
Roth, Philip 40, 140, 143-44
Rouse, Joseph 100
Rousseau, Jean-Jacques 162, 164
Rudolph, Kurt 66
Ryle, Gilbert 86
Sajama, S. 80
Saler, Benson 114, 115
Scharfstein, 22
Schatzki, Theodore R. 57
Schleiermacher, Friedrich 162, 164
Schopenhauer, Arthur 163-64
Schütz, Alfred 81
Seidman, Steven 168, 171-72
Shapin, Steven 182
Showerman, Grant 149
Shweder, Richard 57, 85
Silk, Mark 148
Simon, H. 80
Skorupski, John 158
Slupecki, Jerzy 61
Smith, Jonathan Z. 90, 106-7, 131, 142, 144, 152, 154-55, 163
Smith, Huston 175
Sokal, Alan 21, 136, 139, 156
Solomon, Robert C. 41
Sorell, Tom 168-69
Southard, Robert 151
Sperber, Dan 25, 28
Spiro, Melford 30, 54-55, 133
Stich, Steven 86
Stoller, Paul 39
Strenski, Ivan 119
Sylvan, David 181
Tambiah, Stanley J. 31-32, 34, 37
Tominaga, Nakamoto 68
Trigg, Roger 122
Tsunoda, R. 71
Turner, Jonathan H. 181
Tyler, Stephen 29, 37
Tylor, Edward B. 9, 93, 164
Voltaire 68
Wach, Joachim 145

Wagner, David G. 171-172
Wajsberg, Mordchaj 61
Wallace, Anthony 61
Wansbrough, John 154
Weber, Max 19, 164
Wendland, Paul 155
White, Hayden 164
Whitehead, Alfred North 59

Wiebe, Donald 79, 112, 113, 132
Wilson, Bryan 57, 159
Winch, Peter 22, 25, 37, 159
Wittgenstein, Ludwig 25, 102, 104,
    107, 112, 113, 159-60
Xenophanes 9
Yonan, Edward E. 21
Zadeh, Lofti 61
Zos 142

Index of Subjects

Affectivity 52-56
— and collective representations 55-56
Agnosticism, methodological 114
Anthropology
— and cognitive evaluations 38
— cognitive 78, 80
— cultural 78
Anti-intellectualism 136
Anti-rationalism 29
Arbitrariness - and semantic systems
    58

Beliefs
— about beliefs 105
— and actions 80
— and content 108
— and context 102
— and experience 59
— and objects 104
— and rationality 83, 123
— and rituals 94-95
— as norms and directives 39
— as objective 105-7
— as propositions 158
— as reasons 158
— bases for 102
— counterintuitive 56
— false and rational 158
— irrationality of 55
— 'mythopoeic' 112-113
— ontological commitment to 88
— pragmatist view of 92
— rational assessment of 105
— rational grounds of 100
— religious, about reality 114
— religious as false 114
— semantics of religious 122
— as social products 55

— systems of 82
— systems of traditional   31-32
— traditional 27-28
— true 114
Belief systems
— closed 158
— coherent 157-59
Bias, of conventional expressions 45
Buddhism 68-75

Categories
— in research 57
— status of analytic 35
— validity of 148
Categorization, generative 152
Cognition
— and affection 45
— and collective repre sentations 51
— and cultural development 63
— and developmental psychology 57
— and problem solving 80, 84
— intentional systems of 82
— objective standards of 38
— relation to affectivity 55
Common Sense 85-88
Concepts
— public 102
— public as social facts 118
Confucianism 68-75
Construction vs. discovery 106
Constructionism 13, 16-17, 117, 120-21
— in the Study of Religion 163-164
— methodological 154, 159
— in deconstruction 182
Constructivism, and emotions 54
Creationism 128
'Crisis of representation' 10
Criteria, relevance of 151

Critical rationalism 159
'Critical Spirit' 27
Cultural Translation 157
Culture
— defined 169
— in history 148
'Cultural Copyright' 13
'Cultural Heritage Management' 13,
    120

Darwinism 68
Data — and representations 164
Deconstruction 119, 136
— of religious authority 70
Deism 160-161
Demarcation, the problem of 12, 117,
    127-28
Determinism, linguistic 160
Discourse
— conflations of 11
— religious as 'irrational' 130
— scientific 11, 13
Dreams 155

Emic, and Etic 175
Emotions 41-42
— ambivalence about 54
— and cognition 45
— and cultural categories 53-54
— and cultural propositions 55
— and rationality 54
— folk theories of 53-54, 56
— interpretive functions of 57
— question of universality 56
— reconceptualized in anthropology
    57
Empathy 39, 56, 123, 130
Empiricism
— critique of 58-60, 159
— rejected 181
Enlightenment, the 68-69, 147, 153-54,
    162-63, 166, 170, 173, 176-78, 182
Epistemology 11
— amoral 183

— and anthropology 35
— and cognitive evaluations 35-38
— and language 58
— and politics 168
— and the linguistic turn 16
— and reflexivity 101
— and rules 36
— as social practice 100-7, 120
— as social myth 170
— commonsense and religion 92
— democratization of 13, 16
— egalitarian 178
— no special social scientific 126
— normative 12
— of science 28
— pluralist 127-29
— 'sociological turn' 101-2
— virtues in 128-29
'Erfahrungsraum' 165
'Erwartungshorizont' 165
Esoteric claims, non-rational 139
Essentialism 13, 120
Ethnocentrism 29
Ethnohermeneutics 175-176
Evidence
— and experience 139
— criteria for 139
— establishment of 138-139
— vs. argument 182
Evolutionism 68
Experience
— as complex concept 59
— religious 89, 91
Explanation 174
— 'bottom-up' 91
— linked to interpretation 170
— of religion 161
— 'top-down' 91

Fallibilism 124
Falsification 127, 130, 163
— and verification 62
— blocks to 159
'Family resemblance' - classification

of sciences 127
Fiction — and history 164
Foundationalism 173
Fundamentalism 177-178

'Geisteswissenschaften' 129
'Genealogy' 154
'God's eye view' 16, 101

Hallucinations 82
'Heilsgeschichte' 145
Hellenistic, as category 152
Hermeneutics, 'ethno' 67, 175-176
Hierophanies 87
Historical-critical methods 147
Historical generalization 149
Historicism
— descriptive 146
— forms of 146-149
— 'new' 147-149
— rise of 164
Historicity 12, 15, 106-107, 119, 126
Historiography 145
— and imagination 153
— stereotypes in 152
History
— imagination in 165
— literary representation of 164-165
— natural 160
— theoretical models for 155
— theory of 165
Holism 98, 104
— and meanings 33
'Homo religiosus' 79, 92
Humanities vs. science 173

Incommensurability 103
Individualism 155
'Insider vs. outsider', views 112
Intellectualism 26-28, 31-33, 115
— and Durkheim 94-95
Intentionality 131
Interpretation
— anthropological 35

— humanistic 39
— privileged 120
'Interpretive turn', the 120
Intersubjectivity 13, 38-39, 119, 138
Irrationality — only human 84

Knowledge
— amoral 178
— as 'cultural posits' 121
— as social construct 12
— criteria for obtaining 178
— in social science 180
— scientific 11
— scientific (not universal) 171
— science as privileged 168
— transcultural 178
— vs. truth 177
— unity of 128

Language - as rational 107
Logic
— Aristotelian 61
— differences in 47
— paleo- 57, 61
— trivalued 57, 61-62

Magic 26-27, 57, 61-62, 157
— and cognition 63
— and untestable propositions 62
'Mana' 154
Materialism, eliminative 131
Meaning
— and context 104
— and reference 130
— and significance 173
— 'as use' 104, 112
— social world of 121
Meanings
— implicational 33, 37, 39
— intentional 33, 39-40
Mentality
— 'archaic' 48
— as discursive formations 64
— 'mystical' 48, 54-55

— 'prelogical' 47-49
— 'primitive' 45-49
Metaphysics, in religious discourse 122
Methodology
— dialogical 176
— normative 12
Methods
— and cultural autonomy 75-77
— in Tominaga's work 71
— no formal 124
Models
— cognitive and moral 180
— folk/cultural 80, 85
— generic 85
— in interpretation 85
— mental/cognitive 85
— religious functional 89-92
— religious 80-81, 85, 87-92
— religious ontological 89-90
— types of 85
Modernity 14
— criticized 171
Modernization 164
— and religion 165
Monotheism 162
'Myth of the Framework' 16

'Naive Physics' 79, 84, 90
Natural histories 140
'Natural kinds' 117
Naturalism 111-13, 116
Neoplatonism 50
Nominalism 117
Normativity
— methodological 125
— moral 125

Objectivism — in historiography 146
Objectivity
— as faith 170
— as 'solidarity' 39
— discarded 171
— in social science 126
Ontology — of theoretical entities 91

'Orientalism' 72-77
Origins
— not causal 155
— not privileged 154
'Other Minds' 25
'Other', in history 148

Participation 137, 169
— and rationality 51
— as imitation 60
— (Lévy-Bruhl) 46-51
— in Christian theology 50
— in Platonic Philosophy 49-51
— metaphorical 60
— metonymical 60
Phenomenology
— ahistorical 145
— Husserlian 80
— of religion, three types of 81
Philosophy of history 153
Philosophy, in the Study of Religion
    166
Physicalism 111
Political Correctness 13
Polytheism 161-62
Positivism 11, 99-100, 112, 120, 170
— methodological 111
Positivities, as historical data 154
Postmodernism 12-14, 28-30, 105, 148,
    171
— analyzed 182
— and Foucault 154
— and particularism 174
— and Rationality 14
— critique of 28-30, 177-83
— ethos of 79
— incoherence of 182
— in the Study of Religion 175-76
— in anthropology 172
— theory as conversation 179
'Postmodern science' 100
Propositions
— and rationality 102
— indeterminate 62

Rationality
— and animals 18
— and cognitive adequacy 20
— and commonsense theories 78, 86-87
— and communication 18
— and context 102
— and epistemological dualism 34-38
— and European conventions 26
— and evidence 138-139
— and Foucault's historiography 153-155
— and foundationalism 28
— and interpretation 29
— and logic 44
— and logical universals 25
— and morality 22
— and 'objective knowledge' 20
— and 'Other Minds' 15
— and Postmodernism 14
— and questions of truth 108-110
— and rationalism 28
— and realism 20, 58
— and reasons 18
— and reasonability 130
— and reflexivity 57-60
— and religious beliefs 19, 22
— and religious bias 23
— and ritual 22
— and rules 18, 33-38, 84
— and symbolism 27
— and systemic properties 78, 83
— and the 'exotic' 68
— and truth of religious statements 95-97
— and unambiguousness 130
— and values 14-15
— and Worldviews 15
— as consistency of actions 40
— as cultural creation 41, 44
— as human property 17-18
— as property of language 107
— as social construct 99
— axiomatic 41

— Brown's model of 122
— connotations of 44-45, 56
— critique of 11, 16-18, 28-30, 174
— definition of 40
— dissatisfaction with 170
— divergent 175
— emic 19
— epistemic 86
— evaluative 86
— explanatory role of 78
— fundamentalist 182
— human property 122
— ideal type of 83
— in anthropology 38
— in explanations of religion 78
— in behaviour 78-80
— in cognitive processes 80
— in East Asian cultural history 69, 77
— in religion 15
— in religious systems 79
— in the Study of Religion 38, 79
— institutional 36-37
— instrumental 32
— in the cultural sciences 117
— intentional 36-37
— methodological 84, 95-97
— monist 27
— 'naturalized'? 20
— no criteria of 26
— norms of scientific 40
— not European construct 67-69
— objective criteria of 37
— of action 24
— of action vs. belief 37
— of magic 26
— of religious systems 66
— ontological 83
— particularist 25-26
— polythetic notion of 18
— practical 86
— primary locus of 83
— rationalist 24
— reflexive 20
— relativist 24

— relativized 41-42
— rule, transcending 20
— 'Savage' 93
— scientific 17, 82, 97, 182
— secondary locus of 83
— systemic property 15
— the assumption of 27, 84, 39
— 'thin' 19, 40
— 'underived' 21
— universal criterion of 28
— universals of 34-38
— universal standards of 33-34
— universalist 24-25
— of unreasonable beliefs 157-59
— varieties of 18-20
— versions of 17
— 'very strong' 27
— vs. reason 158
'Rational Choice' 19, 27
'Rationality Debate' 17
Rationalism 177-78
— and critical method 30
— behavioural 38
— defined 38
— product of history 30
— radical 31
Rationalist fundamentalism 178
Realism 103-7, 130
— and Culture 32-33
— and truth 99
— attacks on 105
— conceptual 85
— critique of 16-18, 29
— historical 146, 153
— metaphysical 99
— 'promiscuous' 127-28
Reality, and science 111
Reason 137
— as intelligibility 140
— hegemonization of 182
— no role in social theory 170
Reasons
— as causes 133
— invalid 157

Reduction 10, 12, 117, 126
Reductionism 113, 115
Referentiality 130
Reflexivity 130, 173
— and values 124
— critical 119
— sociological 180
Religion
— and abstract objects 91
— and causality 88
— and commonsense ontology 92-96
— and human nature 160
— and meaning 173
— and 'Naive Physics' 92-96
— and possible worlds 80
— and problem solving 88-92
— and reason 9, 113, 160
— and reduction 147
— and science 111
— as a human creation 115
— as cultural construction 137
— as 'discursive grouping' 154
— as social facts 109, 117
— as 'sui generis' 154
— autonomy of 112
— emotionist view of 162
— 'enlightened' 162
— 'essence' of 147
— functions of 163
— in European history 165
— 'intuitions about' 137
— natural history of 160-62
— not founded in reason 161
— 'of the heart' 162
— origins of 160
— plurality of models 76
— projection 9
— rational beliefs in 116
— referents of 109
— taxonomies of 142-44
— truth, claims in 110-11
— truth of 10
Relativism 16-17, 25, 110, 171, 173, 177-
     78

— and cognitive evaluations 36, 179
— and historical-critical methods 71
— and historical interpretation 146
— and reality 107
— and truth 105
— and value judgments 125-126
— compatible with rationality 17
— compromise with rationalism 30-33
— conceptual 105
— critique of 16
— cultural 10, 12
— cultural and episte- mology 36
— cultural and the 'Other' 72
— ethos of 79
— extreme 30
— historical 68-69, 70, 147
— radical 120-21
— refuted 96-97
— sceptical 119
— strong 11, 101-2, 159-60
— vs. foundationalism 40
Representations, as social facts 121
Romanticism and religion 162
Rules
— and rationality 84, 123
— of reasoning 24

Sacred
— as notion 88
— epistemic background of 88
'Salad Bar Problem' the 90
Science
— and objective knowledge 168-169
— and social context 100-2
— as institution 171
— as interpretive 172
— as 'religion' 137
— delegitimation of 168
— disagreement in 115
— 'disunity' of 126-28
— epistemic goals of 178
— 'incomplete' 118
— pluralist view of 126
— postmodernist view of 171

— progress in 153, 179
— quest for knowledge 183
— relativist critique of 40
— transcultural 183
— unity of 32
— vs. humanities 173
Scientism 128
— critique of 113, 169-171
— vs. relativism 116
Secrecy 155
Semantics 20
— and religious discourse 131
— Davidson's 122
— holist 130
— religious 130
Sharability, of evidence 138
Shinto 68-75
'Situational Logic' 27, 33, 40, 41-42
'Sociological turn' 22, 120
'Survivals' 165
Social facts
— as discourse 118
— reality of 118
Social sciences
— not scientific 169
— undermined 172
Social theory 171, 179
— vs. sociological theory 172
Sociology of knowledge 26, 100-1
— 'strong programme' in 114
Sociology of Religion 108
Sociology of science, critique of 110
Solipsism 103
Study of Religion
— and eurocentrism 68
— and model sciences 12
— and philosophy of religion 161
— and metaphysics 122
— and question of truth and value 66
— and rational constraints 107-10
— and rationality in religion 114
— and scientific practice 129
— and truth-issues 109-10
— anthropological 115

— as identifying religious models 88
— as rational exploration 65-69
— boundary conditions for 126
— cognitive 78
— cognitive approach to 95-97
— cognitive goals of 183
— comparison in 106
— concepts in 117
— constructionism in 106-7
— critical 11
— cumulative 129
— emancipation from theology 167
— identity crisis of 167
— marginalization of 10, 13
— metaphysical paradigms in 163
— methodology and postmodernism
   175-76
— multidisciplinary 67
— neutrality in 115
— no 'special method' 122
— not objective 173
— phenomenological 65
— and philosophical conceptions 164-
   166
— postmodernist challenge to 172
— postmodernist critique of 173-174
— radical programmes in 176
— requirements of a 143
— scientific? 112-13
— vs. theology 161
Subject-object distinction 113-14
Subjectivity
— and 'Meaning' 172
— and religion 162
— objectlike 129
— postmodernist 39
Supernatural
— entities 89
— mechanisms 88
— vs. the natural 95-96
Symbolism 26-28, 32, 109, 159
— and irrationality 27
— and rationality 27
— vs. cognitivism 88

Syncretism 152, 154-55

Tahara - Muslim system of Purity 19
Taxonomies
— of religion 142-44
— and intelligibility 141-42
Theories
— and data 100
— and speculations 153
— as social facts 118-19
— primary and secondary 32
— translation of 104
Theory
— and morality 171
— historiographical 149
— of 'new social realists' 181
— sociological 179-180
'Third World' (of meaning) 20, 37, 119,
   132
Tominaga 68-77
Transcendence, claims, non-sharability
   of 139-140
Transcription Systems
— Wade-Giles 73-77
— Chinese 'pinyin' 74
Truth
— and coherence theory of 159
— and correspondence theory of 159
— and objectivity 132
— and observation 159
— as social construct 101
— claims to 99
Truth claims
— as social facts 122
— in religion 175
— of religion 173
Value judgments, 125
Values
— and facts 14
— and Science 15, 124
— as social facts 120
— in research 14
— in the Study of Religion 11-14

— Rationality of 15
Varnashrama-dharma 19
Verificationism 113
Virtues
— and Science 15
— epistemological 128
— scientific 108

Witchcraft, Zande 43, 62, 157-60
Worldviews 15, 32